THE MUSLIM NEXT DOOR

DR. ALFONSE JAVED

A practical training guide for evangelism and discipleship
with theological and apologetical answers to some of the
most common questions asked by Muslims

ANM
publishers

THE MUSLIM NEXT DOOR

ISBN: 978-0-9715346-8-1 Paperback

Published by:

ANM
publishers

Advancing Native Missions
P.O. Box 5303
Charlottesville, VA 22905
www.AdvancingNativeMissions.com

ENDORSEMENTS

"If you are serious about understanding Islam and sharing Christ with your Muslim neighbors, *The Muslim Next Door* will be a great help to you. I have known Dr. Alfonse Javed for many years and have great respect for both he and his ministry. We work together at Calvary Baptist Church in New York City sharing the gospel with everyone – including Muslims. His book will help equip you to be a more loving, informed and effective witness for Jesus Christ."

Rev. Dave Epstein
Senior Pastor, Calvary Baptist Church, New York City

"'Discipleship precedes any other action.' With insights like these, Dr. Alfonse Javed gives us a treasure trove of practical advice on reaching out to Muslims with the gospel. Writing from an eastern perspective, the author rightly emphasizes both *evangelism* and *discipleship* in ministry to Muslims. The Q & A style makes *The Muslim Next Door* eminently readable."

Rev. Fred Farrokh
Director, Jesus For Muslims Network, Metro New York City

"Paul announced, '*I have become all things to all men, that I might by all means save some.*' Without a doubt Dr. Alfonse Javed shares the apostle's passion to reach those of another culture and it is evident in his book *The Muslim Next*

Door. Dr. Javed provides keen insight and wise counsel for those seeking to share Christ with Muslims without compromising the message of the Cross."

Rev. Gary Frost
President, Concerts of Prayer Greater New York

"I am a Jew who loves Muslims. I love Muslims because I love Jesus the Jewish Messiah. *The Muslim Next Door* helps me to love Muslims in the best way possible. It teaches me how to effectively share the greatest gift I have to give to my Muslim friends, the love of God in Messiah Jesus. Thank you Dr. Javed for helping me to be obedient to my Savior's command."

David Brickner
Executive Director, Jews for Jesus

"It has been one of the most distinct experiences here at Hephzibah House, NYC, to share in the life and ministry of the author, Rev. Dr. Alfonse Javed. God has entrusted many gifts to this man, including a sharp mind with the ability to communicate what God has taught and instilled in him, through His Word, but also through his personal experiences of life. God has no doubt equipped him and placed him in NYC, USA for such a time as this. His book is like him...it has his personal heart throughout it...energetic, compassionate, intelligent, with the sole purpose of honoring Jesus Christ. The writings of this book should be read by American Christians, so that God may use us with greater effectiveness as His witnesses."

Mrs. Lois Ewald
President/Director, Hephzibah House, New York City

"A must read for anyone engage in evangelism to Muslims. Particularly to those that are dedicated to reaching Muslims within our prisons. Islam is not only the fastest growing religion in the world but also in correctional facilities within the United States. *The Muslim Next Door* is primer on how, when and where to share the gospel in terms that are culturally relevant, sensitive and persuasive."

Rafael Lozada, JD
Executive Director / North East, Prison Fellowship

"Having an interest in muslims over 35 years of ministry with international students, this is a very useful resource to the church in North America."

Tim Sigman
Director, New York Metro Area Director, International Student Inc. (ISI)

"When it comes to evangelism with Muslims, there are always many questions to address. Muslims have lots of questions for Christians. Christians have a lot of questions about Muslims. Alfonse Javed's years of experience answering the questions of both Muslims and Christians shines through in *The Muslim Next Door*. The book's dialogical style invites the reader into an intimate question and answer session with an experienced practitioner. The reader will certainly find helpful answers to questions they want, or need, answered."

Chris Clayman
North American Mission Board (SBC), Author, ethNYcity: The Nations, Tongues, and Faiths of Metropolitan New York

"People in general, and Christians in particular, do not know how to react to the growing presence of Muslims in America. *Who are these Muslims? What do they really believe? Should I be afraid of them?* Christians, in addition, struggle with how to befriend Muslims and how to share the gospel with them. In *The Muslim Next Door*, Alfonse Javed provides Christians, in a question and answer format, with the tools to do both."

George T. Russ
Executive Director, Metropolitan New York Baptist Association

DEDICATION

I want to dedicate this book to Christians and Muslims fighting for religious freedom throughout the world. My book serves as a means to acknowledge those who have come to faith under great persecution; specifically those Muslims who have tried to leave Islam, but due to Sharia law (Islamic law that forbids apostatizing) have lost their lives. It is important to note that although there is no record of their deaths due to their faith in Jesus Christ, God knows their sacrifice.

I also want to dedicate this book to Hephzibah House and Calvary Baptist Church in New York City for their commitment to speak the truth with boldness. I particularly commend Pastor David Epstein, the Senior Pastor of Calvary Baptist Church, for his willingness to boldly proclaim the need to reach out to the Muslim world.

Finally, I want to dedicate this book to Christian ministries such as Love For Muslims, (which is an arm of Advancing Native Missions), which have dedicated their time and effort to inform and train people how to witness to the Muslims living among us.

Dr. Alfonse Javed

ACKNOWLEDGEMENTS

I want to thank God for His grace that was given to me. I was not saved through an evangelistic campaign, but by the strong conviction of the Holy Spirit concerning the sin in my life and my desperate need to know Jesus Christ.

I also want to thank the Lord for the freedom I have today in the United States. The freedom of expression available in the United States of America has made it possible for me to write this book. Moreover, it is a great blessing to express my knowledge, understanding and experience without any fear of what might happen to me.

NOTE FROM
THE AUTHOR

This book condemns any deceptive technique to evangelise Muslims. It also condems any Christian effort to bridge the gap between Muslims and Christian by compromising the word of God. Particularly, Chrislam, the Insider Movement, and the Common Creed document signed by Western so called Christian leaders.

PREFACE

It was 2010 when Hephzibah House, a ministry in New York City, opened its doors to me to come and work as a missionary. I honestly did not have any idea how or what I could do to reach out to Muslims in this city. There are over 10 million Muslims from around the world living in North America; New York City is a reflection of every nation, culture, and religion.

Lois K. Ewald, director of Hephzibah House, has dedicated her life as a long time missionary in the city. Lois prayed with me and suggested I continue to pray for the LORD's direction. I started personal evangelism to Muslims by building relationships with unknown Middle Eastern, Arab, and South Asian men working in the streets of New York City.

As time passed, God began bringing new things to my attention. I found that New York City has a very different perspective about religion. For instance, I discovered that Islam is considered an enemy as well as a friend. I realized that church-going Christians were very confused regarding how to address the growing population of Muslims in the city. Thus, no one seemed to have the answer. It is important to point out that there were a number of evangelistic tracks available. However, some were based on a Western perspective of Islam, thus they lacked an accurate understanding of true Islam. Furthermore, several evangelistic tracks simply ignored the fact that Muslims are all about community, *brotherhood*, and family.

I could not find a document written from an Islamic perspective to communicate to Christians how to reach out to Muslims. Thus, I found it imperative to develop a guide for churches, especially in the West, to help them understand

Islam. I came across a number of books which certainly challenge the West to take action. These resources were very informative: they provided warnings about the imminent danger if the West fails to learn about Islam. Moreover, they stressed the need for Christians to develop a solid strategy regarding how to be friends with Muslims and reach out to them with the Good News. However, I failed to place my finger on a book that I could recommend to church leaders which could equip them to engage and impact Muslims living in New York City, throughout the United States and abroad.

I was born and lived for over twenty years in a Muslim country. I believe this gives me sufficient foundational knowledge and experience about Islam as a culture, religion, education system, politics/government and society. I have also lived six years in the West, which provides me with ample experience to enable me to bring both cultures together to address the core of the issue: reaching out to Muslims with the gospel of Christ Jesus.

CONTENTS

INTRODUCTION

MUST READ

In today's world of conflict and change, no one can escape the reality that Islam is spreading very fast. Since 9/11, the Muslim population has doubled in the United States of America. Muslims are building mosques and Islamic centers throughout the country. There is an increasing fear among Americans of the imminent threat of terrorism by Muslims in America. What does Islam teach about terrorism? What is Jihad? What does Islam teach about Christians and Jews? What are the basic beliefs of Muslims? Are all Muslims extremists? How about the ones living among us? Do Muslims hate non-Muslims (specifically Christians and Jews)? Is Islam a religion of peace? These and many other questions will be answered in this book. Understanding Islam is the only way to reach out to Muslims in America and worldwide.

The Muslim Next Door, is a guide for churches and individuals to evangelize Muslims. I do not believe you can evangelize Muslims only through traditional evangelistic approaches. However, a clear understanding of pure Islamic knowledge can make a difference in our relationships with Muslims in our neighborhoods. The Bible teaches us that "God is not willing that any should perish" (1 Peter 3:9 AKJV). If we know that our Muslim neighbors are walking in darkness, we need to step up and reach out to them with the light. Jesus said "I am the light of life" (John 8:12).

Five times a day, faithful Muslims pray to Allah "show us the right path" in Arabic "Ih'dina Sirathwal musthakim." This is the sixth verse of the first Surah or chapter of the Qur'an, and it means, "Show us the straight path." In Islam, there is a traditional saying that 'sirathwal musthakim' is a narrow bridge over hell to heaven which is made out of seven torn pieces of hair. The righteous can pass over the bridge without any trials; but the wicked will go to hell. Jesus said, "I am the way, and the truth, and the life; no one comes to the Father but through Me" (John 14:6 NASB). He also warned us that the path to heaven is narrow; no one can go to heaven except through Him. Romans 3:20 says, "No human being will be justified in his sight by deeds prescribed by the law." Although our Muslim friends are very committed to following their holy book and the commandments of their prophet, they will not be able to get into heaven. The Bible is very clear that no one can go to the Father without Jesus. Paul, in 1 Cor. 2:14, writes, "The man without the Spirit does not accept the things that come from the Spirit of God, for they are foolishness to him, and he cannot understand them, because they are spiritually discerned." 1 Timothy 2:3-4 says God our Savior desires all men to be saved. Thus, the phrase "all men" includes our Muslim neighbors.

This book addresses everything you need to know to witness to a Muslim, whether he or she is a family member, friend, co-worker, classmate, boss, relative, or even a stranger. It provides effective techniques, which have been used for years with an emphasis on reaching those of the Islamic faith. Moreover, the book also includes a section concerning your safety. I understand that some of you are very afraid to talk to Muslims, while others are so fearless that their personal boldness puts them in danger. The section on safety will allow you to avoid any potential danger to you, your co-worker, an evangelist or even your family.

This book provides information on what Muslims believe about the Bible and what they think Christians believe about the Bible. Moreover, it uncovers some of the misunderstandings about the religion of Islam. I have provided both Muslim and Christian perspectives about particular issues, such as the Trinity, the death and resurrection of Christ, the legitimacy of the Bible, as well as guidelines regarding how to handle such issues. This book is an attempt to answer three major Islamic allegations about Christianity:

1. Jesus is not the Son of God (The deity of Christ)

2. The Bible has been changed/corrupted (Validity of the Scriptures)

3. The Death and Resurrection of Jesus Christ (The Good News)

I have spent an enormous amount of time explaining the significance of the validity of the Bible. The reality is if you remove any of these three allegations, the other two will automatically fall to pieces. Thus, I have focused on the validity of the Bible because if you are able to prove this through Islamic sources, including the Quran and Hadith, this provides strong evidence that the Bible is unchanged and without corruption. Moreover, acknowledging the validity of the Bible confirms the deity of Christ and His death and resurrection. Furthermore, I endeavor to follow three steps which I strongly recommend. They are:

1. ● Apologetics
2. ● Education
3. ● Evangelism

Why apologetics?

Apologetics includes how to defend your Christian faith and then present your faith. When you are talking to a Muslim, you cannot present your faith without first knowing how to defend it. Christianity has been attacked by both nominal (and liberal) Christians and non-Christians. There are so many theological issues you need to know before you present your faith to a Muslim. What Muslims believe and why they believe also what they believe about Christianity and the person of Christ is of utmost importance. (For more information on this subject, please refer to my book *Chrislam: Islamic Theology for Christians*.) Once you know how to defend your faith, then you will be able to present your faith.

Why education?

In order to defend and present your faith, you need to receive education regarding the doctrines of your faith. In the case of Muslim evangelism, you need to educate yourself about the history of Islam, the historical relationship between Islam and the West, and about the Quran, the holy book of Muslims. Not only do you need to be educated, but you also need to educate the one to whom you are witnessing. You must know what Islam preaches and teaches. If you know the history of Islam and Christianity, you will be able to share that as part of your witness.

In the West, we think all Muslims who follow the Islamic dress code and eat according to Islamic requirements know everything there is to know about Islam. Unfortunately, the reality is that many Muslims do not know what Islam really teaches. Since most Muslims do not speak Arabic, they do not understand the text of the Quran. Whatever they have been told orally, they have believed for generations. This book provides Qur'anic verses to educate Muslim friends about Islam in order to speak about the person of Christ. I have provided Qur'anic verses in Arabic, Urdu, and English.

Why evangelism?

The book provides evangelistic approaches and techniques, as well as Qur'anic verses in Arabic, Urdu and English that you can use when speaking with a Muslim. In addition, the book includes a number of articles from other authors, with their permission, in regards to Islam in the West. This book is for everyone who is willing to take our Lord seriously. Evangelism can be used in any setting whether you are witnessing to a Muslim or not. However, the special focus of this book is for a Muslim audience. **Personally, I believe our job is not to convert people but to witness to them, and leave the results to the Holy Spirit. Also, we should not compromise on anything that is a contradiction to our Christian beliefs.**

Furthermore, the book is written in a question and answer format that helps the reader to understand commonly asked questions the reader or other individuals may have. Over a period of twelve years, I have collected questions from my visits to different churches and my days teaching at Bible College. They are addressed in this book. All the Qur'anic verses mentioned here contain commentary, or in Arabic *Tafsir*, which is from a Muslim scholar to show how Muslims understand the Qur'anic verses in the 21st century.

Apart from theological and apologetical answers to some of the most commonly asked questions by our Muslim neighbors, this book also encourages the Christian to stay focused on the Scriptures. For example, the Trinity, death, burial and resurrection, and the message of salvation should be very clear. Under no circumstance should one compromise the truth of the Gospel. The cross and Christ should always be the focus of our witnessing. *Insider Movement, Inter-faith dialogue* and many other movements are leaving Christ outside the door when they engage in conversation with Muslims. If one mini-

NO WAY!

mizes the person of Jesus or the Holy Spirit, in any shape or form, one has already left Christianity.

I have tried to provide as many techniques and tools as possible. I would like to remind the reader that no technique or tool is perfect or everlasting. No one ever has or will claim that he has found the formula to convert Muslims. Furthermore, it is not about converting them, but reaching out to them with the Gospel. Besides, it is not our job to convert people. If you are sensitive to the voice of the Holy Spirit, then God will fulfill His promise as it is written, "for the Holy Spirit will teach you in that very hour what you ought to say" (Luke 12:12 NASB).

For example, a Muslim woman called the Manhattan office of *Jews For Jesus*. She asked if there are any Muslims for Jesus. When the call was directed to me, I spoke to her after introducing myself as the director for *Love For Muslims*. The very first comment she made was "I am a Muslim-Christian." Of course, there is no such thing as a Muslim-Christian. Either you are a Christian or you are not. You cannot follow Islam and Christianity at the same time. I used the techniques provided in Chapter 8 of this book to initiate my conversation. I showed her the difference between Muslim salvation and Christian salvation. When I mentioned a few verses from the Qur'an she asked me to hold on for a few seconds because she wanted to open her Qur'an to check the verses. You are encouraged to keep this book handy when you are witnessing to a Muslim because it provides verses from the Qur'an in Arabic and English.

There are many times when the evangelist becomes part of the problem. For example, a leader in a church took my class on Islam **My Neighbor the Muslim.** When I asked the question, "How would you identify whether a person you are talking to is a Muslim or not?" His answer was: "I would say, I notice you have an accent." As much as one might think it would be a good way to identify ethnicity and religious affiliation, it could lead to intimidation. Let's be honest, if I have an accent, I do not want other people to tell me that I have an accent. I would definitely not want a stranger to tell me. After all, you wouldn't tell an overweight person that they are fat.

In addition, another church leader shared how it became offensive to a young Muslim woman from West Africa when she tried to start a nice conversation by saying "Wow! You speak English very well." The response she received was astonishing to her because the young lady screamed, "I went to school, and in

Africa we have schools." I have tried to deal with some similar issues. Starting a conversation with a non-Christian, especially with a Muslim, is a very significant step towards a long-lasting relationship. In a few seconds, either you are accepted or you are rejected.

I pray that this book gives you a clear understanding about Islam and our mandate to reach the Muslim community. I pray that this book becomes a guide for you and your church to reach out to Muslims here in the United States and abroad. My prayer is that you and your church may able to *embrace Muslims with the love of Christ.*

CHAPTER 1

Christian Mandate: Evangelism and Discipleship

This chapter examines some of the very common questions regarding evangelism and discipleship. Moreover, some of the questions regarding discipleship are a little complicated. I must warn you, you might feel a little uncomfortable with the answers. However, sometimes our discomfort can bring us to another spiritual level in our journey with Christ. The focus of this chapter is to provide a clear and precise understanding about the scriptural mandate to evangelize the world and make disciples. Furthermore, I will also briefly discuss the topic of evangelism and discipleship among Muslims. Thus, you or your church can benefit from this chapter in various ways. The questions and answers in this chapter address many of the issues in the Church and in the life of believers. Thus, Pastors, Elders, Deacons, Youth leaders and Sunday School leaders can adopt some of these suggestions to experience rapid growth in the church without compromising the sound doctrines of the Christianity.

Remember
Evangelism is something that every Christian should do, but to evangelize you must conduct an outreach. An outreach is simply a venue or an effort to make yourself available and accessible to those you are trying to witness to. However, the first two elements will be pointless if you fail to make disciples.

Q#1—What is Evangelism?

Answer: You can find hundreds of books on evangelism and most of them give a standard definition of evangelism. Generally, the term refers to the practice of conveying information about a particular set of beliefs to others who do not hold to those beliefs. The term has been commonly used in Christianity as an act of spreading the Good News of Jesus Christ. Jesus Christ, the Son of God, came into this world, died on the cross for the sins of the world. He was buried, rose again on the third day, and ascended back into heaven. He now sits on the right hand of God the Father interceding on our behalf. Those who share such Good News with others are called Christian evangelists. These evangelists communicate their particular beliefs at home, in their neighborhoods, or even overseas. Some evangelists serve as full time missionaries. Many evangelists choose to speak to large or small crowds. According to Colossians 4:2-6, Ephesians 6:19-20, and 1 Peter 3:15, believers are urged to speak the gospel clearly, fearlessly, graciously, and respectfully whenever an opportunity presents itself.

Q#2—Are Muslims familiar with the term *evangelist*?

Answer: This is one of those questions I hear often, and quite honestly I like this question a lot. An Islamic term for evangelism is *TABLIGUE* and the one who performs the duty of *TABLIGUE* is called a *Mubaligh*. In English *mubaligh* is an evangelist. Every Muslim is called to share his or her faith with non-Muslims. Muslims are more eager to tell others about their faith than members of any other religious group. They appear to be very bold in their faith. In most instances, they act very kind but are also aggressive; they will speak to you as if they know everything. Their arguments might feel compelling at the moment, but underneath there is a personal motive to convert you to Islam. However, this does not apply to all Muslims.

In my personal research and experience, I have found that although the Qur'an *Sura* 2:256 says "there is no compulsion in the religion (Islam)," if you leave the religion of Islam you will be cut off from everything and most of the time your life will be in danger. Therefore, once you are brought into Islam, then Muslims believe you are a Muslim for life. Thus, if you attempt to leave your life is endangered. Many of the Muslim evangelists are like those salesmen that rip you off and still you say, "Wow! I can't believe I let them talk me into buying that." They are extremely skilled.

I remember in February 2010, I was looking for a specific camera for my fiancé's birthday. I went to downtown Manhattan in New York City where there are many electronic shops. These shops are mainly owned by South Asians and Middle Easterners. As soon as I entered one shop, I was treated like a prince by the salesmen. Moreover, two salesmen started showing me different cameras, one after another. They were showing so many different cameras that I felt intimidated. I asked them to please not bring out all these cameras from the showcases. I asked the price of a couple of the cameras. The written prices were very high. One was $650.00 and the other one was about $400.00 I thanked them and said that I would like to check the prices at other camera shops and then make a decision. Doesn't that sound logical?

Suddenly, a man behind me, who seemed to be older than my dad, started yelling, "So you are here to waste our time!" One of the men who assisted me at the counter started asking me how much I would pay. Now in this good cop and bad cop game, I found myself becoming very nervous and feeling coerced. I told him I didn't know how much these cameras were really worth. The man said, "How about $180.00." Well, from $600.00 to $180.00 was a pretty big drop in price, yet I still did not know the true/actual price/value. Anyway, long story short, I paid $200.00 including taxes for the camera. The moment I walked out of the shop, I said, "Wow! I can't believe they made me buy this camera!" It was then that noticed the box was open and the camera that I had purchased was a used camera. I returned to the shop within five minutes. To my surprise, the nice salesman was not nice anymore. The man who yelled at me previously, asked me what I wanted. I demanded my money back because they had intimidated me. I was upset, besides the camera was used and I was not satisfied with the product. They were very rude and refused to allow me to return the camera. Furthermore, one man told me: "we're not holding a gun to your head." Well, I still have the camera and the memories of such a horrible ordeal. I decided not to buy anything else from these shops. I buy from reputable stores because I know I can return items easily and will be treated with respect. Oh, I forgot to mention the camera I bought was sold for $80.00 on Amazon.com!

I admire these salesmen for their skills, but at the same time I learned a valuable lesson that *when someone is very nice, gentle and kind to us, we are more vulnerable to accept whatever is being offered. Furthermore, this occurs when our knowledge is very limited compared to the one who is talking to us.*

This story is very similar when it comes to arguing with Muslims. They will not let you check to verify whether or not the information they are telling you is correct. They will keep pounding away until you give in. Although, it seems very pushy, and intimidating it works; their determination and zeal to convert people to Islam encourages them to be more persistent. Therefore, it is important to watch out when one is aggressive or seems very kind just to present his or her personal agenda.

Q#3—Don't you think many Christian evangelists do that, too?

Answer: Good point. I would not defend these evangelists. I have seen many of them. As a matter of fact, I have witnessed this type of evangelism more so in New York City than anywhere else. I call them *Aggressive Evangelists*. They are eager to share but they do not hold to sound doctrine. If you ask them about their church affiliation or leader, most of them claim that they do not need a leader because God is their leader. One must be discipled by someone as well as disciple others. In some cases, I have found these aggressive evangelists preaching the agenda of a cult leader or simply the wrong Gospel. Such Christian evangelists seem to be bold, but are way off target.

Q#4—Should we downplay the message when we evangelize?

Answer: Certainly not. There is one truth and that truth is Jesus. We cannot compromise on the teaching and character of Jesus Christ. No, you should not soften the message, but you should be gentle in your presentation. As an evangelist, you can be passionate but if you are not gentle, people will not see Jesus in you or in your testimony. Jesus' earthly ministry was indeed a model for every Christian missionary and evangelist to come. When I read Matthew, Mark, Luke and John, I hear Jesus in all His compassion and passion. Moreover, I picture Him speaking with passion and a loud voice because there were no microphone and loudspeakers. Thus, in order to talk to thousands of people, Jesus must have spoken very loudly. Yet, He was gentle and kind and people were drawn to Him and followed him wherever He went.

For example, in Matthew 14:13-21 and Matthew 15:32-39, there are two separate accounts about the miracle of Jesus providing food for thousands of people. We know this because Jesus Himself talked about both events in Matthew 16:8-10. In the first account, 5000 people were fed with five loaves and two fish and in the second account with seven loaves and "a few small fish.... 4000 men besides woman and children were fed." Today, when we look at our world in terms of the total number of men vs. women and children, it is very low. It was the same case during Jesus' time. Roughly at least 10,000 people were fed that day.

If I am speaking to a crowd of 10,000 people even with a microphone—I have to have a very loud voice, and must speak at the top of my lungs. I believe there is a very fine balance in yelling and being loud. You can be gentle, kind, and compassionate in a loud voice, but when you yell it scares people away. How could Jesus claim, "Take my yoke upon you and learn from me, for I am gentle and humble in heart, and you will find rest for your souls" (Matthew 11:29) if people did not witness that? Although Jesus was talking spiritually, people witnessed his gentleness and humbleness.

The work of an evangelist is to proclaim the truth and call people to repentance. You can't call for repentance unless you show people what they need to repent from. If you mildly lay down the Scriptures you do not have much chance to call people to repentance. You cannot share the Good News without making people realize that their sin is bad news.

Q#5—What do you suggest?

Answer: First, as a Christian evangelist, you must not compromise sound doctrine. Second, in your effort to reach out to the lost, you must not seek to please people rather than God. Be bold. Tell people the truth according to the Scriptures; without Christ we are already condemned. Once you have done this, then you can communicate the Good News. Let the Scriptures, "the living Word of God," speak to the hearts of sinners.

Let me give you an example. It is clearly stated in Scripture that: *"for all have sinned and fallen short of the glory of God"* (Romans 3:32), and that: *"the wages of sin is death"* (Romans 6:23). That is the bad news but the verse does not end there it continues with Good News: *"but the gift of God is eternal life in Christ Jesus our Lord."*

The Scriptures teach that it was God who reached out to us, not the other way around.

Romans 5:8 *"But God demonstrates his own love for us in this: While we were still sinners, Christ died for us."*

Now the next step according to Scripture is:

Romans 10:9-10 *"If you declare with your mouth, 'Jesus is Lord,' and believe in your heart that God raised him from the dead, you will be saved. For it is with your heart that you believe and are justified, and it is with your mouth that you profess your faith and are saved."*

Romans 10:13 *"Everyone who calls on the name of the Lord will be saved."*

Q#6—What is your definition of evangelism?

Answer: My definition of evangelism is somewhat different from most of the definitions you may find in most books. Furthermore, my definition is not commonly taught in most churches. In my experience, I have found evangelism to be a process of discipleship. Matthew 28:19-20 commands us to make disciples: "Therefore go and *make disciples* of all nations, baptizing them in the name of the Father and of the Son and of the Holy Spirit, and teaching them to obey everything I have commanded you. And lo, I am with you always, even to the very end of the age." So discipleship precedes any other action. However, Mark 16:15 says, "He said to them, "Go into all the world and *preach the good news* to all creation." Looking at both verses, one might point out the difference between *making disciples* vs. *preaching the good news*. Traditionally, an evangelist is someone who goes to spread the fire of the gospel. He or she shares a general message and invites the people to respond by giving their lives to Jesus and by joining a church or group to be discipled in the faith.

This is exactly what MT. 28:19-20 says

However, in Muslim evangelism, it must begin with discipleship, which means building a relationship. The purpose of evangelism is to call people to repentance. Moreover, the purpose of discipleship is to lead people to repentance. You live your life and share yourself with those to whom you are mentoring. Your time, money, food and knowledge are used to guide and nourish your disciples. Evangelism must be discipleship-oriented in order to make Jesus personal to everyone who hears the good news. Islam is man's efforts to please God; and through works, they believe they gain entry into heaven. As Christians, our job is not to convert people but to witness to them. We should not compromise with anything that contradicts our Chris-

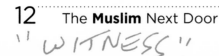

"WITNESS"

tian beliefs. Building relationships through friendship with Muslims must be genuine and unconditional.

Q#7—This is confusing. I thought discipleship comes after one has placed his or her faith in Christ?

Answer: I understand your confusion. It always confuses people because the Christian concept of discipleship is to mentor and train those who profess their faith in Jesus Christ. In the traditional sense, discipleship begins after one accepts Christ and God helps him or her to grow into spiritual maturity. I have no objection to that, but when I say *discipleship* I am referring to the process of developing an honest, trustworthy, and brotherly relationship with the lost person. The same kind of relationship we develop with the one who has accepted Christ to show how to live the Christian life. As I said, evangelism is generally a call to repentance but this kind of discipleship leads to repentance. In my personal ministry, I have seen it happen over and over again. I continue building relationships, continue mentoring and discipling, Consequently, the lost person asked questions and finally accepted Christ. Jesus discipled His disciples first and then asked, "But who do you say that I am?" (Matthew 16:15).

Q#8—What is more important, evangelism, discipleship or outreach?

Answer: I believe they are interconnected, one cannot function on its own. Evangelism-Outreach-Discipleship is like a threefold ministry. Christians must evangelize, but to conduct evangelism you have to have an outreach. Some evangelists use crusades like Billy Graham did throughout his life. Others use holistic ministry such as Samaritan's Purse (Billy Graham's son Franklin Graham) or World Vision. Many local churches plan activities to have access to the lost. Your outreach activities are a platform to evangelize the lost. Putting an event together is an outreach, for example, filling a box with Christmas gifts to send to the less fortunate overseas is an outreach. Moreover, putting a team together to go to meet the needs of indigenous people in a place where natural disaster has devastated the land is also a form of outreach.

Furthermore, medical, food, education, television ministry, all fall under the category of outreach to evangelize the non-Christians. However, all the money, time, and energy that volunteers spend to make such outreaches successful will not bear fruit if there is no substantial plan to disciple the seekers (those who respond to the message of Gospel). In the same way, your evangelism will not do any good for the Body of Christ if you are not discipling those who accept Christ. Therefore, Evangelism-Outreach-Discipleship go hand in hand.

Let's examine a real life scenario. I quickly discovered no one was reaching out to Muslim Pakistanis in New York City. Most missionaries involved in Muslim evangelism are either focused on West African Muslims, Turkish Muslims, or other groups of Muslims from South Asia, but not Pakistanis. In Brooklyn, there is place called little Pakistan. Coney Island Avenue has five mosques that include Islamic centers. In that Muslim community, no church was found. I started praying for the area, and after a few months, God allowed me to meet someone at a pastoral conference in New Jersey. The brother is in seminary and looking for an opportunity to serve God in an unchurched area. When I shared about the need in the little Pakistan area, he committed himself right away to meet me in the area every Tuesday. Since then, another brother has joined us. We have been coming together to pray for the area. We talk to individuals on a one to one basis. However, for evangelism, we have been doing a different outreach. I recognize that I cannot stand in middle of the road and start preaching. First, there is a security issue. Second, the community does not welcome Christians who are speaking out about Christianity. Our vision was to plant a church in that area, so the following steps were needed to plant a church:

- Evangelism: We needed to evangelize the area.

- Outreach: In order to evangelize we had to have a massive amount of outreaches in the area.

- Discipleship: Out of the outreach (evangelistic campaign) we were to make disciples, so that they may become disciple-makers.

Q#9—Are all Christians obligated to evangelize? Is an evangelist also a disciple maker?

Answer: According to the Great Commission, Jesus called us to be disciple makers. I would like to introduce an odd term, *Discipler-maker.* I define a discipler-maker as one who is not only making disciples but also teaching them how to make disciples. To understand the concept of discipler-maker I would like you to look at the Parable of the Talents with a different perspective. The parable can be found in Matthew 25:14-30. The master was pleased with his first two servants because they were faithful in carrying out the unspoken commandment of the master. V.15 indicates a unique aspect of the deal: "to each according to his ability." So the master knew the slaves or servants personally, their work ethic, their education, capability and faithfulness. When the master returned after a long time, he settled his accounts with them. The first two brought forth double what they were entrusted with. The master responded with the same answer to both "Well done, good and faithful servant! You have been faithful with a few things; I will put you in charge of many things. Come and share your master's happiness!" (Matt. 25:14 v. 21 and v. 23). When the one who was given one talent brought forth the talent given to him without any additional profit earned on it, the master was angry with his actions, "You wicked, lazy servant! So you knew that I harvest where I have not sown and gather where I have not scattered seed? Well then, you should have put my money on deposit with the bankers, so that when I returned I would have received it back with interest" (v.26-27).

In this parable, although the master did not give specific job instructions or instruction on what to do with the talents, it was understood. However, Christ gave us clear instructions on how to make disciples.

Q#10—What is a discipler-maker, and how it is different from a disciple maker?

Answer: For a church to grow, it is important for that Church to bring in more people. Many churches have very good programs to attract people. Some churches are still within the boundaries of sound Christian doctrine. Unfortunately, many churches have strayed away from such a concept. However, a disciple maker should be what the Scripture commands us to be. Each Christian has to be entrusted according to his or her ability for discipling. Discipling is the best way to increase congregants and still remain within the boundaries of orthodoxy without turning the Church into a social club. In worldly business terms, it is called Multilevel Marketing (MLM). The church model was introduced by the early church community where each believer was responsible for making disciples and teaching the disciples how to disciple.

The question is whether you were discipled in a way that led you to become discipler-maker. If you have not been discipled to become a discipler-maker, chances are you perhaps have only one or two talents to show to your "master on his return after a long time." You still have time and I believe this book will help you to become a discipler-maker.

Remember

It is good to be a Disciple Maker but it is also great to be Discipler-Maker (producer of disciple makers).

Let's examine your Christian life in light of the Scriptural mandate to make disciples. If you look at your Christian life and try to evaluate your efforts to reach out to the lost, where do you see yourself today? The following chart is an example of a Discipler-Maker who made only three discipler-makers in his/her entire life but brought forth tens of hundreds times more then he was entrusted with.

Where do you see yourself and your church?

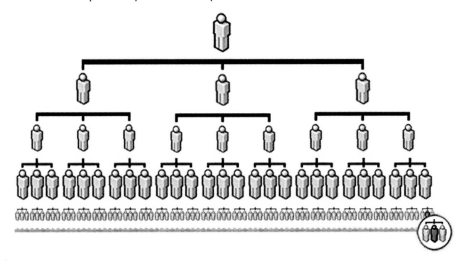

Personal Notes and Comments:

_____

_____

_____

_____

_____

_____

_____

_____

_____

_____

_____

_____

_____

_____

_____

_____

_____

_____

_____

_____

CHAPTER 2

Church Mandate: Missions and Missionaries

This chapter examines Muslim evangelism and missions. There are many questions regarding how Islam is spreading in recent times. Consequently, there are many speculations about the spread of Islam. Some Muslim resources claim there are as many as 1.5 billion Muslims throughout the world. Moreover, Muslims also claim that there are approximately 10 million Muslims in the United States of America alone. Whether the statistics are valid or not, no one can deny that Islam is the fastest growing religion in the world. The Western resources claim that Islam is spread by the sword. The Eastern resources reject such a claim and blame the Western media and literature as responsible for such anti-Islamic teachings.

The questions and answers in this chapter will help Christians to understand what other ways Islam is becoming a dominant religion in the world. There are no swords, yet Islam continues to invade civilization and the cerebral territory of the Western world.

Q#11—How about Muslim missionaries? Do Islamic countries send missionaries to other countries to spread Islam?

Answer: Yes, Muslims are very active in missionary work. They have strategic ways of spreading Islam in the world. In Islam, their mission doctrine is called *Dawah*. Before Arabs found oil, they were focused on aggressive actions and direct war (Jihad) in order to spread Islam. However, since the collapse of the Ottoman Empire, after World War I, all this has changed. The abundance of oil and minerals has provided Muslim nations with new means to reach out to the West and to the non-Muslim world. I have received many testimonies from Muslims in the United States and abroad. Many wealthy Islamic countries use money to manipulate governments and individuals within these governments to promote their branch of Islam in a particular country. Today, we see the West turning into Muslim occupied land through immigration. Who would have ever thought that could be a productive way to invade a land?

One of the missionary approaches in Islam is immigration. In Islam, the term *HIJRAT or HIJRA* is well known because of the prophet of Islam, Muhammad's migration. In his early ministry, he fled from Mecca, the birthplace of Muhammad to Medina (The two most sacred places for Muslims, where they perform the duty of Hajj or 'pilgrimage'). On his return from Medina, he became the ruler of both Mecca and Medina. The prophet Muhammad provided the Immigration or migration model to spread Islam. In the last century, it has been used excessively in Europe, South America, and North America. Today, in Europe, the ratio of the Muslim population to others is 1 to 8. Muammar Gaddafi, an Islamic hero and dictator of Libya, stated if Muslims wait for a couple of more decades, "the whole world will be ours without blowing up buildings and killing others."

Q#12—I heard that Islam is becoming dominant because of reproduction?

Answer: It's not entirely because of reproduction, but reproduction is playing a vital role in making the adherers of Islam the major population of the world. No Muslim will deny the truth that it is God's grace that they are becoming a major religion and it is due to reproduction. Muslims consider that a natural way of making Muslims. In contrast to Christianity, every baby born in a Muslim household receives his confirmation of being a Muslim when he is born. The mullah of the local mosque (sometime a friend or a relative if an Imam is not available) recites certain portions of the Qur'an into the baby's ear. I have met many Muslims who openly consider reproduction God's weapon for making entire world Muslim. The statistics point towards their hope that Muslims will, in a few decades, control Europe. Europe will be no more, but will be a Muslim state because of the reproduction.

Q#13—Do Muslims have mission agencies, and do they support their missionaries?

Answer: Yes, all Muslim and non-Muslim countries have Muslim mission agencies. They are usually called *JAMAT*, which literally means groups. These groups are everywhere and are connected to the main funding agencies on the basis of their Islamic doctrine. Some of them are military-minded groups who operate training centers to actively conduct Jihad. From time to time, when different groups need help with military action, they contact such groups and recruit *Mujahedeen* (the ones who carry out jihad) for their purpose.

For example, during the 1980's, the United States, Saudi Arabia, Pakistan and a few other nations collectively supported some of these groups to fight against the USSR. In recent years, the 9/11 tragedy was a result of such missionary work, and even after that, when the U.S declared war on terrorism, these Muslim groups formed alliances to fight against the UN forces in Afghanistan and Iraq. At the same time, wealthy Muslim countries like Saudi Arabia started investing money in the West for missionary projects. After 9/11, Saudi Prince Alwaleed bin Talal Al-Saud donated $20 million to Harvard University and $20 million to Georgetown University to start Islamic centers. He also gave millions to small schools and colleges to encourage the same thing. Moreover, The Saudi government has spent billions of dollars throughout the world to spread Wahabism. In New York City, all Muslim chaplains in hospitals are Wahabi. Muslim missionaries are responsible for huge conversions among prison inmates. Recently, I was invited by a church for a mission conference, where I had the privilege of meeting a brother who is involved in prison ministry. He asked me why more and more inmates are accepting Islam. He was amazed at the number of converts. I can say with certainty that the missionary and evangelistic efforts of Muslims are at least parallel to Christian efforts, if not stronger.

Q#14—Are there many denominations in Islam, like in Christianity?

Answer: Islam does not call them denominations. They prefer to be known as sects of Islam. There are two main sects in Islam: Shia and Sunni. The Sunni sect comprises 90% the of Muslim population and the Shia sect comprises 10%. However, one can find more than 170 sects in Islam. Each sect considers itself to be the legitimate Islamic religion and tries to promote its own doctrines. For example, the most extreme branch of Islam is Sunni, and Wahabism is part of Sunni Islam. In addition, extreme sects tend to inspire Muslims by reminding them of the glorious time when Islam was at its peak. They call young Muslims to step up and join the mission to bring Islam back to its original glory. For example, during a live coverage of a telethon, organized by Prince Alwaleed bin Talal Al-Saud of Saudi Arabia, a Saudi official named Sheikh Saad Al-Buraik made the following statement:

"I am against America until this life ends, until the Day of Judgment; I am against America even if the stone liquefies. She is the root of all evils. Muslim brothers in Palestine do not have any mercy, neither compassion, on the Jews, their blood, their money, their flesh. Their women are yours to take, legitimately. God made them yours. Why don't you enslave their women? Why don't you wage jihad? Why don't you pillage them?"

Now remember, Prince Alwaleed bin Talal Al-Saud is the very same man who donated large amounts of money to build Islamic centers in the U.S under the cover of peace and harmony. This event was organized to raise money for the Al Quds Intifada (a terrorist group in Palestine).

Many analysts and scholars believe that such ideologies are part of the religious doctrine, which is based on brain washing and indoctrinations. Interestingly enough, Islamic prophet Muhammad once prophesied that there would be 73 sects and all would go to hell except one.

Q#15—Have you ever met any Muslim missionaries?

Answer: In 2003, I was flying to England. I was seated next to a handsome young man. The man was dressed like an Englishman, spoke like an Englishman and looked like an Englishman. After half an hour of conversation, he asked me what I did for a living. I told him I was a missionary and he said "Interesting! I am a missionary too." I was very excited to know that I found someone who had the same interests as I did. I asked him what mission organization he worked with and he replied in Arabic. I was totally shocked. It was because he told me that he was on his mission to England after finishing his training in Pakistan. He would be serving among the English people. It just blew my mind that such a sophisticated man with a modern look was so conservative in his Islamic beliefs. I just could not believe it. There are many

Muslims who choose honorable professions like medical doctors, university professors, and engineers, pilots, priest (Imams), chaplains because they want to use those means to reach out to non-Muslim people.

In the United States of America many of these missionaries work not only in the above-mentioned fields they are also working as diplomats and religious rights activists. They use the constitution of the United States to spread Islam.

Q#16—Does it mean Islam and Christianity are the same?

Answer: There are many similarities in Islam and Christianity, but the fundamental beliefs are entirely different. If we compromise on the deity of Christ, we are not Christians; if Muslims compromise on the deity of Christ, they are not Muslims.

Q#17—Are all Muslim missionaries and evangelists actively involved in Jihad?

Answer: In Islam there are two types of Jihad: *Jihad-Akbar* (Kabir) and *Jihad-Asgar* (Sagir). Akbar is the greater, and Asgar is the lesser. In these Modern times, many Muslim scholars argue that Jihad-Akbar is to fight (or struggle) with one self against such things as: selfishness, unrighteousness, and anything which might urge someone to commit sin. For some reason, Jihad-Asgar has become more popular and has been divided into sub categories. I divide them into two categories: intellectual jihad and military jihad. In the West, many terrorist attacks have been carried out by Muslims who are considered to be military jihadists, while those who plan and provide the resources for these violent acts are called intellectual jihadists. Moreover, Moderate Muslims continue to condemn acts of violence, but many Muslims continue to celebrate the destruction of the West. In many cases the destruction of their own countries, when the counties are under an opposing regime or government is celebrated as well.

Q#18—Which is more dangerous, intellectual jihad or military jihad?

Answer: I firmly believe that intellectual jihad is more dangerous than military jihad. Why? You may argue that the intellectual jihadists are not killing anyone; it is the Military jihadists who are killing others to proclaim the glory of Islam. Yes, you are partially correct. Let me ask you something, what is easier: to protect ourselves when we know who our enemy is and how capable the enemy is, or when we do not know who we are fighting against? Chasing ghosts is not possible. Intellectual terrorists and jihadists are like ghosts. They can be anyone, and they can be anywhere. One of the best examples is the plan to build the mosque at ground zero. They used their constitutional right for freedom and equality. Democracy, which has been the underlying foundation of our nation, has been used by these intellectual terrorists to destroy our democracy and to carry out their impure ambitions.

Q#19—Is there any difference between American Muslims and the non-American Muslims?

Answer: If you are referring to the Nation of Islam, I would like to point out that the majority of Muslims do not even consider the Nation of Islam Muslims. As I previously mentioned, there are many sects of Islam and all claim the other is wrong. For this very reason, Muslims kill each other. However, in America, it is different. American Muslims are an exception in many ways. First of all, they consider themselves exceptional because they reason, read, and rethink Islamic traditions and practices. They have more voice than in any other Muslim country. However, over the last decade, American Muslims have been deluded with many new teachings. It is hard to say whether there are still exceptional cases.

Only 7-10 million Muslims live in America and many of them are first generation immigrants. Some even claim that the Muslims outside of American do not know what true Islam is. That is why they are so violent and do not respect life and do not tolerate other religions. However, billions of Muslims throughout the world consider Muslims in America part of Western propaganda and do not validate what comes from Islamic centers and mosques in the United States.

Q#20—Is there a difference between God and Allah?

Answer: In general, Muslims worship the God of Abraham, Isaac, and Jacob. This is the same God Jews and Christian claim to worship. In Muslim countries, Muslims try to differentiate the God of Christians and Jews from Allah. Moreover, in the United States, many conservative Muslims recommend using the name Allah rather than that of God because He is the God of Christians and Jews. In the East, one can find written material from Muslims to prove that Allah is the true God and that Christians and Jews do not worship him the same. Theologically, in Islam, God is a furious being who is to be feared. A Muslim is forced to do things to satisfy his or her conscience so that he is righteous before God and God is well pleased. The very essence of the Islamic belief system is based on insecurity. You will never know until the day you die and face God whether or not you are allowed to live in His presence. One can distinguish the Islamic God from the Christian God on the basis of Christian and Islamic theology.

Remember

Qur'an 2:98 "Who is an enemy to Allah, and His angels and His messengers, and Gabriel and Michael! Then, lo! Allah (Himself) is an enemy to the disbelievers."

Matthew 5:44-45 "But I say to you, Love your enemies and pray for those who persecute you, so that you may be able sons of your Father who is in heaven; for he makes his sun rise on the evil and on the good, and sends rain on the just and on the unjust."

I know many churches that preach a similar God as Islam believes. Actually in Islamic countries, under the influence of Islamic culture, Christian theology has adopted the Character of the Islamic God. In many ways Christian churches in Islamic countries work like a Mosque and church members act like Muslims, but their believe about the Trinity and the birth of Christ and the resurrection distinguish their theology from Islam.

Islam	Christianity
Furious/ Scary God Forced to do things to please Him	Loving and Kind God Freedom and Choice
Work	Grace
Insecurity of salvation	Surety of salvation

Personal Notes and Comments:

_____

_____

_____

_____

_____

_____

_____

_____

_____

_____

_____

_____

_____

_____

_____

_____

_____

_____

_____

CHAPTER 3

Evangelism: Tools and Techniques

This chapter will help you and your church become more effective evangelists. There are a number of questions that I have been asked over a period of time. I believe each question is very valuable and could help you to learn more about evangelism and the nature of Islam. I have included many different techniques and tools that I have collected and used over the years in my personal evangelism. I have modified some of the most common Christian evangelistic techniques, specifically when dealing with the Muslim population. It is important to recognize the significance of culture: it is just not possible to use the same evangelism techniques to reach out to all ethnic groups. You can use this to train a group of congregants in a seminar or workshop.

Q#21—Are there special evangelistic techniques that you have found to be very useful in reaching out to Muslims?

Answer: There are a number of techniques available for you to use to reach the lost world. The ingredient to a successful approach is to spend twice the amount of time you spend on evangelizing on your knees before God. The hearts of people are under God's control for Jesus said, "I will build My church." We are only instruments; He is an author, doctor and creator. As we spend time on our knees before Him, He prepares the ground for us to reap the harvest. We must be aware of the enemy—spiritual powers and principalities—because the spiritual world is more real than the natural world. The spiritual world is eternal; the natural world is temporary and only a shadow of the real world. Therefore, without God's hand in and upon your work, your eloquent speech, sharp debate, loving attitude and sweet talk will accomplish nothing of eternal value.

> ### Remember!
> Pray more than ever, because evangelizing Muslims requires constant prayer.

Q#22—Who is called to evangelize a Muslim?

Answer: To answer the question, we need to look at the why, when, where, what and how drill. We will discuss how in detail but the following 4W's will help you to remember a few crucial things.

- **Why:** Because Jesus commanded
- **When:** At any and at all times
- **Where:** Starting from your home (neighborhood) to the ends of the Earth
- **What:** Everything you know from the Scriptures about the Good News
- **How:** ?

Q#23—You did not answer "how." Could you please tell me how this can be done?

Answer: To answer the "how," we will need to look into a few different approaches that you might want to adopt in reaching others. **Remember: one set of techniques might not work for every occasion.** Also, depending on your personality you need to find the best fit for you.

The Performer Technique

In this technique, you select a few members of your own team to go to different strategic points in the audience. Choose a speaker with a strong voice and position him or her in such a way that all the audience can see and hear him or her clearly. Therefore, when a question is asked, everyone in the audience is able to hear both the question and the response. Although this manual is developed for the New York City area, it can be used with minor changes in any major city of the world. You can adopt any of the following performance styles:

Subway approach (For overseas readers use this in a Bus or Train)

Have you ever taken time to observe an audience for Christian evangelism while riding a subway? I have seen both males and females among all kinds of ethnic groups in my audience while riding the subway. Diversity makes everything better. Some people are intimidated by other ethnic groups, and often one group is more open to hear about spiritual things while the other is all about the theatrical performance. Regardless of the busy life city people live, most are looking for something with which to occupy them on the train.

I have seen people reading books with absolutely preposterous titles. I have seen many people playing games on their iPods and cell phones, listening to music, surfing the net (if the internet is available), or simply browsing their electronic devices. Furthermore, I have even seen people watching movies or events. On many occasions, performers come through the cars collecting money. A missionary friend told me about a brother in Christ who performs similarly as a form of witness. It is an awesome way to reach the lost. They will listen to you.

Q#24—What should be my opening line to initiate a conversation? Where should I stand or sit while sharing?

Answer: I would begin my evangelizing with something like this: *"Hi! You've seen many performances on this subway car, but I want to give you something you may have never received, and it's free."* I want to encourage you to find a strategic location based on audio and visual appearance. This is absolutely imperative.

You cannot afford missing either one of these natural resources. Audio is actually more important. I would also suggest that you dress nicely because if you look homeless, your audience could be distracted by your appearance and question your authenticity and genuineness rather than the claims of the Christ that you are presenting. That is the last thing you want! Their minds are already weary with everyday life, so your claim must be so appealing with your gestures and approach that it has the power to snap them out of their thoughts. I have encountered a few people in the subway who received more money simply because they were well dressed. Their appearance helped to legitimize their claims. Even someone like me, who operates on donations, was impressed to give something because it came across as genuine and authentic.

Q#25—Is there anything I need to watch out for when using this kind of approach?

Answer: There are many things but first and foremost one must maintain integrity. The next claim you make is powerful. You say, "Actually it's funny that I am here to share with you something that my father has paid for." I can almost guarantee you that through the power of the Holy Spirit and the result of those prayers you have offered before His throne, God will give you honor in the eyes of your audience. Now tell them: "Ladies and gentlemen, I need your attention for 30 seconds." (Important side note—please keep your talk to less than 30 seconds and let one of the team members alert you after 30 seconds). I do not become more and more like Christ in spirit if I forget the concept of time and space. Therefore, I always have a backup plan to hold me accountable to my allotted time. You can choose any sentences as the Spirit leads you because I am sure that you have their attention now.

Another essential step in evangelism is follow-up. Many evangelists feel that when they have shared their faith and people have responded, then their duty is over and now the Holy Spirit will do the follow up. Yes, God is able to do that because Christ promised to build His church. If that is the case, then why are we involved in evangelism? As we have discussed earlier, we are doing it out of our love and gratitude to Him who has set us free from the bondage of sin and slavery, which is eternal death. It is good to share your faith with others but it is very important to follow-up with those who are interested.

Particularly, in the performer technique, you do not get the chance to disciple or go into detail on what to do next. In many cases, people think about what you have spoken and feel convicted. They may want to make their decision but the shortness of time does not allow them to stand up, come up, and even get into a conversation with someone. In performance evangelism, you may not have enough time to give an altar call. Therefore, use the available resources to do the follow-up. For example: pocket-size copies of the Gospel of John are a beautiful resource. They can be obtained through THE

POCKET TEXTAMENT LEAGUE, P.O BOX 800 LITITZ, PA 17543 or www.poletpower.org. The introductory pages of this booklet explain why we are sinners, the ultimate result of sin and the solution. A prayer of confession is found at the end of the gospel. This is an amazing resource you can use for free if you order 30 per month.

In addition, I suggest that you distribute an attractive general brochure about your church. Make something available that you consider would be a healthy way to learn about Christ and Christianity and give it out as a gift. Make sure you point out that it is not an ordinary piece of paper. It could change their lives.

Regarding the 30 second speech, I would suggest that you use current events and situations. Choose something from last night's late show or popular topic in the news media. Just a simple message of salvation works every time. When you conclude your message, your team members should be ready to respond immediately. In my case, I would ask for volunteers to come and share what they think about the current situation and event. You have a very short time, so whatever you do try to make it as brief and relevant as you can. A brother who does this type of evangelism on a regular basis uses personal testimonies to open up the interaction.

Q#26—Is this approach applicable or transferable to other places other than a subway?

Answer: Yes it is. Let's look at another popular place where you can find many people and most likely be able to evangelize using the *Performer technique*.

Square approach (crowd)

This is my favorite method of evangelism. Stand in a crowded place. The ability to select a perfect day and location is crucial for greater impact. Let's say Times Square. Position the performer on a high and prominent spot. Start with some claim, as: "Ladies and gentlemen. I have something very unique to share with you." Look around and observe how many are really listening. Continue: "It is free of charge to you."

Start thanking God for the freedom you have in the United States, how awesome NYC is (or whatever city you are in). Share the brief message of salvation. In this kind of situation, you can share something directly from the

Bible, like 1 Cor. 1:18: "For the message of the cross is foolishness to those who are perishing, but to us who are being saved it is the power of God." or Romans 10:9: "That if you confess with your mouth, 'Jesus is Lord,' and believe in your heart that God raised him from the dead, you will be saved." You can certainly start with a Bible story, a short story, or a benevolent act of Christ. Once you have finished your presentation, invite the audience to ask questions. Be prepared for any question, but it would be ideal if the first question comes from a team member.

Q#27—What if someone doesn't have as much time to learn these techniques? What if they are shy? Is there an easier technique?

Answer: I knew you would look for something easier! There is another technique called *storytelling.*

Storytelling approach

I had the privilege of participating in a *storytelling* training conducted by *Story Runner,* which is a project of Campus Crusade. Story telling is a process of educating and memorizing. In olden days, and still in many places today, oral teaching and learning were quite popular, especially in a city like New York where everyone is in a hurry and has little time to read a whole book. I heard about someone who loved reading books, but for the last fifteen years had little opportunity to read for pleasure. His gigantic collection of books looked very impressive when you enter his reading room. His domestic circumstances changed somehow and he went through an ugly divorce. After a time, he felt it useless to waste his life doing something he didn't enjoy, so he discontinued his regular 9 to 5 job. He had so much free time he began reading his collection of books. Interestingly, he describes the difference between reading a book and listening to a book on audio CD. Fifteen years of doing this enabled him to visualize and almost memorize the stories he heard. Now he prefers listening to a book versus reading a book. It might be different for you, depending on your preference, but the bottom line is that the listening process trains the listener to memorize the story faster.

Long ago, the story tellers were popular. Moreover, good story tellers always tried to be creative in their communication to their audiences. Their stories, as well as their storytelling skills, were the foundation of becoming famous. We still remember some of the stories our grandparents told us. I always ask this question in my workshop, "Do you remember a story that someone told you when you were a young child?" The answer is usually yes. I asked a pastor to share his story in one of the workshops on Muslim evangelism. He shared his story with such passion that we could gain insight into his childhood through his gestures. When you hear a story over and over again, it becomes a part of you; and when you retell the story, it becomes so original that listeners can see that it's genuine. Don't you wonder why God has given us His word in story form? From Genesis through Revelation, God told His personal story, as well as man's response to His story. When Jesus started His ministry, He used parables to reach out to the lost sheep of Israel. He literally told stories to the people.

Q#28—Are there certain rules I should follow when telling a story from the Word of God to a Muslim?

Answer: Certainly there are, regardless of whether or not you are telling a story to a Muslim. It might surprise you that Islam spread through storytelling. Whether it was through art, poetry, songs or tales, storytelling became the foundational tool for spreading Islam. Still, today many Muslims don't know what the Qur'an says or where they can find a verse. Everything they know has come from story lines. Actually, the Hadith, the second most holy account in Islam (after the Qur'an) contains the traditions of Muhammad that have been told and retold. If you go to Pakistan or India, you will find these *Darbars* (Shrines) of old Muslim saints who told stories in song, and poetry. The people come and repeat their sad stories to uplift their faith and sing songs about the deeds of such saints.

Storytelling might seem an outdated approach, but to a Muslim that is the best approach you can use. In the Appendix you can find tips on how to craft a Bible story. When you are telling a story, make sure you follow three rules:

Remember!

Three Rules of Crafting

- Keep it less than 3 minutes—4 minutes maximum
- Use common phrases

- Tell the full story
  - ✦ Permission for omission (story runner rule Campus Crusade).
  - ✦ Bad to Add (story runner rule Campus Crusade).

Q#29—Could you be more specific? Is there any model story to share the Good News?

Answer: The answer is the **20 Step Tale.** It would be easy to remember to run your figures, right hand pinky to left hand; and then reverse, from left hand pinky to right hand. Of course this is suggested, but not required.

Following the above three rules, let me show you the **20 Step Tale:**

1. God's existence
2. Creation of the universe and everything in it
3. Creation of man and woman
4. Disobedience
5. Broken relationship (separation from God)
6. God's Promise (to Abraham)
7. Fulfillment of Promise (many children)
8. Disobedience (Children of Abraham disobeyed)
9. God's promise through Isaiah (message of hope)
10. A promised Savior
11. Fulfillment of Promise (Jesus came as the Savior)
12. Miracles of Jesus (proof that Jesus was the promised Savior)
13. Demon-possessed man's story (to show how demons recognized Him)
14. Promise of eternal life and claim "God and I are the same"
15. Blasphemy and execution
16. Resurrection and the forty days of proof

17. Great commission

18. Baptism (undergoing water, a symbol of turning away from your sins)

19. Jesus' ascension into Heaven and the angel's promise of His return

20. Co-operative worship

The following is the 10 Step Tale (shorter version):

1. Story of Creation

2. Story of Noah

3. Story of Abraham

4. Story of David

5. Story of Promised King through Isaiah

6. Story of Mary

7. Story of Blind Man

8. Story of Crucifixion

9. Story of Resurrection

10. Story of physical appearance before 500 and ascension into the heavens

When you start using the 10 Step Tale, remember that Muslims believe in the first 6 stories almost the same way as we do. This gives you a chance to capture their interest about these stories. It is important to note that Muslims believe that Jesus Christ healed the blind, thus, story 7 is not an issue. The major challenges begin with story 8 through story 10. I guarantee if you use the 3-4 minutes rule, and keep the story interesting by using expressive hand gestures and body language, the person you are sharing these stories with will allow you to finish.

Here are a few suggestions and recommendations. When you share with Muslims, you need to point out the significant parts of the stories. For example, in the Creation account, the most significant part of the story is the creation of the Man *Adam*. You must use your whole body to describe the story. When you say that God created man, say He created him from dirt. At this point, bend down and pretend to pick up dirt from the ground and say God formed man out of that. Second, use your hands as if you are making clay out of dirt and use your fingers, pretending that you are forming a man. Third, bring the imaginary clay man close to your mouth and blow air into the imaginary body, stating that God breathed life into his nostrils.

Now when you are telling the story of the Blind Man, you must use your whole body. Let me explain:

> One day Jesus was walking with his disciples and people were following him. A blind man cried out to Jesus, "Jesus Son of David (here shout over the top of your lungs) have mercy on me." Filled with compassion, Jesus asked him, " what do you want me to do for you?" The man pleaded "that I may see." Jesus took dirt (now bend down, just the way you did for the creation of Man by God. Pretend to pick up some dirt). He spit on it (act it out. You may mention it was moistened) and rub it on the eyes of the blind man. (now at this point you must be little more graphic than usual. You should use your fingers, pretending you are forming eye balls out of clay, and then rub the eyes of you partner to demonstration that Jesus not only gave him eye sight but gave him eyes because he was blind by birth).

When you follow the steps I have described, you are leaving a clue for the audience to wonder if this is the same that God did during creation. The most important component of this story is to present Christ as God while mentioning that Jesus is indeed God.

It is crucial that you act out the Crucifixion story. When you say that Jesus was crucified, stretch your arms posing as if you are being crucified. The key point you must make is the cost of Jesus' own life. Please understand that Muslims skip the crucifixion. They acknowledge that someone was crucified in place of Jesus, most likely Judas Iscariot, but they do not acknowledge that the reason why Jesus was crucified was His personal claim of divinity. Muslims have verse after verse from the Qur'an stating that Jesus never said I am the Son of God. Therefore, it is a perfect opportunity to bring this fact up as communicated in the following passage:

> The Jewish priests were not happy with the popularity of Jesus Christ. He, also, claimed that He was the Son of God. They accused him of many things but primarily of blasphemy. So they crucified him.

Furthermore, it is important to emphasize the resurrection with a special emphasis to the 500 eyewitnesses who saw Jesus after His resurrection. In order to use the 10 Step Tale effectively in reaching out to Muslims, you must mention the resurrection (see the details in the Appendix). If you learn the right techniques and follow the first three rules of crafting, I believe your storytelling can become a major tool in reaching out to Muslims.

> ## Remember
>
> You must ask the following three questions:
>
> - Did you understand the story?
> - Do you have any questions?
> - Can I pray with you?

Q#30—Could you please review the process of storytelling technique?

Answer: Sure! Let's review the process of storytelling. Choose a story from the Bible and let someone read it for you. Normally, in a group of five to seven, if one person reads the story and the others listen, everyone should remember enough fragments of the story to reconstruct it without looking at the story in the Bible. Once you have reconstructed the story, verify it with the story in Scripture to make sure you are not missing the essential parts. Now work on phrases and words that might be difficult for your audience to understand.

For example, Muslims do not know what baptism is, but they do know that water is a cleansing and purifying agent. They are obligated to used water and wash certain parts of the body in a specific way to present their body for prayer and worship before God. Ritual cleansing is very important in many other religions. For instance, the Hindus go to *Ganga and Jamnah* (two rivers in India) to be cleansed before their gods. Other stories you could include are: the story of Naaman, Philip and the Ethiopian treasurer, the life of John the Baptist, and Jesus' baptism. The Holy Spirit in Islam refers to the angel Gabriel, so avoid this term; using God's Spirit would be more appropriate. Rather than using the word 'gospel,' the term 'good news' would be more effective.

Q#31—Is there any other technique?

Answer: There are a few more techniques I have used in everyday evangelism. One of them is the Evangelism Explosion approach. I remember the first time I used the Evangelism Explosion approach after my training when I was studying in Athens. Over a period of time, I made some modifications to avoid some of the questions people may raise in terms of emotional decision vs. genuine decision. The Evangelism Explosion approach follows two diagnostic questions:

#1 **Have you come to a place in your spiritual life where you know for certain that if you were to die today, you would go to heaven, or is that something you would say you're still working on?**

#2 **Suppose you were to die today and stand before God and He were to say to you, "Why should I let you into My Heaven?" what would you say?**

It was my first time away from my family. I was very young and homesick in Greece. These diagnostic questions scared me. What if I died? I would not see my family again. I thought of those people who I shared my faith with. How would they feel when I talked about their death? It also made me think about Muslim friends: the very reason they follow God is because they fear Him. They truly believe if they do not work hard, God will consume them with fire. I also wondered: if I give them the diagnostic questions, will I be able to introduce them to the God of the Bible—a loving and kind God, who is also a Just God? Moreover, many Muslims are not afraid of death. Recently, the suicide bombers who have been captured during their attempts due to the malfunction of their explosives confessed that death for the sake of Allah allows them a free entry into heaven. Therefore, it is wise to avoid such sensitive and theological issues, which may potentially get you off the track. The following verses portray how Islamic teachings threaten an individual to follow Islam.

The Qur'an says in:

Surat Al-'Anfāl (The Spoils of War)—8:27

يَـٰٓأَيُّهَا ٱلَّذِينَ ءَامَنُوا۟ لَا تَخُونُوا۟ ٱللَّهَ وَٱلرَّسُولَ وَتَخُونُوٓا۟ أَمَـٰنَـٰتِكُمْ وَأَنتُمْ تَعْلَمُونَ ﴿٢٧﴾

Sahih International

O you who have believed, do not betray Allah and the Messenger or betray your trusts while you know [the consequences].

Tafsir al-Jalalayn

The following was revealed regarding Abū Lubāba Marwān b. 'Abd al-Mundhir: the Prophet (s) had dispatched him to the Banū Qurayza so that they would submit to his [the Prophet's] authority. But they [Banū Qurayza] consulted with him [as to whether they should cede], and he pointed out to them that a slaughter would ensue— for members of his family and his property were among them: O you who believe, do not betray God and the Messenger, and, do not, betray your trusts, that which has been entrusted to you, in the way of religion or otherwise, while you are aware.

Remember!

Tafsir (commentary) is provided throughout this book to give you an advanced notice how a Muslim person will interpret the verse. Sometimes it helps to know the Muslim perspective regardless of what the verse really says. Also, Tafsir provides some of the Islamic historical background about the verse or passage.

Thus, I came to the realization that although both questions were very challenging, at the same time and to some extent, they are very threatening. If someone receives Christ in order to escape the consequences of his or her sins, wouldn't it be using Him for your personal advantage? Would it be right to use Christ as a token to heaven without having a personal relationship with Him? I believe people need to learn about Him and His love for us in order that they may genuinely love Him as He first loved us. I am not even sure about those who receive Christ under pressure or with the impression that if they do not receive Him, they will die without the Jesus Pass to join the party. Besides, what was Jesus' approach? He was compassionate, humble, meek, kind and always reached out to needy people with comfort, peace and a message of hope.

The 20 Step Tale is the story of His unchanging love. Although people continued to disobey, He faithfully continued His grace by promising and fulfilling those promises. **True repentance happens in the heart, not in the mouth or mind.** Such repentance produces faith in Jesus, which becomes the foundation of the hope that one day we will see Him face to face. When that hope grows in Christ through an everyday relationship with Him, it removes all the insecurities and we become certain that no one and nothing can take us out of His hand. (Rom 8:38-39) With true repentance through His genuine love, we find Jesus as our justification and justifier before God.

God is a loving and just God; therefore, He must punish sins. His holiness can't see even a hint of sin. However, when talking to a Muslim, we have to focus on what Jesus preached and the stories He taught: "love your God" and "love your neighbor." You may be surprised to know that more Muslims have come to Christ because of the message of love than any other way. You can use everyday life stories to form a transition to the Bible.

Q#32—What other techniques do you recommend for evangelism?

Answer: One of my favorite techniques is the **ART-Story approach**. Back in the fall of 2003, I learned another technique through an organization called Open Air Campaigns. The ART-Story approach is the combination of both storytelling and Open Air Campaigns sketch boards evangelism. You don't need to be an artist to use this approach. All you need is a little training for drawing. The training can be provided on request or you can buy a DVD from Open Air Campaigns website: www.oacusa.org.

Remember!

Always remember that Muslims have many similar stories as Christians and Jews, so avoid complicating the stories. Use them as a bridge to introduce the story of Jesus Christ as the promised Savior and Son of God.

Personal Notes and Comments:

_____

_____

_____

_____

_____

_____

_____

_____

_____

_____

_____

_____

_____

_____

_____

_____

_____

_____

CHAPTER 4

Apologetics: Evangelism and Islam

This chapter provides more techniques and tools for evangelism. Now you will see more apologetic approaches to Islamic teaching and claims about Christianity, Christ and the Bible. This chapter will address the very simple things we do or don't do that cause doubts within the mind of a person who may have accepted Christ. Sometimes very minor things can become a gigantic stumbling block for potential followers of Christ.

Q#33—What if there is someone who does not believe in God at all? What should I do if the person is an atheist?

Answer: A conversation between you and an atheist could go like this: (this model questionnaire has been obtained from an online source).

X: I am an atheist and evolutionist. Prove to me there is a God.

Y: I do not think I can do that, because of your presuppositions.

X: Why not?

Y: Because your presuppositions will not allow you to examine the evidence that I present to you for God's existence without bias.

X: That is because there is no evidence for God's existence.

Y: See? There you go. You just confirmed what I was stating.

X: How so?

Y: Your presupposition is that there is no God; therefore, no matter what I might present to you to show His existence, you must interpret it in a manner consistent with your presupposition: namely, that there is no God. If I were to have a videotape of God coming down from heaven, you'd say it was a special effect. If I had a thousand eyewitnesses saying they saw Him, you'd say it was mass-hysteria. If I had Old Testament prophecies fulfilled in the New Testament, you'd say they were forged, dated incorrectly, or not real prophecies. So, I cannot prove anything to you since your presupposition won't allow it. It is limited.

X: It is not limited.

Y: Yes it is. Your presupposition cannot allow you to rightly determine God's existence from evidence—providing that there were factual proofs of His existence. Don't you see? If I DID have irrefutable proof, your presupposition would force you to interpret the facts consistently with your presupposition and you would not be able to see the proof.

X: I see your point, but I am open to being persuaded, if you can.

Y: Then, I must ask you, what kind of evidence would you accept that would prove God's existence? I must see what your presuppositions are and work either with them or against them.

(There are a number of quality websites and articles on how to handle questions from those who advocate atheism, existentialism, deism, humanism, Darwinism, evolutionism, Satanism and etc.)

Q#34—Don't you believe there are many people who love to argue and will continue to argue unless you tell them that they are incorrect?

Answer: This is a very sensitive issue; no one likes to hear that he or she is wrong, especially, if the argument is going on in a public place. However, there are a few ways that you can tell the person that he or she is wrong without offending them. Remember, your role is not to argue, but rather to plant the seed. I learned this from another ministry and, with their permission; I am using their technique for your benefit.

> ## Remember
> Logical fallacy gives you the upper hand.

When you are answering their questions, you might consider asking a very stupid question, such as: "Do I really exist?" According to Matt Slick, "It is true that during a debate on an issue, if you simply point out to your 'opponent' a logical fallacy that he/she has just made, it generally gives you the upper hand." The following is retrieved from (http://www.carm.org/logical-fallacies-or-fallacies-argumentation), and for more apologetic techniques visit this website.

1. Ad hominem—Attacking the individual instead of the argument.

   - Example: You are so stupid; your argument couldn't possibly be true.

   - Example: I figured that you couldn't possibly get it right, so I ignored your comment.

2. Appeal to force—Telling the hearer that something bad will happen to him if he does not accept the argument.

   - Example: If you don't want to get beaten up, you will agree with what I say.

   - Example: Convert or die.

3. Appeal to pity—Urging the hearer to accept the argument based upon an appeal to emotions, sympathy, etc.

   - Example: You owe me big time because I really stuck my neck out for you.

   - Example: Oh come on, I've been sick. That's why I missed the deadline.

4. Appeal to the popular—Urging the hearer to accept a position because a majority of people hold to it.

- Example: The majority of people like soda. Therefore, soda is good.

- Example: Everyone else is doing it. Why shouldn't you?

5. Appeal to tradition—Trying to get someone to accept something because it has been done or believed for a long time.

- Example: This is the way we've always done it. Therefore, it is the right way.

- Example: The Catholic Church's tradition demonstrates that this doctrine is true.

6. Begging the Question—Assuming the thing to be true that you are trying to prove. It is circular.

- Example: God exists because the Bible says so. The Bible is inspired. Therefore, we know that God exists.

- Example: I am a good worker because Frank says so. How can we trust Frank? Simple: I will vouch for him.

7. Cause and Effect—Assuming that the effect is related to a cause because the events occur together.

- Example: When the rooster crows, the sun rises. Therefore, the rooster causes the sun to rise.

- Example: When the fuel light goes on in my car, I soon run out of gas. Therefore, the fuel light causes my car to run out of gas.

8. Circular Argument—See Begging the Question

9. Division—Assuming that what is true of the whole is true for the parts.

- Example: That car is blue. Therefore, its engine is blue.

- Example: Your family is weird. That means that you are weird, too.

10. Equivocation—Using the same term in an argument in different places but the word has different meanings.

- Example: A bird in the hand is worth two in the bush. Therefore, a bird is worth more than President Bush.

- Example: Evolution states that one species can change into another. We see that cars have evolved into different styles. Therefore, since evolution is a fact in cars, it is true in species.

11. False Dilemma—Giving two choices when in actuality there could be more choices possible.

- Example: You either did knock the glass over or you did not. Which is it?

- Example: Do you still beat your wife?

12. Genetic Fallacy—Attempting to endorse or disqualify a claim because of the origin or irrelevant history of the claim.

- Example: The Nazi regime developed the Volkswagen Beetle. Therefore, you should not buy a VW Beetle because of who started it.

- Example: Frank just got out of jail last year; since it was his idea to start the hardware store, I can't trust him.

13. Guilt by Association—Rejecting an argument or claim because the person proposing it likes someone whom is disliked by another.

- Example: Hitler liked dogs. Therefore dogs are bad.

- Example: Your friend is a thief. Therefore, I cannot trust you.

14. Non Sequitur—Comments or information that do not logically follow from a premise or the conclusion.

- Example: We know why it rained today: because I washed my car.

- Example: I don't care what you say. We don't need any more bookshelves. As long as the carpet is clean, we are fine.

15. Poisoning the Well—Presenting negative information about a person before he/she speaks so as to discredit the person's argument.

- Example: Frank is pompous, arrogant, and thinks he knows everything. So, let's hear what Frank has to say about the subject.

- Example: Don't listen to him because he is a loser.

16. Red Herring—Introducing a topic not related to the subject at hand.

- Example: I know your car isn't working right. But, if you had gone to the store one day earlier, you'd not be having problems.

- Example: I know I forgot to deposit the check into the bank yesterday. But, nothing I do pleases you.

17. Special Pleading (double standard)—Applying a standard to another that is different from a standard applied to oneself.

- Example: You can't possibly understand menopause because you are a man.

- Example: Those rules don't apply to me since I am older than you.

18. Straw Man Argument—Producing an argument about a weaker representation of the truth and attacking it.

- Example: The government doesn't take care of the poor because it doesn't have a tax specifically to support the poor.

- Example: We know that evolution is false because we did not evolve from monkeys.

19. Category Mistake—Attributing a property to something that could not possibly have that property.

- Example: Blue sleeps faster than Wednesday.

- Example: Saying logic is transcendental is like saying cars would exist if matter didn't.

Q#35—What are some appropriate questions for Muslims?

Answer: As I have previously mentioned, Muslims do not have the assurance of heaven; therefore, you might start a conversation by asking:

#1 Do you consider yourself a good Muslim?

#2 How do you know that you have enough good deeds that God will allow you to enter into Paradise/Jannat? (Muslim don't have the concept of Heaven.)

The problem with the first question is that you are assuming something that could trouble your whole approach. Let me share another illustration. Pakistani Muslims do not like to be called Indians or Middle Easterners. When people assume all the Muslims are Middle Eastern or Arabic, it upsets them. The worst case is when people assume they know about your religion. I have seen many cases where a person lost control because he felt insulted that the evangelist assumed him or her to be something he was not. For example, during my outreach to Muslims in Queens, I was with my disciple. My disciple initiated a conversation by asking," Are you a Muslim?" Well I do not know if he was upset, but he got very mad for assuming him to be a Muslim. He said, "Just because I am from Bangladesh does not mean I am Muslim. I am Hindu." In my experience it is wise to start with "I assume you are a Muslim, are you not?"

#1 I assume you are a Muslim? Are you?

#2 Do you consider yourself a good Muslim?

#3 How do you know that you have enough good deeds that God will allow you to enter into Paradise/Jannat?

Q#36—Should I ask the person, "What is your religion?"

Answer: Speaking out of my personal experience, this is not polite. Particularly, when it comes to the Muslim community in America. They do not like to be asked about their religious affiliation upfront. Muslims are always afraid of being looked down upon because of the ongoing terrorism activities. It might shut him or her down to continue conversation. So, please do not initiate your conversation with such a question.

Q#37—That makes sense. So tell me more about the Evangelism Explosion approach?

Answer: Well, it is very easy. After confirming whether the person is Muslim or not, you ask the second question. (Use the EE suggested transition to start your answer.) After the third question:

> How do you know that you have enough good deeds that God will allow you to enter into Paradise/Jannat?

Use the following statement: "I thought I had some really good news for you. But after hearing your answer to the second and third question, I know that I have the greatest news you have ever heard."

Q#38—Will it make a difference if the person answers, "Yes I am a good Muslim" or "No, I am not a good Muslim"?

Answer: I believe it would not make any difference. Actually, in my personal experience those who are on the extreme side are easier to witness to. Both extremes: "Yes, I am a good Muslim" and "No, I am not a good Muslim."

Q#39—How come? Both answers contradict each other.

Answer: Exactly, you are right, but one shows the person is very arrogant of his religiosity, and the other shows the person does not practice it at all. Those who are doers show others that they are righteous and when they boast of their righteousness, it shows how hollow they are inside. They are empty and have no peace; therefore they rely on their personal efforts to maintain their religious righteousness. When these two types of people are confronted with the truth presenting a better option of being righteous, they don't feel ashamed because deep inside they know they are pretending to be religious and righteous.

The other group that says, "No, I am not a good Muslim," is simply truthful and is seeking for something that is not as burdensome. The Good News of Jesus Christ does not require works to receive His grace, but a pure heart and repentance before God. It will make perfect sense to such people.

Q#40—Is there any answer between Yes or No?

Answer: Yes, there is! The group who gives *the between answer* are the tough ones to reach with the Gospel of Jesus Christ. They can be identified as "True Muslims or Orthodox Muslims" because of their piety and humility. They answer in very diplomatic ways sometimes with the English phrase "I hope so" or "God Wills" or "I try to" or "I do whatever I can but ultimately it's Him who forgives."

I will come back to talk about these a little later, but now let me complete the answer of your previous question regarding the techniques of EE after diagnostic questions.

X: Do you think that paradise is a precious gift of God which is given to whom He wills?

Y: Yes, I do as a matter of fact.

X: Also, don't you think God is very holy and that the righteousness of man cannot meet the standards of His righteousness/holiness?

Y: Yes, I believe.

X: If He is as holy as Zaboor says (Muslims calls "Psalms" Zaboor; they believe the Psalms are one of the revelations of God which came to David from Allah), there David says that His eye can't see sin. Can sinful man please God with his works?

Let me tell you a little more if you would not mind (ask permission, for it shows whether the person is interested or not). Memorize Ephesians 2:8-9 and when you quote it say: Anjil (Muslims believe the true Gospel which was given to Jesus from Allah was Anjil) "For it is by grace you have been saved, through faith—and this not from yourselves, it is the gift of God—not by works, so that no one can boast."

Q#41—Can I use Romans 6:23?

Answer: Although Romans 3:16, Romans 6:23, and numerous verses are very powerful and certainly can win a soul for God, I suggest you do not use them because they use Christ's name directly. In the early stages, it is wise to hold these verses until a more appropriate time. However, you can say the Anjil teaches, "For the wages of sin is death but the gift of God is eternal life," and leave the rest of the verses just for this time.

Q#42—Could you please give me some real life example or illustration to explain the free gift concept or the concept of grace?

Answer: I am glad that you asked. Actually, EE provides a number of examples. I will give you my version of those few illustrations:

For Free Gift: Let us say a good friend comes to you and gives you a gift. Now you are very thankful for the gift, but you put your hand in your pocket and pull out a ten-dollar bill. (It is important, you share this with someone to act out the illustration. This way the person will stay alert and interact.) Try to give something to the friend who gave you a beautiful gift (stretchout your arm and try to give money to the person you are witnessing to). Do you think your friend will receive the money? No! He would not because it was a gift. Rather, he will be offended. This is exactly how the gift of eternal life is. God wants to give us this gift at no cost to us and when we try to do all kinds of deeds to earn it, it offends Him and insults Him. It disappoints Him because no matter how hard we try we can never be able to pay the price for eternal life. End your illustration with a question. Can a rich person buy a life with his money? You can rephrase this if you want. The point is to challenge the person to realize life cannot be purchased. How then can eternal life be purchased? Our life is a gift of God and our eternal life is a gift of God. The difference is that this life ends, but eternal life never ends.

Q#43—Does the Qur'an teach about the sinfulness of man or original sin?

Answer: The Qur'an or Islamic view of man is different from the Biblical view of man. In Islam, man was made to make mistakes (to sin). God knew that because man has free will, he will sin, and when he commits sin, he will repent and God will forgive him. Therefore, this is a different kind of "original sin." Muhammad the prophet of Islam said:

> *"By Him in Whose Hand is My soul (i.e. God), if you did not commit sins, God would do away with you and come with a race which committed sins. They would seek forgiveness from God and He would forgive them." (Saheeh Muslim #4936)*

Q#44—Does this mean that Muhammad the prophet of Islam believed God created man to sin on Earth?

Answer: That is precisely what the above Hadith says. It means God wants people to sin, and if they do not sin, He will be angry with them. In Islam, there is no purpose of doing good if there is no evil. Evil or sin legitimizes the worship of Allah for forgiveness of sins.

Q#45—Do you have any references from the Qur'an regarding original sin and forgiveness?

Answer: Here are a few references from the Qur'an in reference to sin. The Qur'an is full of verses regarding forgiveness for sin with a notion that God is fine with sin because this way He may continue forgiving. Let's look at a few verses from the Qur'an:

> **"Then Adam received Words (of forgiveness) from his Lord, and he accepted his repentance. Verily, He is the One Who repeatedly accepts repentance, the Most Merciful." (Quran 2:37 MK Translation)**

> **Say: "O 'Ibadi (My slaves) who have transgressed against themselves (by committing evil deeds and sins)! Despair not of the Mercy of Allah, verily Allah forgives all sins. Truly, He is Oft-Forgiving, Most Merciful..."' (Qur'an 39:53 MK Translation)**

Q#46—Does this mean that all Muslims believe that it was God's plan that man commit sin?

Answer: Yes, they believe that if we as human beings don't sin, then whom shall God forgive? In order to practice His forgiveness, He wants them to sin. Thus, human sin was the great and wise plan of God. Moreover, the story of Creation in the Qur'an reveals it in these words:

> **"And (remember) when your Lord said to the angels: 'Verily, I am going to place (mankind) generations after generations on earth.' They said: 'Will You place therein those who will make mischief therein and shed blood,—while we glorify You with praises and thanks (Exalted be You above all that they associate with You as partners) and sanctify You.' He (Allah) said: 'I know that which you do not know.'"** **(Quran 2:30 MK Translation)**

Q#47—That is really interesting. Then I think we should tell them about original sin. Don't they need to know about it?

Answer: I truly believe that they need to know about original sin. The problem is what source can we use? The Qur'an does not talk about original sin rather the Qur'an is in favor of sinning, so God can practice His forgiveness.

Q#48—Why can't we use the Bible? Is it true that Muslims believe in the previous Holy Books?

Answer: Yes, you are right! They do believe in the previous Holy Books: namely, The Torah, Psalms, and the Gospel. But here lies the problem: Muslims believe that the Bible has been changed and corrupted. How can we talk about it when they have rejected the very source on which we base everything we believe? I will tell you how; it is called *"The MUSLIM APPROACH."* We will discuss this in detail.

Q#49—What shall I do then if they do not believe in the Bible? They need to know about original sin so that they can understand the ultimate sacrifice of Jesus Christ.

Answer: The best thing you can do to reach out to a Muslim is do not tell them about original sin at the beginning. Telling them about original sin and God's plan of salvation would raise red flags. Muslims believe that man is a sinner and needs God's forgiveness but not for something Adam did. Therefore they perform five daily prayers, *Namaz* and follow the other four pillars of Islam to simply please God.

Although the Bible teaches in Romans 3:23—**"For all have sinned and fall short of the glory of God"**—it would be better to start with Matthew 5:48—**"Be perfect, therefore, as your heavenly Father is perfect"** (When you quote verses from the Gospels say, "according to *Isa-Al-Mesih…*"). Here it helps to reinsure their insecurity about heaven on basis of works by saying: "Do you see why it is impossible for anyone to get into heaven by their good works?"

Personal Notes and Comments:

_____

_____

_____

_____

_____

_____

_____

_____

_____

_____

_____

_____

_____

_____

_____

_____

_____

_____

CHAPTER 5

Islamic Beliefs: Christian Mandate to Love Muslims

This chapter discusses the basic tenets that make Muslims so righteous before the eyes of men. This was problematic for Jews during the time of Jesus. In their own way, they were righteous and faithful but faithful to a book, traditions, and religion. The grace of God is available for everyone and anyone who desires to seek His will. However, what if good works and deeds of a Muslim are more powerful and evident than the lives of many Christians around them? The chapter will help you to understand the very mind of God and also the very mind of the human to please God. I will continue using different apologetic approaches to deal with some of the critical complications of Muslim disbelief about the deity of Christ.

Q#50—What are the "five pillars of Islam"?

Answer: Let me take one-step back and explain what the "five pillars of Islam" are at this stage. Actually, it is a good example, which we discussed in the storytelling technique. Remember the three principles we learned:

- Keep it less than 3 minutes—maximum 4 minutes
- Use common phrases
- Tell the full story

The second point 'Use common phrases' is just what you are experiencing right now. Because you are not a Muslim or have not been exposed to Islam, you do not know the very basic elements of Islam as a religion.

The religion of Islam stands on five pillars and if you remove any one of the pillars, the building of Islam will collapse. You see what is so common to Muslims has held you back in continuing your dialogue. This is true in the case of Muslims as well as any non-Christians. As Christians, there are many words and phrases we use without noticing if the person we are talking to does not understand. As a matter of fact, this is precisely what happens when we use simple Christian terms such as disciples of Jesus Christ or baptism etc. A listener who is unaware of such terms will hang on to those words and will miss the whole story and consequently you will miss the opportunity to minister to that lost soul.

Q#51—I understand the importance of using simple vocabulary. So what are the pillars of Islam?

Answer: As I said, there are five pillars of Islam. Those pillars of Islam are cohesive with the six basic beliefs of Islam also known as the articles of faith:

FIVE PILLARS OF ISLAM
1. Kalima (Testimony of faith)
2. Salat (Prayer: five times a day)
3. Zakat (Almsgiving)
4. Sawm (Fasting)
5. Hajj (Pilgrimage)

SIX ARTICLES OF FAITH
1. Faith in the unity of God (Towheed)
2. Faith in angels
3. Faith in prophets
4. Faith in books of revelation [The Bible: Turat (Torah) Zabor (Psalm), Angil (the Gospels) and the Qur'an]
5. Faith in an afterlife
6. Faith in destiny/divine decree

Q#52—That sounds like a lot of work to please God. It also sounds like Old Testament teaching. Certainly this is man's effort to please God. Isn't it?

Answer: You are right about that. This is why it is so important to focus on God's holiness as mentioned in my response to question #48. Here are a few more illustrations I learned when I took Evangelism Explosion training courses.

> Illustration 1: Ask the person when thinking of sin what comes to their mind immediately (give the person about 10-20 seconds) and ask, if they are thinking of things like robbery, murder, adultery, etc. Reconfirm with the person by saying: "Isn't it true we think about *BIG SINS*? But a sin is a sin just like a crime is a crime." It is important to engage the listener. Ask the person "how would you define a sin?" Whatever answer you receive, just reaffirm it with the following answer. "Wouldn't you agree that anything that doesn't please God also breaks His law? Things we do that we shouldn't, such as losing our temper, stealing, talking behind someone's back, converting, thinking sinful thoughts, lying, cursing, lust, pride, and hatred—these are sins of commission. Anything we should do but we don't, such as failing to pray or read the God's word or to truly love our neighbor—these are sins of omission. Don't you think these are all sins?

Q#53—Doesn't God forgive all of these sins if we ask for forgiveness?

Answer: You have said "if you ask," It's like magic words but the problem with people who think that they are doing good deeds is they don't understand the concept of forgiveness for their deeds. They consider themselves good on the basis of their good deeds and they tend to forget that they are sinful. Continue your conversation with the person you are sharing your faith with and follow up the question by asking: if you commit three of those minor sins in one day, how many will you commit in a week? (Wait and let the person respond) if the person is unable to calculate then jump in and say: "21 in a week right? If that is the case then how many in a year?" Well, three sins multiplied by 365 days would be 1095 a year. God may give you a healthy life, you may live for a long time. But let's say you get to live an average life of 70, so based on 3 minor sins a day how many would you commit in 70 years? Yes over 70,000 right? If you cannot stand in a court of Law for one crime how do you expect God who is completely just to let you go to paradise with 70,000 plus sins? And some of those are sins you didn't even think you had committed because they were so minor!

Follow up with an immediate question: would you eat an omelet that has been made with five good eggs and one rotten egg? No! Right? So why would you expect God to receive all your goodness with one bad deed? Is it impossible to be holy and pure before God with human effort unless God intervenes and decides to forgive us and give us eternal life.

Q#54—But don't Muslims believe that "If Allah wills it so" they will enter in paradise?

Answer: Very sharp! That is the point of this illustration; to help them to understand that they cannot be good enough to please Him. There is absolutely no way through human efforts that man can enter paradise. It is only through God's will that they can enter into Heaven; so in that case their righteousness and works are not credited towards eternal life. The division between "I do good things that Allah may let me enter" versus "If Allah wills I will enter into heaven" brings a Muslim friend one step closer to accept the truth and to rely on the redemptive work of Christ.

Q#55—Now I understand why you emphasize this so much, because the person needs to look for an answer. If he can't please God through his good deeds and good deeds are not good enough, then what is the answer? How can someone be sure that he or she can enter in paradise?

Answer: Exactly. That is the reason. Once a person is open to investigating other possibilities, it allows us to continue sharing the good news.

God Is Love

God is a loving and kind He forgives. "God is love." (1 John 4:8b)

God is Just

God is also a Just God. Therefore, His justice requires punishment for sinfulness. "Yet He does not leave the guilty unpunished." (Exodus 34:7b)

Q#56—What is the solution to this problem? Even if God wants to forgive us, He can't because He is just.

Answer: The answer is faith.

Q#57—Isn't it the very foundation of Islam's claim that "Faith and deeds go hand to hand? There are six articles of faith and the five pillars of Islam are the required deeds.

Answer: Yes! But the faith Muslims possess is mere head knowledge. Their faith is not in their prophet Muhammad's ability to take them to paradise. James 2:19 says, **"You believe that there is one God. Good! Even the demons believe that — and shudder."** We know that when Jesus cast out the demons of the possessed man they recognized him as the Son of God, who had the power to punish them. They believed that He was the Son of God. Evangelism Explosion gives us an excellent illustration for faith:

Faith is the key that opens the door to paradise. On this key ring (hold up your key ring) there are many keys. Some even look somewhat alike. Yet, when I go to unlock my front door tonight, I could try all of these keys and for except the right one I could not unlock the door. It does not matter how sincere I am in exercising my belief that a different key will open the door. The fact is that only the right key will open the door. The right key to heaven is saving faith. Saving faith is the only key that will open heaven's door. Other keys are head knowledge and temporal faith.

In the world, there are many religions and many religious leaders. None of those leaders claimed to be the door to Heaven. Christ said, **"I am the way and the truth and the life. No one comes to the Father except through me"** (John 14:6), He also said, **"I am the door; if anyone enters through Me, he will be saved, and will go in and out and find pasture"** (John 10:9), and **"I am the resurrection and the life; he who believes in Me will live even if he dies"** (John 11:25).

Q#58—Don't Muslims believe in Christ? I have heard Muslims say without believing in Jesus they are not even Muslim.

Answer: It is true; one of the six articles of faith is having faith in previous prophets. Again, it could be understood by another illustration I borrowed from Evangelism Explosion. Many people know certain historical facts about Jesus. They believe in Jesus the same way they believe in Napoleon or George Washington. They believe He actually existed. They believe He was a real person in history, but they do not trust Him to do anything for them now. The Bible says the devil believes in God (James 2:19). So believing in God's existence is not what the Bible means by saving faith. Muslims not only believe Jesus existed, but that He was a powerful prophet who raised the dead and healed the sick. Therefore, when they are sick, they pray to Jesus. They go to church to get healing. It's like temporal faith.

Temporal Faith (EE explains this with the following illustration)

Temporal faith is another thing that people often mistake for saving faith. When a person trusts in the Lord for finances, you could call that financial-faith. A person may pray and trust the Lord to take care of his family. You could call this family-faith. Many have prayed for a safe trip. You could call that traveling-faith. There is one thing that all of these have in common. They are temporary. For instance, once you reach your destination, you don't need to trust the Lord for traveling-faith. All the things of this world will pass away. They are temporary. But saving faith is trusting in Jesus Christ alone for eternal life.

Q#59—Do you have any other illustrations to explain it? I feel it is a very crucial point to differentiate between having faith in Jesus vs. all other kinds of faiths.

Answer: As a matter of fact, Evangelism Explosion provides another excellent illustration that you can act out in order to make the listener get actively involved.

You believe this chair exists, don't you (point to empty chair)? Do you believe this chair would support me if I were to sit on it? But you see, it's not holding me up for one simple reason: I'm not sitting on it. For the sake of making my point, let the chair I'm sitting on represent me and this empty chair represent Christ. For a long time I believed He existed and He could help me. However, I did not have eternal life because I was trusting in my own good works to get me into heaven. Years ago I repented of my sins and transferred my trust from myself to Jesus Christ—from what I had been doing for God to what He has done for me on the cross (move to the empty chair). By a simple act of faith I transferred my trust from what I had done to what Christ has done for me. When I asked you earlier what you would say to God if He were to ask you, "Why should I let you into My Heaven?" you said, "I try to be good. I try to live a good life. I have been a pretty good person." Who is the only person referred to in your answer? To receive eternal life you must transfer your trust from yourself to Jesus Christ alone for eternal life.

Q#60—I believe now after this illustration, the person would want to ask me about Jesus. How should I respond? I don't want to be pushy.

Answer: It is very wise not to be pushy. Many times very good evangelists drop the ball when they get very excited because of the open door and awesome opportunity. Their conversation and excitement about the Good News makes them forget whom they are talking to. They can easily scare away the person. Dealing with Muslims is very complicated. You can't trust your instincts; you have to rely on God for every step you take. At this point, you have a beautiful opportunity to share the full Gospel but the problem is the recipient might hesitate to accept Christ because of the Person of Christ as both fully man and fully God. I would say to take it slowly and remove the potential obstacles and share the Person of Jesus Christ.

Q#61—Sorry, I didn't understand. What do you mean by the Person of Christ?

Answer: The creed of Islam is "There is no God but Allah and Muhammad is His prophet" it is called *Twheed*. Muslims are misguided about the person of Christ. Many of them believe that Christianity teaches that Jesus was physically the Son of God while Mary is the wife of God. This complication is very difficult to address until the person is already convinced by the Holy Spirit to seek the truth. You have to explain that Christ was not born out of God's union with a woman but He is the second person of God. Not less or more, but equally God. God himself came into the world because no man was able to meet His standards of righteousness and holiness but He Himself. The other way is to use the "**The Muslim Approach**."

Q#62—What if the person is ready and wants to hear about the person of Jesus Christ as God?

Answer: Well, then it is very simple; follow the guidelines provided by Evangelism Explosion tracts to witness to the person or Romans' Road or whatever your church recommends:

Who He is—the infinite God-Man

John 1:1, 14—"In the beginning was the Word, and the Word was with God, and the Word was God. The Word became flesh and made His dwelling among us. We have seen His glory, the glory of the One and Only, Who came from the Father, full of grace and truth."

What He did—He died on the cross and rose from the dead to pay the penalty for our sins and to purchase a place in Heaven for us.

Isaiah 53:6—"We all, like sheep, have gone astray, each of us has turned to his own way; and the Lord has laid on Him the iniquity of us all."

Q#63—Is it important to memorize the verses?

Answer: I would suggest you open the Bible and share the verses from the Scriptures. In this way the person will know that it is written in the Bible. You can also use the Bible to demonstrate a last illustration I would recommend from Evangelism Explosion training. In Islam, it is believed that there are two angels on your shoulders. One is the angel of good and the other one is the angel of evil. One writes all the good deeds and the other writes all the bad deeds. On the Day of Judgment, both books will be put on a scale to measure the weight, and depending on the weight you will receive your reward: Janat (paradise) or Jahnum (hell). Therefore, it is suggested you close your conversation with the following:

Let's imagine that this book in my right hand is a minutely detailed account of my life. Each page details the sin of a particular day—every word I have spoken, every thought that has ever crossed my mind, every deed I've ever done that falls short of God's perfection. Here then (hold up the book) is the problem—my sin (place book in palm of left hand). God loves me (point to your left hand) but He hates my sin (point at the book on top of your left hand) and must punish it.

To solve this problem, He sent His Son into the world (lift up the right hand parallel to the left hand). The Scripture says (quote Isaiah 53:6—as you say the words "laid on Him" transfer the book in one distinct motion from your left hand to your right hand and leave it in the right hand). All of my sins, which God hates, have been placed on Jesus Christ. Finally, when the last sin had been paid for, Jesus said, "It is finished!" This is an interesting word in the original text. It is TETELESTAI, a commercial word which means, "It is paid; the debt is paid." When He died, He was buried in a grave for three days (put the book on your lap); but He rose from the dead and went to Heaven to prepare a place for you and me. Now He offers Heaven—eternal life—to you and me as a gift.

Q# 64—Is there any further step after leading him or her in prayer?

Answer: Please invite him or her to attend a church meeting with you. Lead a Bible study with him or her. Provide a copy of the Bible for him. Tell him or her about baptism, Holy Communion and other Christian traditions, etc. Stay in fellowship with the person and make appropriate arrangements that the person may grow in Christ.

Q#65—I believe you know a lot of Muslims who came to Christ. What attracted them to Christianity? What made them follow Christ?

Answer: One of the most common reasons reported by Muslims regarding why they came to the Lord was through the friendship and personal relationship of a Christian brother or sister. Interestingly enough, I have heard so many claims from Muslims that Christians engage in deception when it comes to evangelizing them. Muslims claim "that Mr. or Miss Christian became my friend to convert me" However, You can have all the apologetic knowledge you need to win a debate with a Muslim but without the direct assistance of the Holy Spirit you will not be able to win a soul. If you hear the testimonies of MBB (Muslim background believers), most of them will tell you that their conversion was the result of the constant and unconditional love they have experienced from a Christian brother or sister, or through a vision or dream directly from God.

Q#66—Are you saying that friendship evangelism is not the right way to evangelize Muslims?

Answer: I believe sometimes friendship evangelism is considered **deceptive evangelism** by Muslims unless it is a genuine relationship. Muslim culture is inspired by the Arabian and Middle Eastern culture where family and tribe are the most important units of the society. Muslims are blessed with an ancient structure of family. Thus, you can find three or four generations in the same house. In Muslim culture, there is no concept of retirement or a home for the elderly. Children are expected to provide care for their aging parents. People give more value to family than anything else. They spend a great deal of time with each other. Therefore, to Muslims being family means everything. In a Muslim neighborhood, the term "neighbor' is never used, other members of the community are referred to as "aunts" or "uncles." When I was living in Pakistan, I considered everyone in my town as an uncle, aunt or cousin. The complaint or misunderstanding is that you became a friend to me; you helped me or provided my needs because you were looking for an opportunity to convert me to your religion. Now here is the thing: if you are forming a friendship (a relationship between you and a Muslim person), be bold about your identity in Christ. Tell the person that you are a Christian and you just want to be a good friend. If possible, let the person know that you are not trying to be a friend to convert him or her. Your honesty and upfront intentions will earn you more respect. Honesty is important in such a relationship (discipleship). It will provide you a ground to stand on when Satan tries to accuse you of being a swindler.

Remember!

Actions speak louder than words, so demonstrate Christian faith through your actions. Do not let your words and actions contradict each other.

Recently, I was asked by a missionary friend to meet with a young Tajik man who was arriving in New York City for the first time. When I met him, he was very grateful and felt that he had someone to talk to. His experience here in the United States was not a very good one. As he arrived at the airport, he lost his money, credit card and other personal possessions. He was homesick when he arrived in Brooklyn. However, he was promised a job, a place to live, internet, TV and other luxuries. Upon his destination, he discovered it was an absolute fraud—no job, no place to live, absolutely nothing! This young man was a Muslim who had never been exposed to Christianity. I was told by the missionary that it is the law in Tajikistan not to share faith with anyone under 16 years old. So the missionary friend never had the opportunity to witness to him.

I went inside the building and demanded to see the manager of the company here in Brooklyn to find out what was going on with this Tajik brother. The manager requested that I find a job for this young man. That same hour, after a quick prayer, I called a Christian camp; if this young man could work in this environment, it would change his life forever. The director of the camp was very gracious, regardless of the lateness of the hour and agreed to give him a job. I was very happy to tell the Tajik man that I had secured a job for him with food and housing. He seemed very happy until I told him it was a Christian camp. He not only refused to go, but he refused to hang out with me because I am a Christian.

He mentioned to my missionary friend that I was very kind and told him of my offer to assist him with his needs. The Tajik man made it very clear; he does not want to continue any friendship with me because I am a Christian. You may have experienced similar situations, but do not worry; you have planted a seed. Hopefully someone will come along to water it. **Remember our Lord and God is the One Who is able to grow it. So trust in the Lord.**

Personal Notes and Comments:

_____

_____

_____

_____

_____

_____

_____

_____

_____

_____

_____

_____

_____

_____

_____

_____

_____

_____

CHAPTER 6

Deceptive Evangelism: Islam and Christianity

This chapter examines some of the accusations concerning the deception in Islam and Christianity. Both religions claim that the other one uses deceptive modes for proselytization. In the previous chapter, I addressed one accusation: "Friendship Evangelism." It is important to emphasize the traditional understanding of friendship evangelism by Muslims is incorrect. A better word for friendship evangelism could be building genuine relationships. The following questions will use many verses from the Qur'an to provide a justification for Muslim Evangelism. It does not mean that you hide the fact that you are a Christian, it simply means you do not initiate your conversation stating upfront that you are a follower of Christ. If the person finds you somewhat different than others and is open to talk, then share. I would say what Paul said "To the Jews I became as a Jew, in order to win Jews. To those under the law I became as one under the law (though not being myself under the law) that I might win those under the law" (1 Corinthians 9:20 ESV).

If you do not feel comfortable with this Muslim evangelistic approach, then please do not do it. The title for the approach is Muslim approach but it does not mean that you are acting as if you are a Muslim. It simply means you are using Muslim beliefs, theology, doctrine, and traditions to make your point that Christ is the Son of God. Moreover, that He is the only way to Heaven and no one can satisfy the wrath of God by his or her righteous acts.

This chapter is one of the shortest chapters in the book as well as one of the most controversial.

Q#67—What is the Muslim approach? Isn't this when you pretend to be Muslim?

Answer: The Muslim approach is when an individual uses Muslim beliefs, tradition, doctrine, and teaching to present the Gospel. It is very difficult, but if you have a grip on Islamic teachings and Christian doctrine, it can be an effective tool in Muslim evangelism. When you are involved in friendship evangelism, a good approach is to leave one or two clues behind that you are a Christian or belong to a church so as one may not accuse you of keeping him or her in darkness. However, when the Muslim you meet is a total stranger, and your time is limited, you don't know if he or she will be open to initiate a conversation about Christ. In that case, it is imperative to receive him or her gladly, and at the appropriate time, or when you are asked, to reveal that you are a Christian. Furthermore, coming from one of the most extreme Muslim countries, I assure you, that the Qur'an uses the word Muslim in the same sense I am asking you to introduce yourself as a Christian. You will not be lying or being dishonest. Qur'an calls all the previous prophets (Adam, Noah, Abraham, Isaac, Jacob, Moses, David, Jonah, Lot, John the Baptist, and Jesus) Muslim. Theologically, *Islam means submission to the will of God and obedience to His law.* The Arabic word "Muslim" literally means "someone who is in a state of Islam (submission to the will and law of God)."

Therefore, in the Qur'an we read that Abraham **"Ibrahim (Abraham) was neither a Jew nor a Christian, but he was a true Muslim Hanifa (Islamic Monotheism—to worship none but Allah Alone) and he was not of Al-Mushrikun (See V.2:105)."** (Âl'Imran 3:67 MK Translation). also, **And they say, "Be Jews or Christians, then you will be guided." Say (to them, O Muhammad Peace be upon him), "Nay, (We follow) only the religion of Ibrahim (Abraham), Hanifa [Islamic Monotheism, i.e. to worship none but Allah (Alone)], and he was not of Al-Mushrikun (those who worshipped others along with Allah— see V.2:105)."** (Al-Baqarah 2:135 MK Translation).

Q#68—Does this mean all the prophets were Muslim?

Answer: A list of prophets who were considered Muslim according to Islam: **"He (Allah) has ordained for you the same religion (Islam) which He ordained for Nuh (Noah), and that which We have inspired in you (O Muhammad SAW), and that which We ordained for Ibrahim**

(Abraham), Musa (Moses) and 'Iesa (Jesus) saying you should establish religion (i.e. to do what it orders you to do practically), and make no divisions in it (religion) (i.e. various sects in religion). Intolerable for the Mushrikun , is that to which you (O Muhammad SAW) call them. Allah chooses for Himself whom He wills, and guides unto Himself who turns to Him in repentance and in obedience."(Ash-Shura 42:13 MK Translation). In Al-An'am 6:84-87 a detailed list of the Biblical prophets described as true Muslims. The Surah states, Ibrahim (Abraham), Ishaq (Issac), Yaqub (Jacob), Nuh (Noah), Dawud (David), Sulaiman (Solomon), Ayyub (Job), Yusuf (Joseph), Musa (Moses), Harun (Aaron), Zakariyya (Zachariah), Yahya (John the Baptist), 'Isa (Jesus), Ilyas, Ishmael, Al-Yash'a (Elisha), Yunus (Jonah) and Lut (Lot).

Q#69—Does this mean Muslims believe that Jesus (ISA AL-MESIH) was a Muslim?

Answer: According to the Quran, the purpose of Jesus 'life was to promote Islam. The Qur'an claims Jesus was a true Muslim (Âl 'Imran 3:84 MK Translation) Say (O Muhammad SAW): "We believe in Allah and in what has been sent down to us, and what was sent down to Ibrahim (Abraham), Isma'il (Ishmael), Ishaque (Isaac), Ya'qub (Jacob) and Al-Asbat [the twelve sons of Ya'qub (Jacob)] and what was given to Musa (Moses), 'Iesa (Jesus) and the Prophets from their Lord. We make no distinction between one another among them and to Him (Allah) we have submitted (in Islam)." Also, "like all the Muslim prophets before him [Jesus], and like Muhammad after him [Jesus], 'Isa was a lawgiver, and Christians should submit to his law" (Âl 'Imran 3:50; Al-Ma'idah 5:48).

The Qur'an claims that the original disciples of Jesus were also true Muslims. And [remember] when I inspired to the disciples, "Believe in Me and in My messenger Jesus." They said, "We have believed, so bear witness that indeed we are Muslims [in submission to Allah]." (Al-Ma'idah 5:111 Sahih International Translation)

The Family of ` Imran (Ali ` Imran) 3:52-53: When Jesus found Unbelief on their part He said: "Who will be My helpers to (the work of) Allah?" Said the disciples: "We are Allah's helpers: We believe in Allah, and do thou bear witness that we are Muslims." (Yusuf Ali Translation)

Q#70—Correct me if I am wrong, the above verses reveal that not only was Jesus a Muslim, but all his disciples were true Muslims.

Answer: Yes, I was very surprised when I read it for the first time that "Not only that Jesus was a Muslim but his followers were true Muslim." Therefore, if we are followers of Jesus, we are true Muslims too. I understand it is not what you want to hear, but this is the justification we find in the Qur'an in terms of using the Muslim Approach to reach out to Muslims. Our interpretation of a Christian being a Muslim is solely based on the meanings of the word "Muslim" in Arabic.

Q#71—I still don't feel comfortable acting like a Muslim. I feel I need to be very bold.

Answer: It is very encouraging that you want to be bold. I certainly encourage you to pursue that. As I previously mentioned, Paul writes, **"To the Jews I became as a Jew, so that I might win Jews; to those who are under the Law, as under the Law though not being myself under the Law, so that I might win those who are under the Law; to those who are without law, as without law, though not being without the law of God but under the law of Christ, so that I might win those who are without law"** (1 Corinthians 9:20-21NASB).

It does not mean that you have to lie about your identity in Christ. It simply means use the opportunity, time and the knowledge you have about Islam to reach out to Muslims. When one considers the explanation of the Quran listed above, it seems legitimate to call yourself Muslim (one who submits to the will of God) but you would rather not. Simply use the time you have on hand before your identify yourself and talk through the pages of Qur'an.

Q#72—Do Muslims use the same approach? Do they engage in deceptive strategies?

Answer: I am glad that you asked this question. First, let me clarify something; in the **"Muslim Approach"** we are not hiding but simply building a bridge. It's like the US military policy "don't ask, don't tell" but when you are asked it is imperative to reveal that you are a Christian, whether you are able to continue witnessing or not.

However, many sects of Islam consider deception a militaristic strategy for Jihad in terms of spreading Islam. Thus, to such Muslims it is perfectly legitimate to deceive or lie for the sake of Allah and Islam. They believe in **Al-taqiyah** (dissimulation) which means showing outwardly something other than what one feels inside. In fact, lying and hypocrisy are skills used in deceiving people. Many Muslims are trained and fully skilled in taqiyah. It's like a poker game. They regard the use of taqiyah as a religious duty for minor and major matters, sometimes of fear as well as times of peace and harmony. Whether this doctrine is widely accepted by the Muslim majority or not is not the question. Those who will use such doctrine feel very comfortable justifying their action of deceiving for the greater good of mankind.

Q#73—What does the Qur'an say about such terms and usage?

Answer: Interestingly enough, the Qur'an calls **ALLAH** *makr meaning deceiver.* Many Muslims use the following verses to justify their actions of lying (hiding truth) and deception particularly to non-Muslims. For example, the Qur'an calls Allah a *makr*:

Qur'an 3:54

(It will read like: *Wamakaroo wamakara Allahu waAllahu khayru al-makireena*)!

Pickthall Translation

And they (the disbelievers) schemed, and Allah schemed (against them): and Allah is the best of schemers. This verse can also be translated as: "**But they (the Jews) were deceptive, and Allah was deceptive, for Allah is the best of deceivers.**"

Qur'an 8:30

Dr. Ghali Translation

And as the ones who have disbelieved were scheming to confine you, or kill you, or to drive you out, and <u>they were scheming, and Allah was scheming; and Allah is The Most Charitable of schemers</u>.

Qur'an 7:99

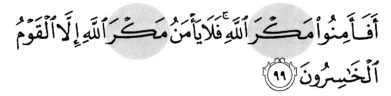

Dr. Ghali Translation

So, do they feel secure against the scheming of Allah? Then none feels secure against the scheming of Allah except the people (who) are the losers. It is also translated as:

"Are they then secure from *Allah's deception (makra Allahi)?* None deemeth himself secure from *Allah's deception (makra Allahi)* save folk that perish."

Qur'an 27: 50

Dr. Ghali Translation

And they schemed a scheme, and We schemed a scheme, and they were not aware. Also translated as: "So they *schemed a scheme: and We schemed a scheme (Wamakaroo makran wamakarna makran),* while they perceived not."

The word for deception/deceiver/scheme is *makr.* The above mentioned Qur'anic verses reveal that Allah (the Creator of heaven and earth) deceived and lied to make his point. Those Muslims who intend to deceive, even for their personal benefit, give many other explanations to justify the above verses.

But the bottom line is this: in a court of law the prosecutor does not ask for detailed answers for such controversial questions. It's yes for yes or no for no. In the above verses, one of Allah's attributes is *makr.*

Q#74—Can I use the Scriptures to talk to a Muslim about Christ?

Answer: Yes. Actually, I call it the **Christian Approach.** In my personal experience, I have found it rather interesting when I initiated a conversation with a Muslim introducing myself as a Christian. If I am in an Islamic country, I have to be very careful in terms of witnessing because almost all the Islamic countries forbid such evangelism. If not forbidden by the law, then the Islamic society forbids it. However, working through the Qur'an is always the best idea. No matter what technique or approach you are using to evangelize a Muslim, you are better off by introducing one or two Qur'anic verses in the beginning of the conversation. One of the most common phrases, "first impression is the last impression," is true even in evangelism. I always use the following verse. The key verse to initiate a good conversation with a Muslim is the following verse from the Qur'an. I recommend memorizing it:

> You will surely find the most intense of the people in animosity toward the believers (Muslims) [to be] the Jews and those who associate others with Allah; and you will find the nearest of them in affection to the believers those who say, "We are Christians." That is because among them are priests and monks and because they are not arrogant. (Al-Ma'idah 5:82 Sahih Translation).

In Islam, Muslims respect a Hafiz (a person who memorizes the Qur'an) and if you quote the Qur'an, it will give you an extra advantage in the conversation. The above verse helps to form common ground to develop relationships with Muslims. I warn you not to get involved in a conversation, which might lead to accusing Jews or an agreement with a Muslim that all Jews are bad. Recently I came across a new phrase: "first comes Saturday and then Sunday." This phrase refers to the Muslim intentions that first they will strike against Jews and then they will come after Christians. Therefore, whatever you do, keep your focus on Christ and don't agree with what a Muslim believes about Jews. We are asked to pray for Jews, not to curse them.

Personal Notes and Comments:

_____

_____

_____

_____

_____

_____

_____

_____

_____

_____

_____

_____

_____

_____

_____

_____

_____

_____

CHAPTER 7

Watch out: Security Issues in Street Evangelism

This is one of the most important chapters. If you have not read the rest of the chapters in depth, I recommend you read this chapter with your full and undivided attention. It is important to recognize that this information may save your life and your group's. This chapter deals with the security measures needed while you are out in the mission field. Remember, the mission field is wherever you are: your mission field can be your own street or somewhere in another country. The following questions and answers will help you to understand some of the unexpected dangers involved in the mission field. When you think you are safe, this might be the time that you are putting yourself in the worst danger you have ever been in. If you have life, you will have more chances to minister. Never lose your life due to ignorance and human self-righteousness.

As Christians, sometimes we are too arrogant. We may say, "well I have never quit anything, therefore, I will not retreat." I pray that you may remain sensitive to the Holy Spirit because there are going to be times when He will ask you to retreat.

Q#75—Is there a strategic plan I should follow when it comes to sharing my faith/engaging in evangelism?

Answer: I have learned several things over a period of time, which I consider very important for evangelism in general. I call them AAA. It is easy to remember because today's "AAA" (Triple A) is famous for its auto and traveling services. When I practice street or friendship evangelism, whether at a mosque, public place, or home, I use the three As:

First, I *A: **assess***, secondly, I stay *A: **alert,*** and at the last, I *A: **acknowledge***. What do I mean by these terms? Let's look at them separately.

1. Assess

In order to explain the term assess, I have to use a personal example. I have ridden a motorcycle most of my life. The Honda 70 is a common transportation in India, Pakistan and a number of other third world countries. I remember the first time my dad allowed me to ride the motorcycle alone. I received my dad's grace through bribing him by washing and polishing the motorcycle. I turned the key to our family's only transportation and kicked the starter lever, pressed the clutch, put the motorcycle in first gear by pressing the gear lever forward, then released the clutch slowly while giving it more gas by rolling the throttle down. During this incredible experience at the age of 12 or 13, I heard someone shout behind me, "WATCH OUT!"

Years later, while at the Valley Forge Motorcycle License Center in Pennsylvania, I heard the instructor emphasizing the word SEE. In my native language, there is one word for both watch and see. Watch and see both can be interpreted as observe. As evangelists, we need to be very good observers. Our mistakes can teach us how to do better next time. Each time we witness and go through the questions and answers phase, we learn a new way to approach our audience. Each time we go to the market place or an evangelism campaign, observation makes us better at evangelism. During my motorcycle instructor's lecture, I learned a new acronym: **S: search; E: evaluate; and E: execute.** It radically changed my evangelism approach.

How? When we go out for evangelism, we are so fired up with zeal, passion and excitement that we do not take time to assess our surroundings. The motorcycle manual states the following in regards of search: "Search aggressively ahead, to the sides and behind to avoid potential hazards even before they arise. How assertively you search, and how much time and space you have, can eliminate or reduce harm." This is exactly what an evangelist should be doing in the field.

Q#76—Do you have a personal experience that you can share?

Answer: During my recent experience in Muslim Evangelism in Queens, I noticed a student, Najima, who is a former Muslim. She was so on fire for the Lord that her boldness could have been a potential hazard. Najima Mohammad is an awesome sister, full of compassion to reach the lost world. She loves to pray and do evangelism. The other day, during our regular street evangelism, Najima and I stopped at a South Asian food place where we ordered two samosas (a fried or baked patty shell filled with vegetables and spices). We had planned to eat this while continuing evangelism, but Najima decided to get some other food which required us to be seated. A young woman sat next to our table. I had noticed the Qur'anic verses on the wall as I was entering in the restaurant so I decided not to interact with the young lady. However, Najima initiated a conversation with a boldness that I do not have. Here is their conversation:

> Najima: *Hi, my name is Najima Muhammad.*
>
> Young lady: *My name is ….*
>
> Najima: *We are here to share about Christ and Christianity.*
>
> Young lady: *Wow! That is different! You are Muslim, and you are sharing about Christ* (and the conversation goes on).

The first rule when you "Assess" and apply "SEE" is: "Search aggressively ahead, to the sides and behind to avoid potential hazards even before they arise." In this scenario, I applied the full SEE and chose not to initiate the conversation with a lady because in Islamic culture this is not the right thing to do. Men do not talk to women. This could have created a problem. Najima not only did an awesome job with proper SEE, she secured an appointment with the storeowner to witnessing to him the following week!

After eating and talking, we continued witnessing in Queens, New York. We walked the streets of Queens every Wednesday. Later that day, Najima greeted a mobile customer service agent standing outside the shop holding a cell phone product to attract more customers. He was accompanied by another man. Both men were in their early 20's. Najima told them that she uses their cell phone service and she is very upset with the cell phone company. As the first man asked her questions about her cell phone, Najima took it as an opportunity to share the Good News. Very respectfully she asked his name and asked if he had a few minutes. Now, here comes SEE. When you are visible, i.e., everybody can see you and you can see them, most likely you are out of EDZ.

Q#77—Wait a minute, what is EDZ?

Answer: It is evangelism danger zone. EDZ is like a blind spot. Think about an experienced driver, who is very alert and aware of the surroundings. Will he switch from one lane to the other without checking his blind spot? No. He would follow the "look over the shoulder" rule to avoid any potential danger. In evangelism, even though you are aware of your surroundings, things are moving very smoothly, and people are interested, if you do not follow the proper technique of "SEE" you are putting other team members in a danger zone. A non-existing threat can suddenly become the potential reason to destroy the whole groundwork for ministry.

In America, God has given us the wonderful gift of the right of free speech. Najima went in and I followed her into the shop. In less than a minute, four Muslim men surrounded us. This is certainly a violation of Assess: SEE. Failure to apply proper SEE techniques put both of us in EDZ. God can bring good from even a bad situation. We prepared them for witness and exchanged the contact information. I intentionally interrupted Najima each time when she tried to witness to them. Please don't get me wrong, I was not afraid, nor did I want to lose the opportunity to witness to them. I was just being careful. We talked about their beliefs and interests. The focus was on them not on us and our conversation showed our genuine interest in knowing them. It prepared the way for our next meeting.

Philippians 2:4 gives an incredible principle for reaching the lost: **"Let each of you look not to your own interests, but to the interests of others."** When we stop focusing on ourselves as someone who is going to win the person to Christ and focus on his or her interests, it will open doors which no one can shut. Often evangelists get so consumed by their desire to win people that they overlook the difference between what they really need as opposed to what they really want. One's character can win more people for Christ than one's argument.

In many evangelistic meetings, during the first "A," assess, I tried to complete SEE before I look at the other two "A"s. After the **search**, the next task was to **evaluate**. When Najima went inside the shop, we evaluated the costs and efforts of sharing. The potential EDZ stopped us to complete SEE by **executing** witness. Once the word is out of your mouth, you cannot bring it back. What is done in the process of witnessing to a Muslim cannot be undone. As previously noted, we have learned that Muslims can deceive for the sake of Allah. Therefore, exaggeration is inevitable, when you are messed up. If you said a, b, c to a Muslim, and if he or she does not agree, then be ready to face the additional d, e, in addition to your original words.

Always follow proper SEE before you compete AAA (SEE).

Remember!
S: Search
E: Evaluate
E: Execute

In Najima's first experience, Assess, Alert, and Acknowledge were successfully applied because of her careful search, evaluation and execution. She failed in the second experience because she failed to complete SEE and subsequently we had to retreat.

Q#78—What is the second A?

Answer: Before, we look at the second A. Let's review all three together just to refresh our memory.

AAA: Assess, Alert, Acknowledge

2. Alert

You never know what might be the result of your successful execution of witnessing and sharing your faith. We never know what is in the heart of a man. Yes, God knows, and He is certainly in control. For you, it is more about staying alert and making the right choices. Would it be wise to choose death or injury when you have the choice to live and witness to thousands of people? The obvious answer is no. It is never wise to put yourself in a dangerous situation.

Christ presented a very critical principle of evangelism. His life is the best role model of evangelism. In His earthly life, Jesus sent out His disciples in groups of two to share the Good News. If one falls, the other will help him to get up. In modern terms it is 'watching each other's back.' In a spiritual sense, when one is witnessing to someone the other can pray for the conversation of the individual. It is also good for security. If something bad happens, an eyewitness (other than you and the Holy Spirit) will give you support in a court of law. It is better to have co-workers of different genders; preferably with some age difference.

In the above-mentioned example, I would not have spoken to the young Muslim lady because she was about my age and of course she was the opposite gender. Najima is older than I am, so the Muslim young lady was not stuck with any suspicions about my relationship with Najima. When Najima initiated the conversation, it allowed me to jump in with a very smooth transition.

In John 15:20 Jesus said, "**...if they persecuted me, they will persecute you also.**" And verse 21, "**They will treat you this way because of my Name, for they do not know the One who sent me.**" We know we will be persecuted; therefore we need to always be alert. In the Islamic faith, dying or giving your life as a sacrifice secures your place in heaven. Our God does not demand such sacrifice because Christ has already paid the price. This life is a beautiful gift of God and our bodies are His temples. We are obligated to reach others with a sincere heart and love for Christ who died for this lost world. Christ said, **"For God did not send his Son into the world to condemn the world, but to save the world through Him. Whoever believes in Him is not condemned, but whoever does not believe stands condemned already because he has not believed in the name of God's one and only Son"** (John 3:17-18 NIV). God loved us first and His love for human kind compelled Him to take the road, which has never been taken by any man for the sake of others. He sent **"his Son to be the atoning sacrifice for our sins"** (1 John 4:10). The world does not know the truth and value of His sacrifice. Christ said, **"So if the Son sets you free, you will be free indeed"** (John 8:36), and when a slave has been given eternal life, he experiences true freedom. Even though the master does not require it, it should be the joy and desire of the slave to share, **"whoever believes in the Son has eternal life, but whoever rejects the Son will not see life, for God's wrath remains on him"** (John 3:36). Like the Samaritan woman at the well, Jesus did not ask her to go and evangelize. She felt obligated out of her excitement about someone who knew everything and potentially could be the Messiah, **"Come, see a man who told me everything I ever did. Could this be the Christ?"** Another example is the blind man whom Christ healed. Out of his love and thankfulness to God he didn't fear but proclaimed the truth, **"One thing I do know. I was blind but now I see!"** (John 9:25).

Q#79—Do evangelists and missionaries often find themselves in evangelism danger zones?

Answer: It happens more than it should. When you act out of love and concern, you might underestimate the danger of unsafe surroundings. Be alert. Christ's personal life shows us that he was always on the alert. Many times Jewish leaders would have laid hands on Him, but they could not because they feared the people. Whenever Jesus addressed their hypocrisy, He chose a spot in the middle of a crowd. He knew the Jewish leaders would not do anything as long as He was surrounded by people who followed Him for His pure teaching. On other occasions, when He was in the midst of a group who disagreed with His claims and tried to persecute Him, Jesus was able to avoid it just simply because He was alert and knew where the emergency "exit door" was. **"They got up, drove him out of the town, and led Him to the brow of the hill on which their town was built, so that they might hurl Him off the cliff. But he passed through the midst of them and went on His way"** (Luke 4:29-30).

Alert means that you are aware of the geographical landscape. Moreover, you are aware of your environment. You need to know where the exits in a building are located and always choose a spot near one. Be aware of your legal and social rights. Ignorance regarding the rules and regulations is not a good excuse. Be aware of what is around you, and how many people are around you. Choose an angle that might help you to see everyone in a room or open area. Your position is crucial in both sharing your faith effectively and avoiding any potential hazard.

The following is a hypothetical situation. You are in a building, which is closed from all sides, and unfortunately all the people are facing the opposite side of the door. In the design below where would you place yourself if the door is the grey side and the people are facing the red side of the box?

A nice, sweet, and kind person such as yourself is sharing your faith with them (of course out of your love). The unexpected may happen. Please remember the rules.

Evangelists do not want to see the evil side of human beings (it's like blind love), especially with in that very nice person with whom they have just shared the Word of God. Reality demands wisdom, as Christ taught his disciples when he sent them out: **"Behold, I send you out as sheep in the midst of wolves; so be shrewd as serpents and innocent as doves"** (Matt 10:16 NASB).

Remember!
Under no circumstances should you let your guard down.

Q#80—Your acronyms are very interesting. They make it easy to remember those things one might forget. Do you have any other useful acronyms?

Answer: I am very happy to describe a couple more. Some time ago, I taught a course entitled "Introduction to Islam" at the **New York School of the Bible** in New York City. I asked my students to follow an acronym that I learned in business school: KISS. *Keep It Simple, Stupid.* One assignment for the final exam of the course was to follow a threefold pattern. First week, find a Muslim person. Once you identify a Muslim introduce yourself to him/her with full honesty, telling him/her that you are a Bible student learning about Islam. Ask the place of his origin, i.e., the name of his home country. Talk about his or her country and culture. Share what you have learned so far in class. Make an appointment for the next week with him/her.

I asked my students to learn about the native country of the person, as well as their personal socio-economical, political and religious struggles. My students were required to meet the person the following week at an appointed time and share some of the interesting things they have learned about his or her country. It is very important to empathize on those points where you feel he/she may have been hurt. For example, in Bangladesh, before it was separated from Pakistan, Pakistani military butchered many Bengalis in their streets on the basis of ethnicity. Every Muslim country has had some painful history, so ask your friend to share some. Finally, encourage him or her to share his Muslim faith and simply listen. Feel free to raise critical questions which are not answered in the religion of Islam e.g. assurance of heaven, after life and how good a person should be to be considered good. The third week my students were required to share their Christian faith. KISS is essential when it comes to long-term relationships. When you share your faith, *Keep It Simple, Stupid.* Share honestly and sincerely, let him think he knows everything and you are learning from him. Build up his/her ego before you shake the foundation of his knowledge and ignorance about Islam and Christianity.

Excess of everything is bad, especially knowledge. Whether the knowledge is correct or incorrect, it can make you think you are sitting on top of the world and nothing else matters to you. You are learning so much that you feel that you know everything about evangelism and you can conquer intellectual religious territory philosophically. You will be surprised to know, soon after you finish your talk, that it is not the knowledge you have that makes you the best evangelistic *soul reaper* but your humbleness before the Holy Spirit.

We are promised to have direct help from our heavenly Father if we are humble before God and let him take over our intellect. As I mentioned earlier, Luke 12:12 writes, **"For the Holy Spirit will teach you in that very hour what you ought to say."** Christ told Peter, **"I will build My church"** (Matt 16:18). Peter was a man who could not even confess his companionship with Christ (Mark 14:66-72) and denied Christ the very night he claimed, **"Even if all fall away, I will not"** (Mark 14:29). He was a man who spent most of his life catching fish and probably had little experience in public speaking. Yet the day came when Peter stood up, filled with the Holy Spirit, and boldly proclaimed the truth: **"...those who gladly received His word were baptized; and that day about three thousand souls were added to them"** (Acts 2:41). Our job as evangelists is to present the truth with boldness and simplicity. Paul writes to the church of Philippi: **"For it is God who works in you to will and to act according to His good purpose"**(Philippians 2:13).

Q#81—Let me review Access and Alert steps. Alright, I am ready, what is next?

Answer: Before we look at the third A, let's review all three together just to refresh our memory—**AAA: Assess, Alert, Acknowledge.** The final and very crucial point in the development of Muslim evangelism or evangelism in general is:

3. Acknowledgement

Think about your life, would you like to be friends with someone who always disagrees with you? If someone is constantly telling me his opinion is right and mine is wrong, no matter what I say, that friendship will probably go nowhere. Most likely I would try to avoid a person who makes me feel that I am always wrong even when the rest of world conforms to my thoughts or opinions. When you are not given the recognition you deserve, it hinders the communication. When we are evangelizing, we must give the person the credit he or she deserves. You may not always agree with him, but search for ways to give him the recognition, which may build the foundation of a strong conversation. For example, a person once asked me about the deity of Christ. He used very humiliating words to question the Trinity, death and resurrection of Jesus Christ and the concept of atonement. "It is nonsense," he said, "to think that God, the creator, died for His creation" he continued. I could have replied, "Sorry, but I disagree." However, I answered humbly, "I agree that it does not make sense that God the Creator would die for His creation." It is important to recognize that you are agreeing with a disagreement, but not confirming that he is right in his assumptions. What you are saying in fact is that the human mind or logic is not able to comprehend the concept of God's grace and mercy toward sinful man. That is absolutely true; our human mind cannot fathom Almighty God. Later in conversation you can refer back to this point to explain His unconditional love for human beings.

Another way to acknowledge someone's tough points, although you totally disagree, is through the simple phrase *I understand what you are saying*. The recognition you are giving is actually nothing more than saying I am listening to you. You did not agree or disagree but it sounds like you agreed where as you did not.

In my personal experience, if you genuinely listen to the Muslim person you are trying to reach; you will be amazed to find many similar things in the Islamic faith. For example, **Islam recognizes Christ as the word of God (now they translate it as word from God), a great healer, a prophet who was without sin, born of a virgin birth, his bodily ascension in heaven**, etc. If we listen carefully and give the proper acknowledgement someone deserves, we will be completing the three AAA's. The completion of AAA will lead to a powerful sharing of your faith without any potential of existing or non-existing harm to you or your fellow workers.

Personal Notes and Comments:

_____

_____

_____

_____

_____

_____

_____

_____

_____

_____

_____

_____

_____

_____

_____

_____

_____

_____

_____

CHAPTER 8

Breaking Down the Walls: Theology of
Sin and Salvation in Islam

This chapter examines some of the issues that you must understand before you engage in Muslim outreach or evangelism. This chapter will help you to understand some of the Islamic cultural issues that evangelists encounter, particularly Western evangelists. Theologically, the chapter will examine the Islamic concept of assurance. Moreover, what assurance the founder of the religion of Islam offers to his followers, and what he said about his own salvation. I will also use some Qur'anic passages to show you Jesus in the Qur'an as well as point out theologically what Muslims believe and why they believe what they believe. The focus of the chapter is to help Christians break down some of the walls that create misunderstandings about Islam and reduce the effectiveness of Christian evangelism.

Q#82—Is it important to learn Arabic to reach out to Muslims?

Answer: It is always good to learn different languages, but in many Muslim countries, even Muslims do not speak Arabic. The second largest Muslim population resides in India and they speak Urdu. However, I recommend that every person who is trying to witness to Muslims learn a few Islamic terms.

Q#83—I thought all Muslims read the Qur'an in Arabic?

Answer: Yes, they do, but it does not mean that they speak Arabic or understand Arabic. I can read and write Arabic because I am from a Muslim country, but I can't understand or speak it. I understand very little. There are very few Muslims who understand the Qur'an, even those who speak Arabic think you need additional education to understand the true meaning of the text in the Qur'an.

If you are using the Muslim Approach in evangelism, then certainly you have to be familiar with various Islamic terms.

If you really have a heart for Muslims you have to take a few steps just like a trained missionary. I know many missionaries who learned a language before they went to their field of missions. Actually, most of my friends are missionaries. Let me share two examples out of hundreds. One of my friends is getting ready to go to a West African country. Apart from raising funds, he is learning about Islam and the Islamic culture, the Qur'an and the Hadiths, the history of Islam and the theology of the Islamic belief system. He grew up in America and has lived here his entire life. Now, at 35 years old, God has called him to minister to Muslims in a West African country. It is imperative as a missionary to Muslims that he or she learns about the culture and language of the country. The point is this: **Islam has its own culture.**

Another friend is serving in Japan. When he was in the US, he hung out with Japanese students and learned about their culture. He knew short phrases before he left for Japan about two years ago. Now he speaks Japanese; and although he has a foreign accent, people appreciate that he speaks their language. They love to talk to him because they find it fascinating.

Ministry to Muslims requires more preparation than the two examples given above. You need to learn about two cultures, the culture of the country and the Islamic culture. You also must learn the language of the people and some of the Arabic phrases to fit into the culture. If you are called to reach out to a Muslim community in your neighborhood, remember you have an advantage being a local missionary because Muslims here in the United States understand Western culture. Yet you need to find some distinctive attributes to relate to them. The following vocabulary would be one unique way.

Here is the list of short phrases that might be very helpful as you prepare for local or global missions among Muslims.

SAY	WHEN
Assalam-u-Alaikum	meet a Muslim
Peace be upon you	
Walaikum Assalam	a Muslim greets you
And peace be upon you	
Assalam-u-Alaikum Wa Rahmatullahi Wa Barakatuh	meet a Muslim
Peace and mercy and blessings of Allah be upon you	
Walaikum Assalam Wa Rahmatullahi Wa Barakatuh	a Muslim greets you
And peace and mercy and blessings of Allah be upon you	
Bismillah	before making a beginning
In the name of Allah	
JazakAllah	for expression of thanks
May Allah reward you	
JazakAllahu Khair	for expression of thanks
May Allah reward you for the good	
BarakAllahu Feekum	responding to someone's thanks
May Allah bless you	
Fi Amanullah	by way of saying good-bye
May Allah protect you	
Subhaanallah	for praising something
Glory be to Allah	
Insha Allah	for expressing a desire to do something
If Allah wishes	
Astaghfirullah	repenting for sins before Allah
I beg Allah for forgiveness	
Masha Allah	for expressing appreciation of something good
As Allah has willed	
Alhamdulillah	for showing gratitude to Allah after success or even after completing anything
Praise be to Allah	

SAY	WHEN
Aameen	the end of a Dua or prayer
May it be so	
Sal Allahu Aleihi Wasallam	whenever saying the name of Prophet Muhammad
Peace be upon him (S.A.W.)	
Alaihi salaam	whenever saying the name of a prophet
Peace be upon him (A.S.)	
Radi Allah Anhu	whenever saying the name of a male companion of the Prophet (Sahabi)
May Allah be pleased with him (R.A.)	
Radi Allah Anha	whenever saying the name of a female companion of the Prophet
May Allah be pleased with her (R.A.)	
Radi Allah Anhum	Plural form of saying companions of the Prophet
May Allah be pleased with them (R.A.)	
Innaa Lillaahi Wa Innaa Ilayhi Raaji'oon	this is uttered as an expression of sympathy of the news of some loss or someone's death
To Allah we belong and to Him is our return	
La Hawla Wala Quwata Illah Billah	during the time of troubles
There is no strength nor power except Allah	
Al Hamdu Lillah	after sneezing
Praise be to Allah	
Yar Hamukallah	someone else sneezes
May Allah have mercy on you	
Fi Sabi Lillah	giving charity
For the sake of Allah	

The above terms were retrieved from http://www.alQuranic.com/articles/mail246.asp. Please feel free to explore the website to learn more.

Q#85—Could you provide an example in dialogue form?

Answer: Sure, **let's get started.**

Assalamu alaikum

Walaikum Assalam

Are you a Muslim?

(If the person is Muslim his answer would be *Alhamdulillah* or simply yes. Please do not assume that everyone who looks like an Asian, Middle Easterner or Arab is a Muslim. Many other minorities live in those areas).

If the answer is yes or Alhamdulillah, your reply always should be *Subhaanallah*, followed by another question: "If you do not mind, may I ask you a question?"

Sure.

Do you consider yourself a good Muslim?

"I hope, I pray every day, I do whatever is the right thing to do…etc." or the answer would be "Alhamdulillah," or "I try to be." Mostly, Muslims tend to be very humble when it comes to religion. So please acknowledge their humbleness; it will bring you one step closer to reaching your Muslim friend.

Subhanallah! (Your answer starting with Subhanallah should draw him.) I am always confused about how good is good enough to be considered a good Muslim before Allah-Tibariko Talla? If one does everything to please God, such as prayers, giving alms, belief in the prophet, reading the Qur'an and performing hajj—is that considered good enough to enter into paradise? And if he does this twenty-four hours a day, seven days a week, and three hundred and sixty-five days per year—is that good enough? But suppose he did three little things wrong per day. In a week he would be guilty of twenty-one wrong things, and in a year he would be guilty of 1,095. If he happened to live for 70 years, he would be guilty of 76,650 sins. Now how would he please a holy God with his sinful life? In a worldly court, one criminal action is enough to charge you guilty of punishment. What if someone is not good enough or even if he is good enough? Either way, what is the future of a Muslim person? What will happen to a Muslim after death? It is the issue of salvation, which is an unknown term among Muslims. Therefore, be careful when you start a conversation about salvation.

Q#86—Do Muslims believe in salvation? If yes, how secure is their salvation? Do they have assurance of salvation, like Christians?

Answer: The most common Muslim response is that Allah knows. No one can know if he will go into paradise or not because Allah will determine it when we die and go before Him. According to Muslims, bad deeds and good deeds will be measured and whatever weighs the most will be rewarded. If the bad deeds side is heavy a Muslim will go to hell; if the good deeds are heavy, then paradise.

(All the Qur'anic verses mentioned in this book contain commentary *Tafsir* from a Muslim commentator to show you how Muslims understand the Qur'anic verses in the 21st century.)

Surat Al-Mu'minūn (The Believers)—23:102 سورة المؤمنون

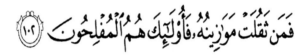

Sahih International Translation

And those whose scales are heavy [with good deeds]—it is they who are the successful.

Tafsir al-Jalalayn (Muslim commentary)

Then those whose scales are heavy, with good deeds, they are the successful, the winners;

The theology of Islam has taken a new direction in recent times. "Islam is a religion of peace" has become a slogan in the aftermath of the terrorist attacks in the West by Jihadists. In order to compete with the Christian theology of salvation and atonement apart from works, Muslims have adopted the Catholic theology of purgatory with the hope that God will show His mercy toward Muslims and let Muslims enter if they do their best to please Him. There is also a belief that all those Muslims who will not be given permission to enter paradise will go to a special place where they will finish their punishment and come back to paradise. However, Allah says:

Surat Al-Baqarah (The Cow)—2:105

مَا يَوَدُّ ٱلَّذِينَ كَفَرُوا۟ مِنْ أَهْلِ ٱلْكِتَٰبِ وَلَا ٱلْمُشْرِكِينَ أَن
يُنَزَّلَ عَلَيْكُم مِّنْ خَيْرٍ مِّن رَّبِّكُمْ ۗ وَٱللَّهُ يَخْتَصُّ
بِرَحْمَتِهِۦ مَن يَشَآءُ ۚ وَٱللَّهُ ذُو ٱلْفَضْلِ ٱلْعَظِيمِ ﴿١٠٥﴾

Sahih International Translation

Neither those who disbelieve from the People of the Scripture nor the polytheists wish that any good should be sent down to you from your Lord. But Allah selects for His mercy whom He wills, and Allah is the possessor of great bounty.

Tafsir al-Jalalayn (Muslim commentary)

Those disbelievers of the People of the Scripture and the idolaters, from among the Arabs (al-mushrikīna, 'idolaters', is a supplement to ahl al-kitābi, 'People of the Scripture', and the min, 'of', is explicative), do not wish that any good, any Inspiration, should be revealed to you from your Lord, out of envy of you, but God singles out for His mercy, [for] the office of His Prophet, whom He will; God is of bounty abounding.

The verse shows that God's grace and mercy is not for everyone, but for whom He chooses. Then how can someone in Islam be assured of paradise at all? Whether they do good deeds or bad, it is still God's will whether or not He forgives. Christianity has a similar theology regarding the elected ones. However, in Christianity, God allows humanity to practice free will. (I understand that not all Christians believe in free will). Under free will, people have the option to respond positively or reject the message of salvation. If they repent and ask forgiveness in the name of Jesus, they are assured of entrance into heaven.

Q#87—Did the Islamic prophet Muhammad claim that he was sinless, as Jesus claimed? No one was able to prove that Jesus had any sin within Him.

Answer: Actually, it is just the opposite of his claim. The founder and prophet of Islam, Muhammad was asked by Allah to repent of his sins: it means he was sinful and needed repentance. Many Muslims do not like such a statement; it is considered blasphemy because according to Islamic teaching, the prophets were innocent.

Q#88—If the prophet Muhammad was not sinful, then certainly he can't forgive the sins of others, like Jesus did.

Answer: It is so obvious to you because you understand the authority of Jesus as the one who forgave the sins of sinner. But Muslims do not understand that because their leader and prophet Muhammad never claimed that he was more than a prophet. There are many verses throughout the Qur'an that indicate that the prophet of Islam was asked to pray for forgiveness of his sins.

In the **Qur'an 40:55** Allah asked Muhammad to ask for forgiveness for his sins.

Surat Ghāfir (The Believer)—40:55

فَٱصۡبِرۡ إِنَّ وَعۡدَ ٱللَّهِ حَقٌّ وَٱسۡتَغۡفِرۡ لِذَنۢبِكَ وَسَبِّحۡ بِحَمۡدِ رَبِّكَ بِٱلۡعَشِيِّ وَٱلۡإِبۡكَٰرِ ۝

Sahih International Translation

So be patient, [O Muhammad]. Indeed, the promise of Allah is truth. _And ask forgiveness for your sin_ **and exalt [Allah] with praise of your Lord in the evening and the morning.**

Tafsir al-Jalalayn

So be patient, O Muhammad (s). Surely God's promise, to grant victory to His friends, is true—for you and whoever follows you are among such [friends]. And ask forgiveness for your sin, so that you will be emulated in this [by your community], and glorify, perform prayer, continuously, with praise of your Lord at night—which means after sunset—and in the early hours: the five prayers.

Surat Al-Fatḥ (The Victory)—48:1-2

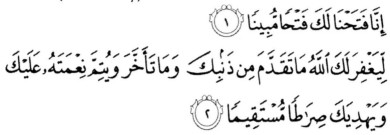

Sahih International Translation

Indeed, we have given you, [O Muhammad], a clear conquest that Allah may forgive for you what preceded of your sin and what will follow and complete His favor upon you and guide you to a straight path.

The following commentary by a Muslim scholar gives a clearer picture of Muslim understanding of the above verse.

Tafsir al-Jalalayn

Verily We have given you, We have ordained [for you] the conquest (fath) of Mecca, and other places **in the <u>future by force</u>, as a result of your struggle, a clear victory,** *[one that is]* **plain and manifest** *that God may forgive you, by virtue of your struggle, what is past of your sin and what is to come, of it, so that your community might then desire to struggle [like you] — this [verse] also constitutes a justification of the [concept of the] infallibility (ʿisma) of prophets, peace be upon them, against sin, by way of a definitive rational proof (the lām [in li-yaghfira, 'that He may forgive'] is for [indicating] the ultimate reason [for the conquest], so that the content [of this latter statement] constitutes an effect and not the cause), and that He may perfect, by way of the mentioned victory, His favour to you and guide you, thereby, to a straight path, upon which He will confirm you — and this [straight path] is the religion of Islam;*

Q#89—Do more references about the Islamic prophet Muhammad's state of sinfulness exist?

Answer: In Islam, there are two major holy sources for guidance. First, the Qur'an, and secondly, the traditions of Muhammad called Hadiths. One of the authentic sources for the traditions of Muhammad by Bukhari states: "Narrated Abu Huraira: … What do you say in the pause between Takbir and recitation? The Prophet said, O Allah! Set me apart from my sins (faults) as the East and West are set apart from each other and clean me from sins as a white garment is cleaned of dirt (after thorough washing). O Allah! Wash off my sins with water, snow and hail." *Bukhari* vol.1:711, p.398 and *Bukhari* vol.1:7, 19,781; vol.6:3; vol.8:319, vol.8:407 prior.

Q#90—What about the Islamic prophet Muhammad's own salvation? Was he sure of what would happen to him after his physical life ended?

Answer: The short answer is no. He was not sure what would happen to him when he died. Still today the followers of Islam do not have any assurance either. Here are a few verses where the prophet of Islam, Muhammad, didn't know what Allah would do to him.

Surat Al-'Aḥqāf (The Wind-Curved Sandhills)—46:9

قُلْ مَا كُنتُ بِدْعًا مِّنَ ٱلرُّسُلِ وَمَآ أَدْرِى مَا يُفْعَلُ بِى وَلَا بِكُمْ إِنْ أَتَّبِعُ إِلَّا مَا يُوحَىٰٓ إِلَيَّ وَمَآ أَنَا۠ إِلَّا نَذِيرٌ مُّبِينٌ ﴿٩﴾

Sahih International Translation

Say, "I am not something original among the messengers, <u>nor do I know what will be done with me or with you</u>. I only follow that which is revealed to me, and I am not but a clear warner."

Tafsir al-Jalalayn (Muslim commentary)

Say: 'I am not a novelty, unprecedented, among the messengers, that is to say, [I am not] the first to be sent [by God as His Messenger]. Already many of them have come before me, so how can you deny me? Nor do I know what will be done with me or with you, in this world: will I be made to leave my [native] land, or will I be slain as was done with [some] prophets before me, or will you stone me to death, or will the earth be made to swallow you as [it did] deniers before you? I only follow what is revealed to me, that is, the Qur'ān, and I do not invent anything myself. And I am only a plain warner, one whose warning is plain.

Q#91—Do Muslims acknowledge that their prophet didn't have any assurance?

Answer: Muslims reject that argument, but the evidence from the Qur'an and Hadiths are available regardless of their objections. Some Christian scholars argue if it would have been in the power of Muslims, they would proclaim the Islamic prophet Muhammad is alive. This is actually what they believe. Well, that is another theological debate for another time. The Qur'an 46:9 clearly states Muhammad did not have any hope for him or his followers in terms for the future. Modern interpretation tends to turn the argument from future knowledge (after life) to the present world (Muhammad's life time on earth). However, verse 46:9, in its context shows the full picture that all the messengers (prophets) before Muhammad didn't know their future. Thus, when the Islamic prophet Muhammad said, *"I am not special,"* it acknowledges that he did not know his future either. To him, and the whole Muslim community, the only hope they have is in the final day of judgment. Moreover, Muslims believe this is the day when God will open the books and weigh their deeds or simply show his mercy and grace. Until that day, no one really knows what will happen in the afterlife.

Q#92—Can you provide the other references with respect to the Islamic prophet Muhammad's lack of assurance regarding his afterlife?

Answer: As I mentioned earlier, Saheeh Bukhari is the second most holy and authentic source after the Qur'an for Muslims. You must understand that Islam is very different from Christianity. In many ways it's like Judaism where the founder or the leader claimed to hear the voice of God and received revelation from God for his people. However, both religious founders/leaders were entirely dependent on the mercy of God. The Prophet Mohammad's traditions (Hadith) conforms it by describing a story: Narrated 'Um al-'Ala:

> An Ansari woman who gave the pledge of allegiance to the Prophet that the Ansar drew lots concerning the dwelling of the Emigrants. 'Uthman bin Maz'un was

decided to dwell with them (i.e. Um al-'Ala's family), 'Uthman fell ill and I nursed him till he died, and we covered him with his clothes. Then the Prophet came to us and I (addressing the dead body) said, "O Abu As-Sa'ib, may Allah's Mercy be on you! I bear witness that Allah has honored you." On that the Prophet said, "How do you know that Allah has honored him?" I replied, "I do not know. May my father and my mother be sacrificed for you, O Allah's Apostle! But who else is worthy of it (if not 'Uthman)?" He said, "As to him, by Allah, death has overtaken him, and I hope the best for him. By Allah, though I am the Apostle of Allah, yet I do not know what Allah will do to me." By Allah, I will never assert the piety of anyone after him. That made me sad, and when I slept I saw in a dream a flowing stream for 'Uthman bin Maz'un. I went to Allah's Apostle and told him of it. He remarked, "That symbolizes his (good) deeds." [*Bukhari* Volume 5, Book 58, Number 266].

Q#93—Do Muslims have any hope in the afterlife?

Answer: Yes, if they accept Jesus Christ. The Qur'an teaches salvation based on works. Muslims hope that on the last day God will show His mercy and grace and let them enter into paradise. There is no doubt that God is all merciful and gracious. God has already showed His grace and mercy in Christ, and through Christ, the grace of God saves the person for eternal life. Once a person receives Christ as personal Savior, he or she is saved forever, and is forgiven once and for all. God is all-forgiving, but the Qur'an teaches conditional forgiveness.

Here are a few verses from the Quran dealing with work-based salvation:

Surat Ash-Shūraá (The Consultation)—42:26

$$\text{وَيَسْتَجِيبُ ٱلَّذِينَ ءَامَنُوا۟ وَعَمِلُوا۟ ٱلصَّٰلِحَٰتِ وَيَزِيدُهُم مِّن فَضْلِهِۦ}$$
$$\text{وَٱلْكَٰفِرُونَ لَهُمْ عَذَابٌ شَدِيدٌ ﴿٢٦﴾}$$

Sahih International Translation

And He answers [the supplication of] those who have believed and done righteous deeds and increases [for] them from His bounty. But the disbelievers will have a severe punishment.

Tafsir al-Jalalayn (Muslim commentary)

And He answers those who believe and perform righteous deeds, He grants them what they ask for, and He enhances them of His bounty. And as for the disbelievers, for them there will be a severe chastisement.

Surat Al-Mā'idah (The Table Spread)—5:9

وَعَدَ اللَّهُ الَّذِينَ ءَامَنُوا وَعَمِلُوا الصَّـٰلِحَـٰتِ لَهُم مَّغْفِرَةٌ وَأَجْرٌ عَظِيمٌ ﴿٩﴾

Sahih International Translation

Allah has promised those who believe and do righteous deeds [that] for them there is forgiveness and great reward.

Tafsir al-Jalalayn (Muslim commentary)

God has promised to those who believe and perform righteous deeds an excellent promise: they shall have forgiveness and a great wage, that is, Paradise.

Surat Al-'Anfāl (The Spoils of War)—8:29

يَـٰٓأَيُّهَا الَّذِينَ ءَامَنُوٓا إِن تَتَّقُوا اللَّهَ يَجْعَل لَّكُمْ فُرْقَانًا وَيُكَفِّرْ عَنكُمْ سَيِّـَٔاتِكُمْ وَيَغْفِرْ لَكُمْ وَاللَّهُ ذُو الْفَضْلِ الْعَظِيمِ ﴿٢٩﴾

Sahih International Translation

O you who have believed, if you fear Allah, He will grant you a criterion and will remove from you your misdeeds and forgive you. And Allah is the possessor of great bounty.

Tafsir al-Jalalayn

The following was revealed regarding his [Abū Lubāba's] repentance: O you who believe, if you fear God, by turning [in repentance] to Him and in other ways, He will grant you a [means of] separation, between yourselves and what you fear, so that you will be delivered, and absolve you of your evil deeds, and forgive you, your sins; and God is of tremendous bounty.

Another translation states the same verse as, **"O you who believe! If you are careful of (your duty to) Allah, He will grant you a distinction and do away with your evils and forgive you; and Allah is the Lord of mighty grace,"** (**8:29**, online, trans. by M.H. Shakir).

Q#94—It seems from above reference that Allah shows his grace. Does it mean Muslim believe in grace like Christians do?

Answer: How can grace and works coexist? In Islam, it's all about rewards, not of grace. It cannot be grace if someone has to work for it. If my father tells me, "Son, today I will drive you to the theater to watch a new movie," I would thank him, and as a sign of my gratitude, I would try to please him with no strings attached. However, if my father says, "Son, today I will drive you to the theater to watch a new movie if you do X, Y, and Z," then it is not grace; rather it is conditional grace. I must do something for him and in return he will drive me to the theater. No gratitude is needed, there is no need to feel thankful because I earned going to the movie. If he could not take me to the theater, I could demand it because he owes me. It is like a business transaction.

If that were the case between God and man, then we are equal to some extent. We could be arrogant and prideful. If I were entering paradise to enjoy my afterlife due to my good works, God would not have any say because I earned it. Why would judgment be necessary? It would just be an automatic reward system. It should be credited to my account, and I should by pass any judgment of God. For example, the Qur'an Surah 29:14 confirms that one receives grace and forgiveness through deeds:

Surat Al-Ḥujurāt (The Rooms)—49:14

۞ قَالَتِ ٱلْأَعْرَابُ ءَامَنَّا ۖ قُل لَّمْ تُؤْمِنُوا۟ وَلَٰكِن قُولُوٓا۟ أَسْلَمْنَا وَلَمَّا

يَدْخُلِ ٱلْإِيمَٰنُ فِى قُلُوبِكُمْ ۖ وَإِن تُطِيعُوا۟ ٱللَّهَ وَرَسُولَهُۥ لَا يَلِتْكُم مِّنْ

أَعْمَٰلِكُمْ شَيْـًٔا ۚ إِنَّ ٱللَّهَ غَفُورٌ رَّحِيمٌ ۝

Sahih International Translation

The Bedouins say, "We have believed." Say, "You have not [yet] believed; but say [instead], 'We have submitted,' for faith has not yet entered your hearts. <u>And if you obey Allah and His Messenger, He will not deprive you from your deeds of anything. Indeed, Allah is Forgiving and Merciful.</u>"

Tafsir al-Jalalayn commentary

The Bedouins—a group of men from among the Banū Asad—say, 'We believe', we affirm the truth in our hearts. Say, to them: 'You do not believe; but rather say, "We have submitted," we are outwardly compliant; for faith has not yet entered into your hearts', hitherto; however, it is expected of you. Yet if you obey God and His Messenger, by [embracing] faith and in other ways, He will not diminish for you (read ya'litkum or yalitkum, by making the hamza an alif) anything of your deeds, that is, of the reward for them. God is indeed Forgiving, to believers, Merciful, to them.

Surat Al-'Aḥzāb (The Combined Forces)—33:70

يَٰٓأَيُّهَا ٱلَّذِينَ ءَامَنُوا۟ ٱتَّقُوا۟ ٱللَّهَ وَقُولُوا۟ قَوْلًا سَدِيدًا ۝

Sahih International Translation

O you, who have believed, fear Allah and speak words of appropriate justice.

Tafsir al-Jalalayn

O you who believe, fear God and speak words of integrity, what is proper.

Surat Al-'Aḥzāb (The Combined Forces)—33:71

يُصۡلِحۡ لَكُمۡ أَعۡمَـٰلَكُمۡ وَيَغۡفِرۡ لَكُمۡ ذُنُوبَكُمۡ وَمَن يُطِعِ ٱللَّهَ وَرَسُولَهُۥ
فَقَدۡ فَازَ فَوۡزًا عَظِيمًا ﴿٧١﴾

Sahih International Translation

He will [then] amend for you your deeds and forgive you your sins. And whoever obeys Allah and His Messenger has certainly attained a great attainment.

Tafsir al-Jalalayn (Muslim commentary)

He will rectify your deeds for you, He will accept them, and will forgive you your sins. And whoever obeys God and His Messenger has verily achieved a great success, he has attained his ultimate goal.

Q#95—I don't understand. If Muhammad was not sure about his salvation and didn't know what will happen to his people, was he really a prophet?

Answer: This is a very complicated question and Muslim friends will be angry with you if you question Muhammad's prophethood. Actually, according to Shar'ia Law (Islamic law), you should be put to death for questioning Muhammad's prophethood. Here is what I have learned over a period of time: In Christianity, we face the dilemma of false prophets, thus, there is standard procedure to test the prophethood of a person who makes such a claim. First, a prophet is called 'prophet' because he prophesies and secondly, every prophet who came told his nation about the future and hope to come. Regarding the life of the Islamic prophet Muhammad, there is no concrete evidence that he ever prophesied. Moreover, all the previous prophets performed miracles, but in case of the Islamic prophet Muhammad, there is no evidence to support that he performed a clear miracle. Muslims say the Qur'an itself is a miracle. Interestingly enough, some Muslims believe that Muhammad once split the moon in two halves.

Q# 96—Where would Muslims find the answer of salvation?

Answer: If someone asks, "Where is the answer?" As Christians we know that in Christ we have full assurance of our salvation. We believe that "...by grace you have been saved through faith; and that not of yourselves, it is the gift of God..." (Eph. 2:8-9). The difference between having assurance and not having assurance is like saying I am traveling from Boston to New York City where I have to teach Bible school on Monday. I decide to leave on Sunday, but because I was busy, I failed to get a ticket in advance. The flight was sold out when I went to buy the ticket and I was placed on standby. People around me were relaxed and happy because they held confirmed tickets in their hands. However, I paced back and forth as I anxiously waited to see whether I would be called to board the plane, and be able to teach at the school. I would wonder, "What if they fill the plane and a seat is not available. What would I do then?" 1 John 5:13 says, "These things I have written to you who believe in the name of the Son of God, so that you may know that you have eternal life." Muslims have no concept of eternal life. Human works can never be sufficient to please a holy God. Isaiah 64:6 says, **"All of us have become like one who is unclean, and all our righteous acts are like filthy rags; we all shrivel up like a leaf, and like the wind our sins sweep us away."**

The Good News is that we do not have to work for our salvation. More importantly, even if we did, it would never be enough to earn the right to heaven. Therefore, Jesus became the answer to every question. God took upon Himself flesh and became a human being that we, by faith, might enter into God's presence. He died for our sins and rose again from the dead (1 Cor. 15:1-4). In Romans 8:3-4, Paul explains the weakness of humanity: **"For what the law was powerless to do in that it was weakened by the sinful nature, God did by sending his own Son in the likeness of sinful man to be a sin offering. And so he condemned sin in sinful man, in order that the righteous requirements of the law might be fully met in us, who do not live according to the sinful nature but according to the Spirit."** He fulfilled all the Law, which no man could fulfill. He continues in 2 Cor. 5:21: **"He made Him who knew no sin to be sin on our behalf, so that we might become the righteousness of God in Him"** (NASB). God is the one who initiates the process of salvation and He is the one who provides the assurance. **"He made**

Him who knew no sin to be sin on our behalf, so that we might become the righteousness of God in Him" (I Peter 1:5, New Living Translation, 2007).

According to 1 Peter 1:9, it is through faith: **"For you are receiving the goal of your faith, the salvation of your souls"** (NIV, 1984). Because we are sinners, we cannot please an infinitely holy God on our own. Furthermore, because we can never fulfill the Law of God perfectly, and because God's eyes are too pure to look upon evil, salvation must be totally by grace. **"For by grace you have been saved through faith, and this is not from you; it is the gift of God; it is not from works, so no one may boast"** (Eph. 2:8, 9, NAB). Thus, if we want to be considered perfect before God, and receive eternal life, then salvation must be the work of God and God alone.

Personal Notes and Comments:

_____

_____

_____

_____

_____

_____

_____

_____

_____

_____

_____

_____

_____

_____

_____

_____

_____

_____

_____

CHAPTER 9

Muslim Beliefs: Corruption in the Bible

This chapter is an apologetic approach to some of the most difficult questions Muslim friends have. Moreover, this is a very crucial step toward becoming a more effective evangelist and apologist to Muslims. It is important to remember that there are good and bad people everywhere. Moreover, there are moderates and fanatics. You can find such people in any nation, any religion or even among those who do not believe in God. However, when it comes to religion, there are beliefs and concepts that become impossible to resolve.

In Islam, there are three things that are impossible to resolve but if you are well prepared and you are patient, meek, kind, not aggressive you may able to break through some of the thick walls. In most parts of the civilized world, you have opportunity to have debates and conversations to present your side of the story. This chapter is a brief survey of some of the significant verses dealing with major allegations against Christianity. **You must know the Bible before you study the Qur'an.** The Qur'an speaks about many of the same prophets and individuals we have in the Bible.

The important point is this: the Qur'an claims that all those prophets received a part of the revelation from God, but Muhammad was given the complete revelation. They believe that there is a book in Heaven, the Book, which is God's book in seventh heaven where God resides. In the past, God took portions of the Book and gave it to prophets for particular nations. However, God took the entire book and gave it to Muhammad through

Gabriel. Thus, Muslims believe that the Qur'an is the exact copy of The Book in heaven. Furthermore, remember when the Qur'an mentions "The People of the Book," it means the text is referring to Jews and Christians.

Q#97—When it is so clear from the Qur'an and Hadith, why don't Muslims read the Bible and seek the truth? What are the major differences between Muslims and Christians?

Answer: It would be very simple if a Muslim could read the Scriptures and understand and believe them. However, Muslims reject the authenticity of the Bible. They consider the Bible changed and corrupted. Thus, it is difficult to use the Bible as a reference to guide or disciple a Muslim. Even if you convince a Muslim that he needs the assurance of salvation, three objections will not allow him to place his faith in Jesus Christ.

These are the three objections:

1. **The Bible has been changed and corrupted.**

   Muslims believe that the Bible has been changed. The fundamental belief that "There is no god but Allah and He has no son," makes them think that the Bible has been changed. They consider it blasphemy to call Jesus God's Son. Also the same problem has another argument, which is the second objection.

2. **Jesus never claimed that He was the Son of God.**

   Speaking from the Qur'anic references about Jesus, Muslims claim that Jesus never said that He was the Son of God. They believe it was added later to the Scriptures by man, therefore the Bible is corrupted. Thus, the concept of atonement, that Jesus died on the cross for the sins of the whole world, becomes easy to deny. So, the third objection is:

3. **That Jesus did not die, He was lifted up into heaven before they arrested Him and someone else was crucified in his place. Since He never died, therefore, there was no reason for resurrection.**

If you are able to prove the authenticity of the Bible before you try to resolve the other objections, then you can answer the rest of the questions through the Bible. According to Shamoun in his article on http://www.answeringislam. org/Shamoun/aboutbible.htm

"We must also point out that the idea of the Bible being corrupted was first promoted by Ibn Khazem (d. 1064 A.D.), as a means of avoiding the obvious contradictions between the Bible and the Quran. Believing that the Quran could not possibly have been corrupted, he then assumed that it was the Bible that underwent textual modifications. This, he felt, must have been the case (cf. Gerhard Nehls, *Dear Abdallah*, Letter 2)."

The Qur'an is full of verses that disprove such a claim. In fact the Qur'an proves the Bible is a trustworthy and reliable source. However, the dust of historical lies continues to cover and hide such a truth from the Islamic world. This is done in such a way that no one challenges the Qur'an and its teachings. Thus Ibn Khazem's assumptions became the easy answer to any objection or efforts to investigate the authenticity of the Qur'an. If the scales to measure the truth and validity are broken, then assumptions and guesses can be trusted. The question is this, where would you go to prove the validity of the Gospel, and that Jesus, the incarnated God, came into this world to die for the sin of the world and rose again on third day, if the original proof of evidence (the Bible) has been considered an incorrect account by Muslims? Probably the crime scene with available objects that are assumed to be the only true evidence would be the best place to start. Muslims believe in the Qur'an and cannot deny the authority of what is written in it. Thus, using the scriptures they believe are true, and proving the truthfulness and authenticity of the Bible would be the best way to go.

Q# 98—How can I prove the authenticity of the Scriptures by using the Qur'an?

Answer: When Christians or Jews talk to Muslims using the Bible as a reference, even an illiterate Muslim will respond with the following statement: "The Bible has been changed." The problem Muslims face today is deeply rooted in their history; therefore, it is important to know something about the history of Islam and the Qur'an before understanding the Qura'nic verses. (For details knowledge about the history of Islam, please see my hand-book, *My Neighbor the Muslim*). During Muhammad's time, many Jews and Christians lived in Yasrub (modern day Medina). Because they were rich and religious, they regarded the Arabs as inferior and ignorant (with no knowledge) of the true God.

Muhammad had a very unfortunate childhood. Arab society was divided among tribal chiefs called *Sardars*. Muhammad's mother, Aamina, was married to Abdullah, son of Abd al Muttalib. Soon after the wedding, the bridegroom traveled by caravan to Al-Sham (modern day Syria). During the trip, Abdullah fell sick and died. Later, when Muhammad was six years old, his mother Aamina died. When Muhammad was ten years, two months and ten days old, he was taken into custody by his Uncle Abu Taleb, who sold merchandise from his caravan. Here Muhammad came in contact with Christians and Jews from all over the Arabian Peninsula. Evidently, Muhammad was able to hear the Scriptures as a young boy. Later he was able to take frequent trips to Sham, first with his uncle Abu-Taleb and later as his first wife, Khatija's, employee. This time period "furnished more grist for his thinking and contemplation as he came to know more of the doctrines and rituals of the people of Al-Sham. At Busrah, he came into contact with Syrian Christianity and their monks and priests, some of whom were Nestorian. Perhaps those very priests discussed with him the religion of Jesus which had by then divided itself into several sects and parties" (retrieved from WPONLINE.ORG).

Historically, Nestorius and his teachings were condemned as heresy at the First Council of Ephesus in 431A.D and the Council of Chalcedon in 451A.D, leading to the Nestorian Schism in which churches supporting Nestorius broke with the rest of the Christian Church. Those teachings became the major source of Qura'nic references.

Q#100—Are there verses in the Qur'an that prove that the Bible has never been changed or corrupted?

Answer: Yes, Indeed. Let's look at a few Qur'anic verses followed by verses from the second most popular source the Hadiths to answer that question:

Surat Al-'An`ām (The Cattle)—6:34

وَلَقَدْ كُذِّبَتْ رُسُلٌ مِّن قَبْلِكَ فَصَبَرُوا عَلَىٰ مَا كُذِّبُوا وَأُوذُوا حَتَّىٰ أَتَىٰهُمْ نَصْرُنَا وَلَا مُبَدِّلَ لِكَلِمَٰتِ اللَّهِ وَلَقَدْ جَاءَكَ مِن نَّبَإِ الْمُرْسَلِينَ ٣٤

Sahih International Translation

And certainly were messengers denied before you, but they were patient over [the effects of] denial, and they were harmed until our victory came to them. And none can alter the words of Allah. And there has certainly come to you some information about the [previous] messengers.

Tafsir al-Jalalayn (Muslim commentary)

Messengers indeed have been denied before you—herein is a consolation for the Prophet(s)—yet they endured patiently the denial and the persecution until Our victorious help came to them, through the destruction of their peoples, so be patient until the victorious help comes to you through the destruction of your people. There is none to change the words of God, His promises, and there has already come to you tidings of the messengers, [tidings] through which your heart can be at peace.

Urdu In

اور تم اور تم سے پہلے کبھی کبھی پیغمبر جھٹلائے جاتے رہے تو وہ تکذیب اور ایذا پر صبر کرتے رہے یہاں تک کہ ان کے پاس ہماری مدد پہنچتی رہی اور خدا کی باتوں کو کوئی بھی بدلنے والا نہیں۔ اور تم کو پیغمبروں (کے احوال) کی خبریں پہنچ چکی ہیں (تو تم بھی صبر سے کام لو)

The Qur'an claims that no one can alter God's Word. If that is the case, and Muslims believe that the Bible is God's Word (at least before they assumed it was altered or corrupted), then how can the Word of God be changed. **The Word of God is unalterable.** Either God is not the God He claims to be, the God who never changes and whose Word never changes, or He has no power

ـect His Word from changes. If He is who He says, and if He has the ــwer to protect His Word, then the message He gave to Moses, Jesus and other prophets is the same and cannot and will not change.

Let's see more references from the Qur'an to understand why the Bible is not changed or corrupted. Also, read the commentary by an authentic Muslim commentator.

In **Jonah (Yunus)—10:64**

لَهُمُ ٱلْبُشْرَىٰ فِى ٱلْحَيَوٰةِ ٱلدُّنْيَا وَفِى ٱلْأَخِرَةِ ۚ لَا تَبْدِيلَ لِكَلِمَٰتِ ٱللَّهِ ۚ ذَٰلِكَ هُوَ ٱلْفَوْزُ ٱلْعَظِيمُ ﴿٦٤﴾

Sahih International Translation

For them are good tidings in the worldly life and in the Hereafter. No change is there in the words of Allah. That is what is the great attainment.

Tafsir al-Jalalayn (Muslim commentary)

Theirs are good tidings in the life of this world: in a hadīth verified by al-Hākim this has been explained as [referring to] a propitious vision which an individual might have or [a vision] which another might have of that person; and in the Hereafter: Paradise and reward. There is no changing the Words of God, no failing of His promises; that, mentioned, is the supreme triumph.

Urdu In

ان کے لیے دنیا کی زندگی میں بھی بشارت ہے اور آخرت میں بھی۔ خدا کی باتیں بدلتی نہیں۔ یہی تو بڑی کامیابی ہے

The above verse clearly states that God's Word does not change. He is unchangeable and whatever He has said will stay the same. Since the Bible is His written word (just as Muslims believe the Qur'an is), it is unchangeable.

Surah Yunus verse 94 is another proof. If the Bible is changed or corrupted, why would Allah ask the Islamic prophet Muhammad to ask Jews and Christians if he has doubt about what he has been given?

Surat Yūnus (Jonah)—10:94

فَإِن كُنتَ فِى شَكٍّ مِّمَّآ أَنزَلْنَآ إِلَيْكَ فَسْـَٔلِ ٱلَّذِينَ يَقْرَءُونَ
ٱلْكِتَٰبَ مِن قَبْلِكَ لَقَدْ جَآءَكَ ٱلْحَقُّ مِن رَّبِّكَ فَلَا تَكُونَنَّ مِنَ
ٱلْمُمْتَرِينَ ۝

Sahih International Translation

So if you are in doubt, [O Muhammad], about that which We [Allah] have revealed to you, <u>then ask those who have been reading the Scripture [the Bible] before you.</u> The truth has certainly come to you from your Lord, so never be among the doubters.

Tafsir al-Jalalayn (Muslim commentary)

So, if you, O Muhammad(s), are in doubt concerning what We have revealed to you, of stories—hypothetically speaking—then question those who read the Scripture, the Torah, before you, for it is confirmed [therein] with them and they can inform you of its truth. The Prophet(s) said, 'I have no doubt, nor will I question'. Verily the Truth from your Lord has come to you; so do not be of the waverers, [of] those who have doubts about it.

Urdu In

گر اگر تم کو اس (کتاب کے) بارے میں جو ہم نے تم پر نازل کی ہے کچھ شک ہو تو جو لوگ تم سے پہلے کی (اُتری ہوئی) کتابیں پڑھتے ہیں ان سے پوچھ لو۔ تمہارے پروردگار کی طرف سے تمہارے پاس حق آچکا ہے تو تم ہرگز شک کرنے والوں میں نہ ہون

In 10:94, Allah is commanding Muhammad the founder and prophet of Islam that if he has any doubt about the Qur'an, ask the Jews and Christians about the truthfulness of what is written in the Qur'an, based on its similarity to Jewish and Christian teachings. Now if the Bible was corrupted or altered why would Allah emphasize that the Bible is a reliable source before God to confirm the truthfulness of Qur'an?

The following Surah Taha verse 133 talks about the previous holy books (the Old Testament and the New Testament) and miracles. If the Bible was corrupted why would Allah use it as the reference?

Surat Ṭāhā (Ta-Ha)—20:133

وَقَالُوا۟ لَوْلَا يَأْتِينَا بِـَٔايَةٍ مِّن رَّبِّهِۦٓ ۚ أَوَلَمْ تَأْتِهِم بَيِّنَةُ مَا فِى ٱلصُّحُفِ ٱلْأُولَىٰ ﴿١٣٣﴾

Sahih International Translation

And they say, "Why does he not bring us a sign from his Lord?" <u>Has there not come to them evidence of what was in the former scriptures?</u>

Tafsir al-Jalalayn (Muslim commentary)

And they, the idolaters, say, 'Why does he, Muhammad(s), not bring us a sign from his Lord?', of the sort which they request. Has there not come to them (read ta'tihim or ya'tihim) the clear proof, the statements, of what is in the former scriptures? the tales contained in the Qur'ān relating to past communities and [the details of] their destruction for denying the messengers?

Urdu In

اور کہتے ہیں کہ اور کہتے ہیں کہ یہ (پیغمبر) اپنے پروردگار کی طرف سے ہمارے پاس کوئی نشانی کیوں نہیں لاتے۔ کیا ان کے پاس پہلی کتابوں کی نشانی نہیں آئی؟

Remember!

This verse shows two major arguments we hear today from our Muslim friends. First, according to Muslims, the Islamic prophet Muhammad did show miracles, which according to this verse is false. Second, the verse authenticates the previous Scriptures (the Bible).

Q#101—Why do Muslims believe that the Qur'an is not changed? It makes more sense that if the previous revelation (God's spoken word) can be altered, then what stops the later revelation from being changed?

Answer: That is a very valid argument. If God says His Word never changes, how can it change? And if it changed once, it can change again. The truth is this: that His Word never changes. He is an unchangeable God; He is God because He never changes.

In defense of the authenticity of the Qur'an, Muslims hold pride in the fact that Allah said he would protect the Qur'an. Muslims claim that Christians and Jews did not receive such a promise. Therefore, they claim the Bible got corrupted. However, the argument remains the same regarding the character of God and His first promise. If God said His Word never changes and then His Word changed, there is no credibility in the promises and the statements of God. Let us examine the main verse Muslims use to defend the validity of the Qur'an and see whether the promise is exclusive to the one message (as Muslim say of the Qur'an) or to all the messages (the Bible: Torah, Zabor, Injil).

Surat Al-Ḥijr (The Rocky Tract)—15:09

Zikar

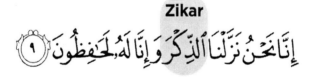

Sahih International Translation

Indeed, it is We who sent down <u>the Qur'an [Zikar]</u> and indeed, We will be its guardian.

Tafsir al-Jalalayn (Muslim commentary)

Verily it is We (nahnu emphasizes the subject of inna, or [functions as] a separating pronoun) Who have revealed the Remembrance, the Qur'ān, and assuredly We will preserve it, against substitution, distortion, additions and omissions.

Urdu In

بے شک یہ (کتاب) نصیحت ہمیں نے اُتاری ہے اور ہم ہی
اس کے نگہبان ہیں

Q#102—In the Bible, God promised the same in Matthew 5:18, Isaiah 55:01, and Revelation 22:18-19. What is special about the Qur'anic promise?

Answer: As I previously mentioned, this is a sincere effort on the part of Muslim scholars to keep the Qur'an unquestionable (out of their reverence to the word of Allah). However, let me share regarding this main verse in terms of divine protection of the Qur'an. In the English translation, **it says the Qur'an; but in both Arabic and Urdu, it does not say the Qur'an.** The Arabic word in the verse is *Alzikera* and in Urdu it's simply translated as advice. If you look at the Arabic word, you will be surprised to know that throughout the Qur'an Alzikera is used to describe the Bible. For example,

Surat An-Naḥl (The Bee)—16:43

Zikar

وَمَآ أَرْسَلْنَا مِن قَبْلِكَ إِلَّا رِجَالًا نُّوحِىٓ إِلَيْهِمْ فَسْـَٔلُوٓا أَهْلَ ٱلذِّكْرِ
إِن كُنتُمْ لَا تَعْلَمُونَ ﴿٤٣﴾

Sahih International

And We sent not before you except men to whom We revealed [<u>Our message 'Zikra'</u>]. So ask the people of the message if you do not know.

Tafsir al-Jalalayn

And We did not send before you anything other than men, to whom We revealed, and [sent] not angels: 'So ask the followers of the Remembrance, those knowledge-

able in the Torah and the Gospels; if you do not know', that, then they know it, and you are more likely to believe them than the believers are to believe Muhammad(s),

Urdu In

اور ہم نے تم سے پہلے مردوں ہی کو پیغمبر بنا کر بھیجا تھا جن کی طرف ہم وحی بھیجا کرتے تھے اگر تم لوگ نہیں جانتے تو اہل کتاب سے پوچھ لو

Surat Ghāfir (The Believer)—40:53-54

وَلَقَدْ ءَاتَيْنَا مُوسَى ٱلْهُدَىٰ وَأَوْرَثْنَا بَنِىٓ إِسْرَٰٓءِيلَ ٱلْكِتَٰبَ ﴿٥٣﴾

هُدًى وَذِكْرَىٰ لِأُوْلِى ٱلْأَلْبَٰبِ ﴿٥٤﴾

Yusuf Ali Translation

We did aforetime give Moses the (Book of) Guidance, and We gave the book in inheritance to the Children of Israel. A Guide and a <u>Message</u> [Zikra] to men of Understanding.

Tafsir al-Jalalayn (Muslim commentary)

And verily We gave Moses the guidance, the Torah and miracles, and We made the Children of Israel, after Moses, heirs to the scripture, the Torah, as a guidance, to guide, and as a remembrance for people of pith, a reminder for possessors of intellect.

Surat Al-'Anbyā' (The Prophets)—21:48

وَلَقَدْ ءَاتَيْنَا مُوسَىٰ وَهَٰرُونَ ٱلْفُرْقَانَ وَضِيَآءً وَذِكْرًا لِّلْمُتَّقِينَ ﴿٤٨﴾

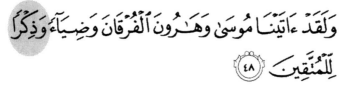

Yusuf Ali Translation

In the past We granted to Moses and Aaron the criterion (for judgment), and a Light and a Message [Zikra] for those who would do right,

Tafsir al-Jalalayn (Muslim commentary)

And verily We gave Moses and Aaron the Criterion, the Torah that discriminates between truth and falsehood, and [between] what is lawful and unlawful, and an illumination, by it, and remembrance, an admonition therein, for those who are wary of God,

Urdu In

اور ہم نے موسیٰ اور ہارون کو (ہدایت اور گمراہی میں)
فرق کر دینے والی اور (سرتاپا) روشنی اور نصیحت (کی
کتاب) عطا کی (یعنی) پرہیز گاروں کے لئے

Surat Al-'Anbyā' (The Prophets)—21:105

Zikar

Yusuf Ali Translation

Before this We wrote in the Psalms, after the Message [Zikra] (given to Moses): My servants the righteous, shall inherit the earth." (Direct quote from Psalms)

Tafsir al-Jalalayn (Muslim commentary)

Certainly We wrote in the Scripture, (al-zabūr) means 'the Book', that is, the revealed Books of God, after the Remembrance, meaning the Mother of the

Book (umm al-kitāb), which is [kept] with God: 'Indeed the land, the land of Paradise, shall be inherited by My righteous servants'—[this promise] applies to all righteous ones.

Urdu In

اور ہم نے نصیحت (کی کتاب یعنی تورات) کے بعد زبور میں لکھ دیا تھا کہ میرے نیکوکار بندے ملک کے وارث ہوں گے

It is fascinating to see the very word over and over again used by the Qur'an to describe the Bible. This proves that the verse was not exclusive to Qur'an but all the Word of God, whatever He said from day one.

Q#103—If Muhammad knew the truthfulness of the Bible, why didn't he ask his followers to obey it?

Answer: Interesting enough, the Islamic prophet Muhammad not only knew about the truthfulness of the previous scriptures (namely the Bible), he was asked to consult with Christians and Jews about the questions he and others have about the Qur'an.

In **Surat Al-'Anbyā' (The Prophets)**—21:7

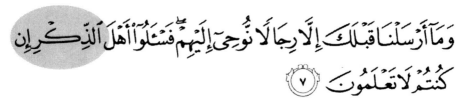

Yusuf Ali Translation

Before thee, also, the messengers We sent were but men, to whom We granted inspiration [Zikra]: If ye realize this not, ask of those who possess the Message.

Tafsir al-Jalalayn (Muslim commentary)

And We sent none before you other than men to whom We revealed (read nūhī or yūhā, '[to whom] it is revealed') and [We sent] not any angels. Ask the People of the Remembrance, those with knowledge of the Torah and the Gospel, if you do not know, this; for they will know it. Since you are more likely to believe them, than the believers are to believe Muhammad(s).

Urdu In

اور اور ہم نے تم سے پہلے مرد ہی (پیغمبر بنا کر) بھیجے جن کی طرف ہم وحی بھیجتے تھے۔ اگر تم نہیں جانتے تو جو یاد رکھتے ہیں ان سے پوچھ لو

The Qur'an not only uses the word AlZikra in reference to the Bible, but it also commands them to consult with Christian and Jews if they have any questions concerning Mohammad and his teaching because they already have the Scriptures from Allah. It proves the authenticity and the claim of Allah in Al-Hija to protect the Bible.

Q#104—If there are so many proofs about the authenticity of the Bible, even in the days of Muhammad, then where does this claim of today's Muslims stand?

Answer: This is what is called taking things out of context and using them for personal benefit. Many Muslims use part of the Qur'anic verses to falsify the Bible. For instance the following verse:

Surat Al-Baqarah (The Cow)—2:79

فَوَيْلٌ لِّلَّذِينَ يَكْتُبُونَ ٱلْكِتَٰبَ بِأَيْدِيهِمْ ثُمَّ يَقُولُونَ هَٰذَا مِنْ عِندِ ٱللَّهِ لِيَشْتَرُوا۟ بِهِۦ ثَمَنًا قَلِيلًا ۖ فَوَيْلٌ لَّهُم مِّمَّا كَتَبَتْ أَيْدِيهِمْ وَوَيْلٌ لَّهُم مِّمَّا يَكْسِبُونَ ﴿٧٩﴾

Yusuf Ali Translation

Then woe to those who write the Book with their own hands, and then say:"This is from Allah," to traffic with it for miserable price!—Woe to them for what their hands do write, and for the gain they make thereby.

Tafsir al-Jalalayn (Muslim commentary)

So woe, a severe chastisement, to those who write the Scripture with their hands, that is, fabricating it themselves, then say, 'This is from God' that they may sell it for a small price, of this world: these are the Jews, the ones that altered the description of the Prophet in the Torah, as well as the 'stoning' verse, and other details, and rewrote them in a way different from that in which they were revealed. So woe to them for what their hands have written of fabrications; and woe to them for their earnings, by way of bribery (rishan, plural of rishwa).

Urdu In

تو ان لوگوں پر افسوس ہے جو اپنے ہاتھ سے تو کتاب لکھتے ہیں اور کہتے یہ
ہیں کہ یہ خدا کے پاس سے (آئی) ہے ، تاکہ اس کے عوض تھوڑی سے قیمت
(یعنی دنیوی منفعت) حاصل کریں۔ ان پر افسوس ہے ، اس لیے کہ (بے اصل
باتیں) اپنے ہاتھ سے لکھتے ہیں اور (پھر) ان پر افسوس ہے ، اس لیے کہ ایسے
کام کرتے ہیں

Q#105—What is the true picture of this mistaken verse?

Answer: Now if you look at the part of the verse alone, it can be used to falsify the Bible, but if you read the verse before 78 it tells the full story of those who are writing the scriptures.

Surat Al-Baqarah (The Cow)—2:78

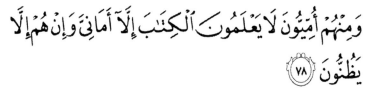

Yusuf Ali Translation

And there are among them illiterates, who know not the Book, but (see therein their own) desires, and they do nothing but conjecture.

Tafsir al-Jalalayn (Muslim commentary)

And there are some of them, the Jews, that are illiterate, unlettered, not knowing the Scripture, the Torah, but only desires, lies which were handed down to them by their leaders and which they relied upon; and, in their rejection of the prophet hood of the Prophet and fabrications of other matters, they have, mere conjectures, and no firm knowledge.

Urdu In

اور بعض ان میں ان پڑھ ہیں کہ اپنے باطل خیالات کے سوا (خدا کی) کتاب سے واقف ہی نہیں اور وہ صرف ظن سے کام لیتے ہیں

The full story we receive from verse 78-79 is that there were some Jews in Yeserb (Medina), or generally, in Arabian Peninsula, who were forging the scriptures for their personal benefits. However, throughout the Qur'an we find references where Quran talks about the rest of the Jews and Christians who have kept themselves pure from such sin. For example:

Surat 'Ālī 'Imrān (Family of Imran)—3:113-114, 119

ليْسُوا سَوَآءً مِّنْ أَهْلِ الْكِتَبِ أُمَّةٌ قَآئِمَةٌ يَتْلُونَ ءَايَتِ اللَّهِ ءَانَآءَ الَّيْلِ وَهُمْ يَسْجُدُونَ ﴿١١٣﴾

Yusuf Ali Translation

Not all of them are alike: Of the People of the Book are a portion that stand (For the right): They rehearse the Signs of Allah all night long, and they prostrate themselves in adoration.

Tafsir al-Jalalay (Muslim commentary)

Yet they, the People of the Scripture, are not all alike, equal; some of the People of the Scripture are a community upright, with integrity, adhering to the truth, such as 'Abd Allāh b. Salām, may God be pleased with him and his companions, who recite God's verses in the watches of the night, that is, during its hours, prostrating themselves, performing prayer (wa-hum yasjudūn, 'prostrating themselves', is a circumstantial qualifier).

Urdu In

یہ بھی سب ایہ بھی سب ایک جیسے نہیں ہیں ان اہل
کتاب میں کچھ لوگ (حکم خدا پر) قائم بھی ہیں جو رات
کے وقت خدا کی آیتیں پڑھتے اور (اس کے آگے) سجدہ
کرتے ہیں

Surat 'Āli 'Imrān (Family of Imran)—3:114

يُؤْمِنُونَ بِاللَّهِ وَالْيَوْمِ الْأَخِرِ وَيَأْمُرُونَ بِالْمَعْرُوفِ
وَيَنْهَوْنَ عَنِ الْمُنْكَرِ وَيُسَارِعُونَ فِي الْخَيْرَاتِ وَأُولَٰئِكَ مِنَ
الصَّالِحِينَ ﴿١١٤﴾

Yusuf Ali Translation

They believe in Allah and the Last Day; they enjoin what is right, and forbid what is wrong; and they hasten (in emulation) in (all) good works: They are in the ranks of the righteous.

Tafsir al-Jalalayn (Muslim commentary)

They believe in God and in the Last Day, enjoining decency and forbidding indecency, vying with one another in good works; those, described in the way God has mentioned, are of the righteous, and some of them are not like this and are not righteous.

Urdu In

(اور) خدا پر اور روز آخرت پر ایمان رکھتے اور اچھے کام کرنےکو
کہتے اور بری باتوں سے منع کرتےاور نیکیوں پر لپکتے ہیں اور یہی
لوگ نیکوکار ہیں

Surat 'Āli 'Imrān (Family of Imran)—3:119

وَإِنَّ مِنْ أَهْلِ الْكِتَابِ لَمَن يُؤْمِنُ بِاللَّهِ وَمَا أُنزِلَ إِلَيْكُمْ وَمَا
أُنزِلَ إِلَيْهِمْ خَاشِعِينَ لِلَّهِ لَا يَشْتَرُونَ بِآيَاتِ اللَّهِ ثَمَنًا قَلِيلًا
أُولَٰئِكَ لَهُمْ أَجْرُهُمْ عِندَ رَبِّهِمْ إِنَّ اللَّهَ سَرِيعُ
الْحِسَابِ ۱۱۹

Yusuf Ali Translation

And there are, certainly, among the People of the Book, those who believe in Allah, in the revelation to you, and in the revelation to them, bowing in humility to Allah: They will not sell the Signs of Allah for a miserable gain! For them is a reward with their Lord, and Allah is swift in account.

Tafsir al-Jalalayn (Muslim commentary)

Verily, there are some among the People of the Scripture who believe in God, like 'Abd Allāh b. Salām and his companions and the Negus, and what has been revealed to you, that is, the Qur'ān, and what has been revealed to them, that is, the Torah and the Gospel, humble before God (khāshi'īn is a circumstantial quali-fication of the person of [the verb] yu'min, 'who believe', and takes into account the [potentially plural] sense of man, 'who'), not purchasing with the verses of God, which they have before them in the Torah and the Gospel pertaining to the descrip-tions of the Prophet(s), a small price, of this world, by concealing them for fear of losing their supremacy, as others, like the Jews, have done. Those — their wage, the reward for their deeds, is with their Lord, [a reward] which they will be given twice over, as [stated] in the sūrat al-Qaṣaṣ [Q. 28:54].

God is swift at reckoning, reckoning with the whole of creation in about half a day of the days of this world.

Urdu In

اور بعض اہلِ کتاب ایسے بھی ہیں جو خدا پر اور اس (کتاب) پر جو تم پر
نازل ہوئی اور اس پر جو ان پر نازل ہوئی ایمان رکھتے ہیں اور خدا کے آگے
عاجزی کرتے ہیں اور خدا کی آیتوں کے بدلے تھوڑی سی قیمت نہیں لیتے یہی
لوگ ہیں جن کا صلہ ان کے پروردگار کے ہاں تیار ہے اور خدا جلد حساب لینے
والا ہے

During Muhammad's time, which was after 600 A.D, the correct and authentic Bible was available. If the Bible was not changed until Muhammad's time, then the Bible we have today is the same as during Muhammad's time. The First Council of Nicaea met in A.D 325 to settle the divinity of Christ once and for all. The council of Christian bishops convened in Nicaea in Bithynia (present-day İznik in Turkey) by the Roman Emperor Constantine I in A.D. Historically, when Constantine defeated Emperor Licinius in 323 AD, he ended the persecutions against the Christian church. Shortly afterwards, Christians faced trouble from within: the Arian controversy began and threatened to divide the church. The problem began in Alexandria as a debate between the bishop Alexander and the presbyter (pastor, or priest) Arius. Arius proposed that if the Father begat the Son, the latter must have had a beginning, that there was a time when he was not, and that his substance was from nothing like the rest of creation.

The Council of Nicaea, a gathering similar to the one described in <u>Acts 15:4-22</u>, condemned the beliefs of Arius and wrote the first version of the now famous creed proclaiming that the Son was "one in being with the Father" by use of the Greek word "homoousius."

> We believe in one God, the Father Almighty, maker of all things visible and invisible; and in one Lord Jesus Christ, the Son of God, the only-begotten of his Father, of the substance of the Father, God of God, Light of Light, very God of very God, begotten, not made, being of one substance (*homousion*) with the Father, by whom

all things were made, both which be in heaven and in earth, who for us men and for our salvation came down and was incarnate and was made man. He suffered and the third day he rose again, and ascended into heaven. And he shall come again to judge both the quick and the dead. And [we believe] in the Holy Ghost.

And whosoever shall say that there was a time when the Son of God was not, or that before he was begotten he was not, or that he was made of things that were not, or that he is of a different substance or essence [from the Father] or that he is a creature, or subject to change or conversion—all that so say, the Catholic and Apostolic Church anathematizes them.

Q#106—Interesting, I heard from a Muslim friend that the Qur'an came from heaven and Muhammad delivered it to Muslims, unlike the Bible, which was written by men who were inspired by GOD.

Answer: This is one of the big misconceptions of Muslims. Many people believe that God provided the Qur'an like a book from a printing press. Thus, the Qur'an was not collected by Muhammad, and was not written by him. Mohammad spoke and his followers remembered what he said. One of the authentic traditions in Islam states:

Abu Bakr As-Siddiq sent for me when the people of Yamama had been killed (i.e., a number of the Prophet's Companions who fought against Musailama). (I went to him) and found 'Umar bin Al-Khattab sitting with him. Abu Bakr then said (to me), "Umar has come to me and said: "Casualties were heavy among the Qurra' of the Qur'an (i.e. those who knew the Quran by heart) on the day of the Battle of Yalmama, and I am afraid that more heavy casualties may take place among the Qurra' on other battlefields, whereby a large part of the Qur'an may be lost. There-fore I suggest you (Abu Bakr) order that the Qur'an be collected." **I said to 'Umar, "How can you do something which Allah's Apostle did not do?"** 'Umar said, "By Allah, that is a good project."Umar kept on urging me to accept his proposal till Allah opened my chest for it and I began to realize the good in the idea which 'Umar had realized." Then Abu Bakr said (to me). 'You are a wise young man and we do not have any suspicion about you, and you used to write the Divine Inspiration for Allah's Apostle. **So you should search for (the fragmentary scripts of) the Qur'an and collect it in one book."** By Allah, if they had ordered me to shift one of the mountains, it would not have been heavier for me than this ordering me to collect the Qur'an. **Then I said to Abu Bakr, "How will you do something which Allah's Apostle did not do?"** Abu Bakr replied, "By Allah, it is a good project." Abu Bakr kept on urging me to accept his idea until Allah opened my chest for what He had opened the chests of Abu Bakr and 'Umar. So I started looking for **the Qur'an and collecting it from (what was written on) palmed stalks, thin white stones and also from the men who knew it by heart,** till I found the last Verse of Surat At-Tauba (Repentance) with Abi Khuzaima Al-Ansari, and I did not find it with anybody other than him. The Verse is: 'Verily there has come unto you an Apostle (Muhammad) from amongst yourselves. It grieves him that you should receive any injury or difficulty..(till the end of Surat-Baraa)' (At-Tauba) (9.128-129) Then the complete manuscripts (copy) of the Qur'an remained with Abu Bakr till he died, then with 'Umar till the end of his life, and then with Hafsa, the daughter of 'Umar." *Volume 6, Book 61, Number 509, Narrated Zaid bin Thabit. Hadids*

Q#107—Is there any historical evidence where Muhammad himself used the Bible as a authentic source to teach, preach or judge people?

Answer: (Bukhari, the Muslim's second most trustworthy and holy source of instruction states): According to the *Mishkat al-Masabih*, Book XVI, ch. I, p. 758: Abdallah b. Umar said that the Jews came to God's messenger

[Muhammad] and mentioned to him that a man and a woman of their number had committed fornication. He asked them what they found in the Torah about stoning and they replied that they should disgrace them and that they should be beaten. `Abdallah b. Salam then said, "You lie; it contains instruction that they should be stoned to death, so bring the Torah." They spread it out, and one of them put his hand over the verse of stoning and read only what preceded it and what followed it. `Abdallah b. Salam told him to lift his hand and when he did so the verse of stoning was seen to be in it. They then said, "He has spoken the truth, Muhammad; the verse of stoning is in it." The Prophet then gave command regarding them and they were stoned to death. In another version it says that he told him to lift his hand and that when he did so, the verse of stoning was clearly in it. The man then said, "It contains the verse of stoning, Muhammad, but we have been concealing it from one another." He then gave command regarding them and they were stoned to death. (Bukhari and Muslim) Now the question is this: If the Bible was corrupted or changed then why would Islamic prophet Muhammad use the very Scriptures to judge the case?

Q#108—I do not understand. If it is so crystal clear, then why do Muslims claim that the Bible has been corrupted and changed?

Answer: It is because the Qur'an does talk about the distortion of the Torah by some of the Jews. As previously mentioned in Question 91, that is because when you take the Qur'anic text out of context, you can misuse it. I provided Qur'anic chapter 2:78-79 for my argument. If you read Surah 2:75 by itself you would misunderstanding the verse:

Surat Al-Baqarah (The Cow)—2:75

أَفَتَطْمَعُونَ أَنْ يُؤْمِنُوا لَكُمْ وَقَدْ كَانَ فَرِيقٌ مِنْهُمْ يَسْمَعُونَ كَلَامَ اللَّهِ ثُمَّ يُحَرِّفُونَهُ مِنْ بَعْدِ مَا عَقَلُوهُ وَهُمْ يَعْلَمُونَ ﴿٧٥﴾

Sahih International Translation

Do you covet [the hope, O believers], that they would believe for you while a party of them used to hear the words of Allah and then distort the Torah after they had understood it while they were knowing?

This is the verse that is commonly used to develop a case against the validity of the Bible. But if one sets his or her heart even as a Muslim to find the truth and reads the previous two verses in the same chapter, it is clear that it was limited to a few people who were making changes in the Scriptures for their personal gain. Moreover, most of the Christians and Jews were following the true Word of God.

This is precisely why the Qur'an not only asks the prophet of Islam to consult the Bible and invites those who have doubts about the Qur'an to check the text of the Bible. The story in the Qur'an and the teachings in the Qur'an were the same as the teaching of the Bible. **Furthermore, the Qur'an encourages Christians to obey what is written in the Bible. Why would Qur'an ask them to do that if the Bible was corrupted or changed?** Look at the following verse from the Qur'an:

Surat Al-Māʾidah (The Table Spread)—5:68

قُلْ يَٰٓأَهْلَ ٱلْكِتَٰبِ لَسْتُمْ عَلَىٰ شَىْءٍ حَتَّىٰ تُقِيمُواْ ٱلتَّوْرَىٰةَ
وَٱلْإِنجِيلَ وَمَآ أُنزِلَ إِلَيْكُم مِّن رَّبِّكُمْ وَلَيَزِيدَنَّ كَثِيرًا مِّنْهُم مَّآ
أُنزِلَ إِلَيْكَ مِن رَّبِّكَ طُغْيَٰنًا وَكُفْرًا فَلَا تَأْسَ عَلَى ٱلْقَوْمِ
ٱلْكَٰفِرِينَ ﴿٦٨﴾

Yusuf Ali Translation

Say: "O People of the Book! ye have no ground to stand upon unless ye stand fast by the Law, the Gospel, and all the revelation that has come to you from your Lord." It is the revelation that cometh to thee from thy Lord, that increaseth in most of them their obstinate rebellion and blasphemy. But sorrow thou not over (these) people without Faith.

In the above verse, Christians are commanded in the Qur'an to continue holding on to the Scriptures if they want to succeed on the day of the judgment. This verse again invalidates the claim of Muslim about the corruption of the Scriptures.

Q#109—Is it very clear, according to the Muslims' holy book Qur'an, that the Bible was corrupted or changed during Muhammad's time, even a portion of it.

Answer: Yes, but I would say at least the correct and pure Bible was available otherwise Muhammad would not use the Bible. Remember that Christian history will tell us during that time there were many heresies. Today you can still find some of them and many new ones. Christianity has been under attack from first century AD, the message has been the same that do not hear the false doctrine.

Here is another example from the Qur'an regarding the availability of the pure and correct Bible during Muhammad's time.

Surat Al-Mā'idah (The Table Spread)—5:13

$$
\text{فَبِمَا نَقْضِهِم مِّيثَاقَهُمْ لَعَنَّاهُمْ وَجَعَلْنَا قُلُوبَهُمْ قَاسِيَةً ۖ}
$$

$$
\text{يُحَرِّفُونَ ٱلْكَلِمَ عَن مَّوَاضِعِهِۦ ۙ وَنَسُوا۟ حَظًّا مِّمَّا ذُكِّرُوا۟}
$$

$$
\text{بِهِۦ ۚ وَلَا تَزَالُ تَطَّلِعُ عَلَىٰ خَآئِنَةٍ مِّنْهُمْ إِلَّا قَلِيلًا مِّنْهُمْ ۖ فَٱعْفُ عَنْهُمْ}
$$

$$
\text{وَٱصْفَحْ ۚ إِنَّ ٱللَّهَ يُحِبُّ ٱلْمُحْسِنِينَ ﴿١٣﴾}
$$

Sahih International Translation

So for their breaking of the covenant We cursed them and made their hearts hard. They distort words from their [proper] usages and have forgotten a portion of that of which they were reminded. And you will still observe deceit among them, except *a few of them.* **But pardon them and overlook [their misdeeds]. Indeed, Allah loves the doers of good.**

Although it uses the word 'few,' it still talks about the true Christians and Jews during Muhammad's time.

Q#110—Do we have the old manuscripts of the Bible?

Answer: Ron Rhodes, in his book *Islam: What You Need to Know*, provides key points regarding the issue. He writes:

1. We possess well over 5,300 partial or complete New Testament manuscripts that attest to its reliability and accurate transmission. The variants in these manuscripts deal mostly with trivial issues (one manuscript might say "Christ Jesus" instead of "Jesus Christ").

2. There are 86,000 quotations of the New Testament by the early church fathers. Because of this, all but 11 verses could be accurately reconstructed even if we had no manuscript copy. (See, *The Complete Book of Bible Answers*) [Harvest House Publishers, 1997].

3. As for the Old Testament, in the Dead Sea Scrolls discovered at Qumran in 1947 we have Old Testament manuscripts that date about a thousand years earlier (150 B.C.) than the other OT manuscripts previously in our possession (which dated to A.D 980). When one compares the two sets of manuscripts, they are practically identical, with very few changes. The fact that there are two sets of OT manuscripts-some dating long before the Muslim claim of biblical corruption (150 B.C.) and some dating long after (A.D 980) and the fact that the two sets of manuscripts are practically identical proves the incredible accuracy of the Old Testament's manuscript transmission.

Remember!

You have established solid ground on the basis of two arguments: first, that salvation is possible only through God's grace, not through the works of man and second, the authenticity of the Bible. You now have the opportunity to open the Bible and share what God says about the free gift of eternal life.

Let us review the questions that you must ask:

Salvation Issues:
1. Are you a good Muslim?
2. How sure are you that you will enter in paradise?

The Bible Issue:
1. When did the Bible change or alter?
2. Was it before Muhammad or after him?
3. Do you know the reference where it says that the Bible has been changed?

The following chart shows how it will close the doors for a Muslim to run around and not confront the original issue for his or her salvation. As you follow the above question by using the following chart, I would encourage you to remember the Christian Church Creed, as well as the dates. Historically, the **First Council of Nicaea** was a council of Christian bishops that convened in Nicaea in Bithynia (present day Iznik in Turkey). It was arranged and brought together by the Roman Emperor Constantine I in 325 A.D. Its main accomplishments were settlement of the Christological issues of the relationship of Jesus to God the Father. The Council was gathered together to settle the issue of Trinity once for all. The Second Council worked with the first Creed, with only minor changes. The following is a comparison of the Church Creed. Both were written down and believed long before Islam came.

FIRST COUNCIL OF NICAEA (325 AD)	FIRST COUNCIL OF CONSTANTINOPLE (325 AD)
• We believe in on God, the Father Almighty, Maker of all things visible and invisible.	• We believe in one God, the Father Almighty, Maker *of heaven and earth, and* of all things visible and invisible.
• An in one Lord Jesus Christ, the Son of God, begotten of the Father [the only-begotten; that is, of the essence of the Father, God of God], Light of Light, very God of very God, begotten, not made, being of one substance with the Father.	• And in one Lord Jesus Christ, the *only-begotten* Son of God, begotten of the Father *before all worlds*, Light of Light, very God of very God, begotten, not made, being of one substance with the Father;

FIRST COUNCIL OF NICAEA (325 AD)	FIRST COUNCIL OF CONSTANTINOPLE (325 AD)
• By whom all things were made [both in heaven and on earth];	• by whom all things were made;
• Who for us men, and for our salvation, came down and was incarnate and was made man;	• who for us men, ad for our salvation, came down from heaven, and was incarnate *by the Holy Ghost of the Virgin Mary*, and was made man;
	• *he was crucified for us under Pontius Pilate*, and suffered, and was buried, and the third day he rose again, *according to the Scriptures, and ascended* into heaven, *and sitteth on the right hand of the Father.*
• From thence he shall come to judge the quick and the dead.	• from thence he shall come again, *with glory*, to judge the quick and the dead;
	• *whose kingdom shall have no end.*
• And in the Holy Ghost	• And in the Holy Ghost, *the Lord and Giver of life, who proceedeth from the Father, who with the Father and the Son together is worshiped and glorified, who spake by the prophets.*
• [But those who say: 'There was a time when he was not;' and 'He was not before he was made;' and 'He was made out of nothing,' or 'He is of another substance' or 'essence,' or 'The Son of God is created,' or 'changeable,' or 'alterable'— they are condemned by the holy catholic and apostolic Church.]	• *In on holy catholic and apostolic Church; we acknowledge one baptism for the remission of sins; we look for the resurrection of the dead, and the life of the world to come. Amen.*

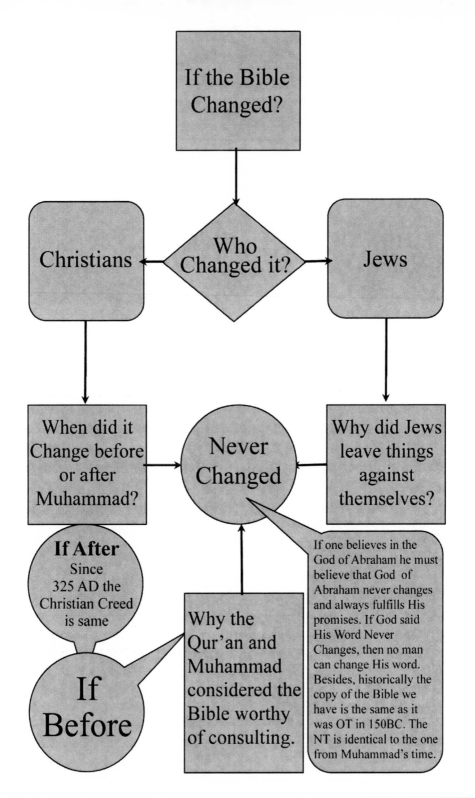

The flowchart contains the following elements:

If the Bible Changed?

↓

Who Changed it? (decision diamond)

← **Christians**   **Jews** →

Christians →

When did it Change before or after Muhammad?

Jews →

Why did Jews leave things against themselves?

Never Changed (center)

If After — Since 325 AD the Christian Creed is same

If Before

Why the Qur'an and Muhammad considered the Bible worthy of consulting.

If one believes in the God of Abraham he must believe that God of Abraham never changes and always fulfills His promises. If God said His Word Never Changes, then no man can change His word. Besides, historically the copy of the Bible we have is the same as it was OT in 150BC. The NT is identical to the one from Muhammad's time.

Personal Notes and Comments:

_____

_____

_____

_____

_____

_____

_____

_____

_____

_____

_____

_____

_____

_____

_____

_____

_____

_____

_____

_____

_____

CHAPTER 10

Islamic Teachings: Sharia Law, Mosque, and Jihad

In this chapter, you will learn some of the simple yet complicated teachings of Islam. In America, the major issues regarding Islam and Muslims include Sharia, which is the Islamic Law, the Mosque, the worship place for Muslims, particularly Islamic centers, and the concept of Jihad. My intention is not to evoke hatred, but to inform the Western audience why a Muslim young man who has many reasons to live is willing to blow himself up. In many of the Islamic countries, the issue of extremism has become a major issue. Approximately 65 Islamic nations are worried about the future and struggling to overcome the issue of Jihadists. Moreover, whether these countries are moderate or conservative, they are threatened by those Muslims who do not agree with their government policies. But more importantly, these governments have a different Islamic view than some of the Jihadists.

There are many Muslim countries where Sharia law is being practiced. In some Islamic countries, it is practiced on a limited scale and in others it is practiced as the law of the land. Either way, the Islamic law has marginalized human rights in the Islamic world. An Islamic society cannot function without Sharia. In the 21st century, the most modern Islamic countries are some of the most fundamental countries. In these countries women can't drive, can't go out by themselves, can't meet other people at public places, the minorities can't practice their religion freely etc. Sharia dictates for Islamic countries and society. Western society has been practicing freedom and democracy for a long time and threatens Islamic culture and society.

The Western society is afraid, too. What if Muslims in the West outnumber the non-Muslims in the West? What if the growing population of Muslims in the West would have enough numbers to demand amendments in the law? Already, in many Western countries Muslims control portions of the countries and practice Sharia. Statistics make clear that in a few years Muslim immigrants in Europe will be the major people group. They will outnumber the Europeans. What if that continues and reproduction in Muslim families in the United States of America or immigration of Muslims in the USA increases the Muslim population? Will they be able to make changes in the constitution of the United States of America and force Sharia law?

Finally, Muslims are building Mosques and Islamic centers everywhere, which is considered by Americans as the first step toward starting a militaristic Islam in the United States of America. There are now more Muslims in the United States than Methodists. Soon there will be more Muslims in the United States than Jews. At the present rate of growth, within the next decade there will be more Muslims in the United States of America than Presbyterians.

Therefore, the topic of the Mosque will be studied to see what the Mosque is, and what are some of the traditional uses of the Mosque. Furthermore, we will examine the Islamic schools, the Madrasah. Fear is growing not only because of the news reports coming from Muslim countries, but because Muslims in United States are increasingly building mosques. Eighty percent of the mosques in the United States have been constructed within the past 15 years.

Q#111—You mentioned Shari'a law (Islamic law), what is it?

Answer: Shari'a law is the foundation of the practice of Islam. It is Islamic law based on the Qur'an, and Hadith. The word Shari'a means 'way' or 'path'. Muslims all over the world regard the Shari'a law as very sacred; however, each sect of Islam uses it differently. Muslims change the interpretations of Shari'a law, depending on what country and culture you are in. "Fiqh" jurisprudence is a secondary source other than the Qur'an and the Hadiths, which is used to interpret and extend the application of Shari'a to questions not directly addressed in the primary sources. Perhaps this is the very reason why, in the United States of America, if you leave Islam or if you say something against the prophethood of Muhammad or question Islam, you would not be executed as Shari'a law requires in Islamic countries. The interpretation of Shari'a law is what turns someone into a moderate, traditional or fundamental Muslim.

Q#112—Do we have Shari'a law (Islamic law) in the USA or in the West?

Answer: No, we do not have Shari'a law in the United States. However, the Muslims have been asking for this in the West. There are many countries where a form of Shari'a law has been practiced. For example, in Canada, there are many Muslims, and they demanded that the government practice Shari'a law when it comes to dealing with the divorce of Muslims. In Islam, the man has all the authority. If husband and wife have an argument and the husband decides to leave her, he does not need any document in order to prove anything. He can simply say three times, "I divorce you, I divorce you, I divorce you" and it is considered done. If the husband comes back to his senses after an hour or two and realizes that he did it out of anger, according to Shari'a, he is not married anymore. He has to remarry his wife. Well, it's not that simple to divorce and then go to the Muslim priest *Mullah* and get married again. The husband has to let her go officially. He cannot marry her unless she marries someone else first. That marriage must be consummated. Then once that husband divorces her, the original husband is able to marry her again. Many new defenders of the Islamic faith are rejecting this practice. However, the Qur'an 2:229-230 says, "Divorce is permissible twice, so if a husband divorces his wife he cannot after that, remarry her until after she has married another husband, and he has divorced her.

Many Western Islamic organizations are using the constitution of the country to legalize some of the practices Islam encourages. One of the reasons is that many western women are getting married to charming Muslim men and these men cannot afford to use Allah's given right through Shari'a law to control their wife. The Qur'an says, "As to those women on whose part ye fear disloyalty and ill-conduct, admonish them, refuse to share their beds, **beat** them" (4:34). A famous saying of Muhammad about women is, "I was shown the Hell-fire and that the majority of its dwellers are women" (Saheeh Bukhari: 29 304, 1052, 1462, 3241, 5197, 5198, 6449, 6546).

One of the best ways to reach out to Muslims is through women. Women know the treatment Islam prescribes, and they are the first teachers for their children. Muslim children would grow in wisdom and knowledge of the Lord if the Muslim mothers come to Christ. This is an awesome opportunity for Christian women to do something, which unfortunately Christian men are forbidden to do. Christian men cannot talk to Muslim women, and witnessing to them is just an impossible thing.

Q#113—What is apostasy and what are the legal ramifications according to Shari'a law (Islamic law)?

Answer: In Islam, apostasy is one of the reasons why many Muslims who want to leave Islam don't. Apostasy is simply leaving Islam. Actually, many Muslim countries require that a person who leaves Islam be approached by the family members to invite him back in the circle of Islam. If he/she refuses to come back to Islam, a group of people will reach out to him/her with the same word. When the invitation is rejected again, then the man or woman is punishable by death. A fatwa will be issued to kill the person.

The following is a fatwa issued by Al-Azhar University, Cairo. The fatwa states, "Since he left Islam, he will be invited to express his regret. If he does not express regret, he will be killed according to the rights and obligations of Islamic (Shari'a) law." This particular man had converted to Christianity. Once you are a Muslim, it is hard to leave Islam and if you are born in a Muslim family, you do not have a choice because if you leave Islam the family members will kill you. This is one of the controversial subjects we are facing in the 21st century. Some of the Muslim leaders argue that there is not a verse in the Qur'an supporting such killing.

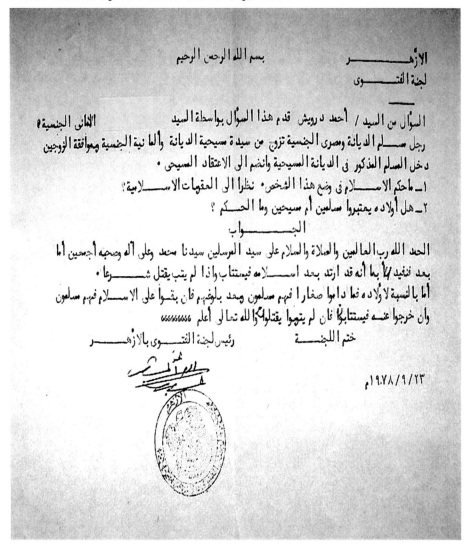

Q#114—I heard that someone was killed in the United States because he left Islam and accepted another religion. Has this actually happened?

Answer: Here in the USA, we have freedom of religion. The constitution of the country protects the right of people to choose whatever religion they want to practice. However, many incidents have happened behind closed doors here on our soil in the name of Shari'a law. The murder of Hossam Armanious, his wife, Amal Garas, and their daughters are a good example. They were a Coptic Christian family in New Jersey who were killed by fanatic Muslims.

Q#115—Previously, you have spoken about Jihad, and honestly I am always afraid to talk to Muslims because I think they may kill me or my family members. Am I just being paranoid or is this normal?

Answer: Don't be afraid, because most Muslims are forced to follow Islam because it is a one-way deal. When we do not talk to them or simply avoid them, it is like accusing them of being killers. I remember once I put a promotion video online to raise funds for Pakistan flood relief and someone's comment on the video came with a user ID "islamisnotgood," and also "Don't give money to the Christian killers—God punishes the sinner." My response to him was: "islamisnotgood brother, I am a Christian and you would be surprised to know that my whole family has been persecuted. I am here in the USA because I was forced to leave my country under false accusations. Christ told us that we will be persecuted for our faith, therefore as a Christian, we are ought to just keep loving and serving without seeking any reward or recognition. Thanks for the post though." I understand all the recent attacks by Muslims make them the bad group. One author by the name David Ibrahim writes in his book *Mirage* the following:

Some of the facts

1.5 BILLION Muslims in the world

280 [sic] Million Americans

5 1/2 Million Israelis Surrounded by 350 Million Arab Muslims!

Fact

90%-95% OF ALL THE CONFLICTS ON THIS PLANET TODAY INVOLVE MUSLIMS FIGHTING NON-MUSLIMS OR EACH OTHER!

There are many troublespots around the world, but as a general rule, it's easy to make an educated guess at one of the participants: Muslims vs. Jews in "Palestine," Muslims vs. Hindus in Kashmir, Muslims vs. Christians in Africa, Muslims vs. Buddhists in Thailand, Muslims vs. Russians, etc.

When you read facts like these, it is easy to think that all the Muslims are violent and want to kill anyone that comes their way. Nevertheless, let's not forget those who do not want to be Muslims, but have to be, because they were born into the Islamic religion. To them, when we constantly hate Muslims, we are not setting a good example either. In the first century, Christianity spread because of their forgiving spirit, selflessness, kindness and genuine love for others, even for those who persecuted them.

My point is this, that if you follow those principles of "SEE," which I mentioned in the beginning of the book, and be watchful, you will be secure and will successfully witness to others. As I said earlier, the best thing in America is freedom of speech and religion. Therefore, use this freedom to proclaim the truth of the Scripture. God is with you and He will protect you. Do not be afraid.

Q#116—Could you talk about major and minor Jihad? Are there subdivisions of such Jihads?

Answer: Jihad is an obligation for every true Muslim. The Qur'an 2:126 says, "Jihad is ordained for you (Muslims) though you dislike it, and it may be that you dislike a thing which is good for you and that you like a thing which is bad for you. Allah knows but you do not know." In the West, Muslims, by using concept of taqiyah (as we discussed earlier), are propagating a new definition of Jihad. Just like the new teaching that Islam is a religion of peace, they have subdivided jihad into various forms and categories. 47:35 states, "So be not weak and ask not for peace while you are having the upper hand." Some of the categories are as follows:

1. Jihad against one's self

2. Jihad against unbelievers

3. Jihad against corrupt Muslims

4. Jihad against hypocrites

5. Jihad against Satan

6. Jihad of the heart

7. Jihad by the hand

8. Jihad by tongue

Ibrahim provides a list of some of the methods Muslims are using in the West and all over the world to conduct such jihads. They are as follows:

1. Jihad of word: Powerful speeches and arguments to challenge people to accept the authority of Islam. Sometimes the statements are threatening and other times flattering.

2. Jihad of deception: It is simply to confuse the opponent; a lie under oath can be justified by this type of Jihad.

3. Jihad of the Sword: This is the most well-known form of jihad. The difference is that, in modern days, Muslims prefer using advanced weaponry.

4. Jihad of Taxation: Where Muslims are in power they force non-Muslims to pay more taxes. It was practiced in the early days of Islam, and therefore, today most of the Arab and the Middle Eastern countries have few or no non-Muslims. They either left the country or converted to Islam for the sake of an easy life.

5. Jihad of Slavery: It may not seem that non-Muslims are slaves in Muslim countries today, but they are not even allowed to ask for their rights as human beings. Some of the worst examples are sexual slavery.

6. Jihad of Shari'a Law: The forcing of Shari'a law in predominantly Muslim countries.

7. Jihad of Polygamy: By having more than one wife, Muslims can have more children, who will eventually dominate the population of that country.

8. Jihad of the Spirit: The belief that when a Muslim dies his/her spirit fights for the spread of Islam.

9. Jihad by Immigration: This is one of the major ways through which the Muslims are taking over the West.

Most of the above-mentioned methods could be summed up in one method called "Silent Jihad." **In the West, the issue of morality or the lack thereof, has opened doors for Islamic Jihadists to sneak in with their fabricated teachings of Islam. Daid Witt and Mujahid El Masih present their theory on silent Jihad. They show how "Nine M's" have served Muslims better than any other means of Jihad.**

> ## Remember!
>
> Nine M's that have served Muslims better than any other means of Jihad are: Moral dilemma, Merchant, Marriage, Money, Mosque, Madrassas, Media, Mysticism, and Migration.

Q#117—Would you please tell me about their place of worship? Why do they face a certain direction? And what is the importance of the Mosque in Islam?

Answer: The Islamic Mosque is certainly not like the church building, synagogue, or temple. In Islam, the Mosque has a unique character and place. It is the house of Allah and a place where all major decisions are made concerning the Islamic community, as well as decisions concerning those who are outside the Islamic community. Historically, Muslims used to perform their prayers five times a day facing Solomon's Temple, just like the Jews. This is also the era when Muhammad was trying to find favor and recognition among monotheist religions (Judaism and Christianity) as the prophet of Islam.

The meaning of Masjid, the Arabic word for Mosque, is derived from *sajada and means* prostrate. However, it is certainly not restricted to worship. During Muhammad's time, and even after his death, the Mosque was used for political, educational, social, judicial, economical and military purposes. There are a number of Mosques in the world, which are considered to be more sacred than others. Moreover, some have more significance than others. A few examples include: the Ka'aba in Mecca, Al-Nabawi Mosque in Medina, and Al Aqsa in Jerusalem.

The reward/blessing system:

- One prayer at the Ka'aba is worth one hundred thousand times more than a prayer performed anywhere else.

- One prayer at Al-Nabawi is worth one thousand times more than a prayer performed anywhere else.

- One prayer at Al Aqsa (Doom of the Rock) worth five hundred times more than a prayer performed anywhere else.

There are a number of other mosques that offer rewards to Muslims if they pray at that particular location. A mosque earns its value (how many points or rewards a person gets by performing prayer at the mosque) entirely on the basis of historical importance such as who founded it, what sect founded it, and what political, religious, educational, economical, and evangelistic/missionary achievements were accomplished by it. One of the duties of Muslims as a nation (all the Muslims in the world are one nation under Islam) is to turn this world into a Mosque. The Mosque also refers to a distinction between believers and non-believers; Muslims and non-Muslims. Since the Mosque is the house of God, Muslims are obligated to turn the whole world into a Mosque.

In order to make the whole world Allah's house, Muslims use Mosques to claim the land. If Muslims erect a Mosque, it is not like any other building that can be taken down at any time. This is one of the dangers of building a Mosque. Muslims as one nation will fight for the existence of the Mosque. This is just like the support the Palestinians get from the rest of the Muslim world to maintain the existence of Al-Aqsa in Jerusalem. In addition, in the West, once Muslims receive a legal right to construct a Mosque, according to the historical concept of a Mosque, they receive legal authorization to run all its institutions, such as political, religious, educational, social and economical.

Q# 118—Could you explain why or how Muslims become so radical?

Answer: There is nothing that specifically makes a Muslim become radical. Muslims are people just like you and me. For every opinion one might have, there is always another individual who strongly opposes that idea. Both sides usually claim to sit with the best arguments, the real facts and correct worldview. Ironically, both sides regard the other as being indoctrinated, blind to the obvious and utterly idiotic. Most people only expose themselves to that which matches their own worldview because it is uncomfortable to do otherwise. Specifically, when it comes to religious beliefs such inclination surpasses all the logical, physical, historical and supernatural explanations. The facts, the evidences, and the truth about a religious worldview are merely subject to the will of a person. One's personal perception about the world, inner satisfaction about the belief, outer reaction to the society, and the understanding of truth, will lead him or her to a strong conviction. Moreover, it is that conviction that results in a radical step to eliminate any threat to his or her belief by any means possible.

Under the influence of religious conviction, Muslims seek to purify the land and make the earth a house of Allah. Thus this will be a place where everyone is a Muslim, resulting in one big family. Muslims willfully acquire a philosophical argument to justify their actions to enhance the religious ideology and propagate their belief.

Dr. Randy Borum, a Professor in the College of Behavioral and Community Sciences at the University of South Florida, identifies a four-stage process whereby individuals develop extremist beliefs. A group or individual first identifies some sort of undesirable state of affairs; then frames that event or condition as unjust; then blames the injustice on a target policy, person, or nation; and then demonizes the responsible party so that aggression seems justified. Nevertheless, by definition extremism is any political theory favoring immoderate, uncompromising policies.

Q#119—What is "Postmodernism"?

Answer: Until recently, Western Civilization—our freedom, and our faith— was attacked by intellectual struggles such as Atheism, Deism, Existentialism, Humanism, Darwinism, Evolutionism, etc. Atheism says there is no God, period. Deism believes there is in existence a supreme being, a creator quote and quota"god" who created everything and then left it alone. Basically, Deists believe there is no interference of a supernatural being in human life. Existentialism assumes that people are entirely free and thus responsible for what they make of themselves. I do not have time to go through them all, but the point is this, no worldviews of previous movements have dared to threaten our society. They were merely an attempt to look at the world and interpret life.

However, in this era of Postmodernism, where everything is supposedly relative, "tolerance" is the new excuse for rejecting right and wrong. In the absence of Absolute truth (Christ), there is no realistic scale to measure what is right and wrong. Paul writes to the Church of Rome in Rom 3:20, "For 'no human being will be justified in his sight' by deeds prescribed by the law, for through the law comes the knowledge of sin." So the law was a way to measure what is right and what is wrong. But postmodernists believe that there isn't such a thing as absolute truth. A postmodernist views the world outside of themselves not as being in error, but that other people's truth is truth to them and it should not be objected or rejected. Therefore, no one has the authority to define truth or impose upon others his idea of moral right and wrong. Thus, in Western mentality, it should not be a big deal if Islam claims to be the only true and acceptable religion in the world.

Moreover, Postmodernists believe that the West's claims of freedom and prosperity continue to be nothing more than empty promises and have not met the needs of humanity. They believe that truth is relative and truth is up to each individual to determine for himself or herself. They do not attempt to refine their thoughts about what is right or wrong, true or false, good or evil.

Postmodernists reject any and every policy that comes from the United States of America because of her capitalism. They believe capitalism intends to keep the poor poorer and the rich richer. Therefore, Muslims have philosophical reasons to hate the West, particularly America. They are obligated to convert everyone to Islam and impose Sharia Law (Islamic law), so for a Muslim it is very easy to take the four steps (stages) identified by Dr. Borum in the last question.

Q#120—It seems you are very biased because you do not look at the good in Islam. What about the verses about peace, care and charity?

Answer: All religions preach peace, love, moral values, ethics, respect etc. Yes, Islam does too, but it is limited to those who are in the circle of Islam. Nevertheless, there are 109 verses that call Muslims to war with nonbelievers. Regarding the peace verses, if you put the Qur'an in a chronological order, you will find that all the peace verses in the Qur'an are from the early revelation (as Muhammad claimed), whereas in his later life all the revelations deal with war, the Jihad killing of infidels.

For instance, when Muhammad started his new movement, he encouraged nonbelievers to freely consider Islam. We can read about it in Sura 2:256 where it says, "Let there be no compulsion in religion." Later, however, when he gained some power and had resources to enforce what he believed, he developed a very harsh attitude toward non-Muslims. The Qur'an 9:5 says, "Fight and slay the idolaters wherever you find them, and seize them and besiege them, and lie in wait for them." What may be considered crimes against the state and crimes against God are dealt with in Surah 5:33, "The punishment of those who wage war against God and his apostle, and strive with might and main for mischief through the land is: execution, or crucifixion, or the cutting off of hands and feet from opposite sides, or exile from the land" Although, Jews and Christians are called People of Book, in Surah 5:5 and 5:19 it says, "but that does not mean that Muhammad had any regards for them;" Surah 5:14 says, "Christians are enemies" and 5:51 says "and Muslims were not to have Christians and Jews as friends."

Q#121—Why is Islam not like any other religion?

Answer: I do not consider Islam simply a religion. Let me explain with an illustration. Previously we talked about how Islam teaches the dominion of Allah and the religion of Islam as the only acceptable religion in the whole world. Moreover, every Mosque is modeled after the first Mosque in Medina "Masjad-e-Nabwi" which is called The Prophet's Mosque. As previously mentioned, according to the Qur'anic reference, Q#102, every Muslim is supposed to follow the role model of Muhammad. He used the mosque for the following purposes, Madrasah (Traditional Islamic education centers), Military (to plan where to attack in order to invade land), Political (to discuss the political issues, particularly diplomatic issues), Governmental (Muhammad, and later his followers, used the Mosque as headquarters to govern the state), Economical (Islam has a unique banking system where interest is considered as sin), Court/Legislation (to impose Sharia law, an Islamic law to determine and define crime and punishment for crime), Social and religious (where people come to gather as a society and worship). The following diagram presents a clear picture of the Mosque and the *Deen* religion of Islam.

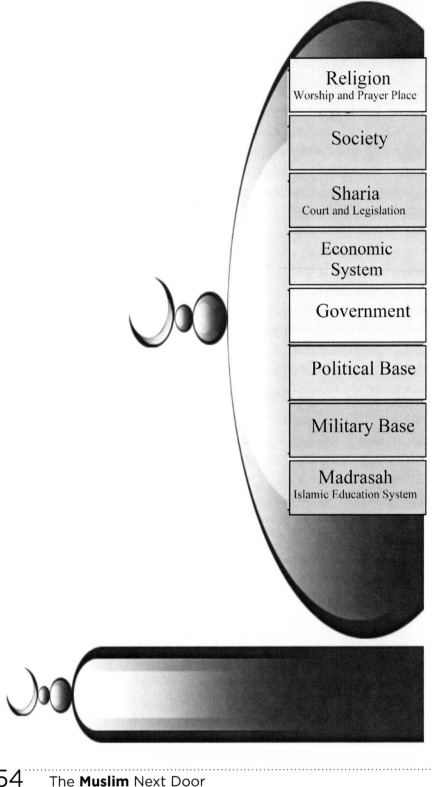

Religion
Worship and Prayer Place

Society

Sharia
Court and Legislation

Economic
System

Government

Political Base

Military Base

Madrasah
Islamic Education System

Personal Notes and Comments:

CHAPTER 11

Jesus in the Qur'an: The Person of Jesus and the Holy Trinity

This chapter deals with the person of Christ, and what the strong defenses against Christian teachings are. First, Jesus in the Qur'an is a good man, a highly respected prophet and a miracle worker. However, he is certainly not the Jesus you and I know. Thus, it is our responsibility to be wise and, like Paul on the Mars Hill, use the beliefs of Muslims to communicate to them about the Christ you and I believe in. Jesus is the one who can save our Muslim friends. Furthermore, the Jesus Muslims know cannot save because he was merely a man. Besides, Jesus in the Qur'an never died. When you talk about Christ, you must address the issue of the Trinity. Therefore, this chapter will provide some simple steps to address that issue.

I strongly agree with Ron Rhodes and his quick reference guide to minister to Muslims, *Islam: What You Need to Know*. He presented ten points to minister to a Muslim friend or family member. One of the ten points is to mention the Qur'an. He writes, "The Quran enjoins every true Muslim to believe in and honor all the prophets of God. Therefore, urge the Muslim to consider the truth-claims of Jesus Christ." We learn so much about the Qur'an and Islam. I am confident that if you take what you have learned so far by reading this book, you should be able to talk about Jesus from the Qur'an. As I mentioned previously, when you are talking to a Muslim, you must start with a reference to what is written in the Qur'an. Also, after providing the validity of the Bible or by simply creating curiosity in a Muslim you may able to find an opportunity to share what the Bible teaches about Christ.

Q#122—Shouldn't I know more about what the Qur'an says about Jesus?

Answer: This will take some time to explain because the Qur'an says so much about Jesus that an entire book could be written. Let me use one of the responses that I found online. I will compare a Muslim response to a Christian response. Actually, when you are witnessing to a Muslim, it is inevitable that the person will give you the interpretation and view he/she has received from the Muslim mullah or family, friend and relative. There are very few people who are willing to read the Qur'an with an open heart to see exactly what it says about Jesus. Thus, those who read and seek the truth come to know the truth and truth makes them free.

The following italic font is my response to the interpretation and explanation of the Muslim belief about what the Qur'an says about Jesus. For a full-length copy of the article go online to http://www3.sympatico.ca/shabir.ally/new_page_24.htm. The Qur'an tells us a lot of wonderful things about Jesus. As a result, believers in the Qur'an love Jesus, honor Him, and believe in Him. In fact, no Muslim can be a Muslim unless he or she believes in Jesus, on whom be peace.

This is a fact, all over the Muslim world, and Muslims believe it. Previously, I have discussed this briefly. It can be used to our advantage and also to our disadvantage. Muslims tend to wander around and keep changing the topic. When you initiate a conversation and after such answers that the Qur'an gives about Jesus, ask how can a Muslim be a Muslim without believing in Him? You need to remember even the demons believe in Him, they give Him honor, in fact they tremble before His name. The acknowledgement of Jesus by Muslims is not enough. They need to know why he came to the earth and why it was crucial that he gave His life for the sins of all mankind. They have never heard about atonement or salvation so they could not know until you share with them.

So take advantage of the situation and the claim that a Muslim makes about Jesus in the Qur'an. Do not let the Muslim take control of the situation and take you another direction with such a claim. Be firm, and politely say, "Isn't it interesting that you can't be Muslim without believing in Him," then go on and use the "20 tale" approach to start evangelizing.

The Qur'an says that Jesus was born of a virgin, that he spoke while he was still only a baby, that he healed the blind and the leper by God's permission, and that he raised the dead by God's permission.

It is a fact that the Qur'an is full of such references. Here are three different translations from the Qur'an:

> **YUSUFALI:** *Behold! The angels said: "O Mary! Allah giveth thee glad tidings of a Word from Him: his name will be Christ Jesus, the son of Mary, held in honour in this world and the Hereafter and of (the company of) those nearest to Allah;*

> **PICKTHAL:** *(And remember) when the angels said: O Mary! Lo! Allah giveth thee glad tidings of a word from him, whose name is the Messiah, Jesus, son of Mary, illustrious in the world and the Hereafter, and one of those brought near (unto Allah).*

> **SHAKIR:** *When the angels said: O Marium, surely Allah gives you good news with a Word from Him (of one) whose name is the : Messiah, Isa son of Marium, worthy of regard in this world and the hereafter and of those who are made near (to Allah).*

What then is the significance of these miracles? First is the virgin birth, where God demonstrates his power to create in every way. God created everyone we know from a man and a woman. But how about Adam, on whom be peace? God created him from neither a man nor a woman, and Eve from only a man, but not a woman. And, finally, to complete the picture, God created Jesus from a woman, but not a man. *Not the full truth… It is a deceptive answer and Muslims throughout the world believe in it. They compare the birth of Jesus Christ with the creation of Adam. Actually, they consider Adam's creation a greater miracle because he was created neither man nor women. However, the truth is this there is difference and similarity between both men. F. W. Grant writes the following:*

> *It is the first epistle to the Corinthians alone, and in the same passage, which gives us the two important terms, so closely related as they are to one another, of "Second Man" and "Last Adam" (15:45, 47). The one looks backward; the other forward. The "Second Man" implies that*

before Him we have only the first man, repeated and multiplied, in his descendents; now a new type has appeared; and that this, which is the full and final thought of man, may become the true heir of the inheritance, the "Second Man" is the "Last Adam." He is the "last" not "second," because plainly there is no other to succeed Him. "The Last Adam" (in opposition to "the first man Adam," (who "became a living soul") becomes "a Spirit giving life." (online sources: http://www.biblecentre.org/topics/ fwg_crowned_christ_7_last_adam.htm)

His answer is very profound and corrects some of the misunderstanding Muslim theologians carry with them by considering the virgin birth of Jesus Christ merely a miracle. It was not just a miracle. It was the power of God, and His humility to come into this world to restore the lost world back to Himself. I encourage you to read the rest of his article on this topic. It will enlighten you on the Muslims' understanding of the virgin birth of Jesus Christ. Muslims support their misunderstanding on the basis of the following Qur'an reference: **"The similitude of Jesus before Allah is as that of Adam; He created him from dust, then said to him: "Be:" and he was"(Quran 3:59).** *But the fact is that this verse simply says, "similitude," which means similarity. In terms of Jesus' miraculous birth, the Qur'an says:* **"So eat and drink and cool (your) eye. And if you see any man, say, 'I have vowed a fast to (Allah) Most Gracious, and this day I will not enter into any talk with any human being.' At length she brought the (babe) to her people, carrying him (in her arms). They said: "O Mary! truly an amazing thing you have brought! "O sister of Aaron! your father was not a man of evil, nor your mother an unchaste woman!" But she pointed to the babe. They said: "How can we talk to one who is a child in the cradle?" He said: "I am indeed a servant of Allah: He has given me Revelation and made me a prophet;" "And He has made me blessed wheresoever I be, and has enjoined on me Prayer and Charity as long as I live;" "(He) has made me kind to my mother, and not overbearing or miserable"** *(Qur'an 19:26-32). The verse also says that Jesus was sent by Allah as prophet, to serve Him, which leads to the next point.*

What about the other miracles? These were to show that Jesus was not acting on his own behalf, but that he was backed by God. The Qur'an specifies that these miracles were performed by God's permission. This may be compared to the Book of Acts in the Bible, chapter 2, verse 22, where it says that the miracles were done by God to show that he approved of Jesus. Also, note that Jesus himself is recorded in the Gospel of John as having said, **"I can do nothing of my own authority"** (5:30). The miracles, therefore, were not done by his own authority, but by God's authority.

Again, not the whole truth, the miracles were the proof of his unique apostleship. Miracles were signs so that many may believe. Even if we accept the claim that Muslims make, then what answer do Muslims have in regards to the apostleship of Muhammad? He did not perform any miracles like Jesus. Does it mean he was not backed by Allah? Muslims use the following biblical verse to support their theology, "... This command I (Jesus) received from my Father" (John 10:18). If so, then they need to accept that He was the Son of God who was fulfilling the will of His Father on this earth. In the same chapter John 10:30 states, "I and the Father are one." Yes, he was using the authority of His Father because the Father and the Son are one. Muslims say that Jesus never claimed that He was the Son of God by using the following verse from the Qur'an:

*"And behold! Allah will say: "O Jesus the son of Mary! Did you say to men, 'worship me and my mother as gods in derogation of Allah'?" He (Jesus) will say: "Glory to You! Never could I say what I had no right (to say). Had I said what is in my heart, though I do not know what is in Yours. For You know in full all that is hidden. "Never said I to them anything except what You commanded me to say, to wit, 'Worship Allah, my Lord and your Lord'; And I was a witness over them whilst I dwelt amongst them; when You took me up, You were the Watcher over them, and You are a Witness to all things" (Qur'an 5:116-7). How come Muslims fail to notice so many references where Jesus claimed not only to be Son of God, but also as the second person of the Trinity. For example, John 8:58 is another example. Jesus declared, "I say unto you, **before Abraham was, I am."** See John: 4:26, 8:24, 8:28, 8:58, and 13:19.*

What did Jesus teach? The Qur'an tells us that Jesus came to teach the same basic message which was taught by previous prophets from God— that we must shun every false god and worship only the one true God. Jesus taught that He is the servant and messenger of that one true God, the God of Abraham. These Qura'nic teachings can be compared with the Bible (Mark 10:18; Matthew 26:39; John 14:28, 17:3, and 20:17) where Jesus teaches that the one He worshipped is the only true God. See also Matthew 12:18; Acts 3:13, and 4:27 where we find that his disciples knew him as the Servant of God.

Misleading about Jesus, but true about what the Qur'an teaches, as I have already mentioned the full verse earlier in **Quran 5:116-7.** *Although the Qur'an teaches that Jesus was teaching what the previous prophets taught, the claim Muslims make about the Biblical references to support their Qur'anic beliefs are entirely false and misleading.* The disciples of Jesus knew that Jesus was Son of God and they worshiped Him. "When they saw Him, they worshiped Him; but some were doubtful" Matthew 20:17. The Apostle Paul tells us that Jesus "is the image of the invisible God, the firstborn of every creature: For by him were all things created, that are in heaven, and that are in earth, visible and invisible, whether they be thrones, or dominions, or principalities, or powers: all things were created by him, and for him: And he is before all things, and by him all things consist" (Colossians 1:15-17). John 1:1 says, "**the Word was God.**" John 1:14 says, "**And the Word was made flesh**, and dwelt among us" and John 10:36 says, "Do you say of Him, whom the Father sanctified and sent into the world, 'You are blaspheming,' because I said, 'I am the Son of God'?" The thrust is this—"Let this mind be in you which was also in Christ Jesus, who, being in the form of God, did not consider it robbery to be equal with God, but made Himself of no reputation, taking the form of a bond-servant, and coming in the likeness of men" (**Philippians 2:5-7**).

The Qur'an tells us that some of the Israelites rejected Jesus, and conspired to kill him, but Allah (God) rescued Jesus and raised Him to Himself. Allah will cause Jesus to descend again, at which time Jesus will confirm his true teachings and everyone will believe in him as he is and as the Qur'an teaches about him.

According to the Qur'an, Jesus was never crucified. Therefore, Muslims do not believe in the teaching of atonement. According to them, Muhammad is dead and is still buried whereas Jesus who is alive and resides in heaven will come back. If that is the case, ask them who they want to be with as a Muslim—with a man who is dead and not promised to come back or the One who is alive and resides into heaven and will come back? In regards to Christ's ascension, when Jesus was about to be lifted up to the heavens He said to his disciples, " "**All authority has been given to Me in heaven and on earth.**" (**Matthew 28:18**). *The death of Jesus and His resurrection is the basis of Christianity; if He would not have died then His miraculous birth would have been useless, and if Jesus would not have resurrected we would have no hope for salvation.* The Scriptures says, "**For if we believe that Jesus died and rose again, even so God will bring with Him those who have fallen asleep in Jesus**" (1 Thessalonians 4:14) "**And if Christ has not been raised, then all our preaching is**

*useless, and your faith is useless" (**1 Corinthians 15:14**), and other references—
Ps. 73:13; Isa. 49:4; Gen. 8:8; Mt. 15:9; Ac. 17:31; Gal. 2:2; Jas. 1:26 2:20.*

According to Muslims Jesus is the Messiah. He is a word from Allah, and a spirit from Him. He is honored in this world and in the hereafter, and he is one of those brought nearest to Allah.

It is a fact that Qur'an addresses Jesus as Messiah, Word from/of God, and Spirit of God (recently Muslims have been promoting a different translation: a spirit from God). It really does not matter what we believe that God really says and how Muslims interpret the text from the Qur'an, the point that really matters is that we should not bring any statement out of Qur'an that might become a hindrance for us. If you do not want to be trapped in your own net, then please be advised what Muslims really believe. You can always go online and submit a question at www. answer.yahoo.com and definitely, you will get some response from a Muslim about the beliefs we think Muslims have. In this regard whether the Qur'an says Jesus is the Word, and Spirit of God, a Muslim by the name Asgar responded as following: (http://answers.yahoo.com/question/index?qid=20081218075910AAM41uu).

1. JESUS (PBUH) "IS A WORD FROM ALLAH" NOT "THE WORD OF ALLAH" the Qur'an mentions in Surah Ali 'Imran Chapter 3 verse 45

   "Behold! The angels said: O Mary! Allah giveth thee glad tidings of a Word from Him: his name will be Christ Jesus. The son of Mary, held in honour in this world and the Hereafter and of (the company of) those Nearest to Allah."

   Jesus (pbuh) is referred in the Qur'an as a word from Allah and not as 'the word of Allah.'

   "A word" of Allah means a message of Allah. If a person is referred to as "a word" from Allah, it means that he is a Messenger or a Prophet of Allah.

2. THE TITLE OF A PROPHET (PBUH) DOES NOT MEAN THAT IT EXCLUSIVELY BELONGS TO THAT PROPHET (PBUH)

   Different titles are given to different prophets (pbuh). Whenever a title is given to a prophet (pbuh), it does not necessarily mean that the other prophets do not have the same character-istic or quality. For e.g. Prophet Abraham (pbuh) is referred to in the Qur'an as Khaleelullah, a friend of Allah. This does not indicate that all the other Prophets (pbuh) were not the friends of Allah. Prophet Moses (pbuh) is referred to in the Qur'an as Kaleemullah, indicating that God spoke to him. This does not mean that God did not speak to others. Similarly when Jesus (pbuh) is referred to in the Qur'an as Kalimatullah, "a word from Allah," it does not mean that the other Prophets were not "the word," of Allah.

3. JOHN THE BAPTIST (PBUH) IS ALSO CALLED "A WORD" OF ALLAH

Yahya (pbuh) i.e. John the Baptist (pbuh) is also referred to in the Qur'an as Kalimatullah i.e. a word of Allah in Surah Ali 'Imran, Chapter 3, verses 38-39

"There did Zakariya Pray to his Lord, saying: "O my Lord! Grant unto me from Thee a progeny that is pure: for Thou art He that heareth prayer! While he was standing in prayer in the chamber, the angels called unto him: "Allah doth give thee glad tidings of Yahya, witnessing the truth of a Word from Allah, and (be besides) noble, chaste, and a Prophet—of the (goodly) company of the righteous."

4. JESUS (PBUH) REFERRED AS RUHULLAH—A SPIRIT OF ALLAH

Jesus (pbuh) also never referred to as Ruhullah "a spirit of Allah" but as a spirit from Allah in Surah Nisa Chapter 4 verse 171 *"O People of the Book! Commit no excesses in your religion: nor say of Allah aught but the truth. Jesus Christ the son of Mary was (no more than) a Messenger of Allah, And His Word, which He bestowed on Mary, and a Spirit proceeding from Him: so believe in Allah and His Messengers. Say not 'Trinity': desist: it will be better for you: for Allah is One God: glory be to Him: (Far Exalted is He) above having a son. To Him belong all things in the heavens and on earth. And enough is Allah as a Disposer of affairs."*

5. SPIRIT OF ALLAH IS BREATHED IN EVERY HUMAN BEING

A spirit from Allah does not indicate that Jesus (pbuh) is God. The Qur'an mentions in several places that Allah breathed into the human beings "His Spirit" in Surah Al-Hijr, chapter 15 verse 29 in Surah Sajdah, chapter 32 verse 9 Surah Al Hijr Chapter 15 verse 29 *"When I have fashioned him (in due proportion) and breathed into him of My spirit, fall ye down in obeisance unto him."*

Surah Sajdah Chapter 32 verse 9 *"But He fashioned him in due proportion, and breathed into him something of His spirit. And He gave you (the faculties of) hearing and sight and feeling (and understanding): little thanks do ye give!"*

Jesus was a man who spoke the truth, which he heard from God. This can be compared with the Gospel According to John where Jesus says to the Israelites: "You are determined to kill me, a man who has told you the truth that I heard from God" (John 8:40).

Again, not the truth. Even in the same chapter John 8, Jesus claimed to be before Abraham was born and that God is His father and His father God and He Himself are witness for the truth he was preaching. But let's examine the Qur'an's resources to see whether Jesus was just "a man" or a perfect man and perfect God.

The Qur'an says, "I bring you a sign from your Lord. From clay I will make for you the likeness of a bird. I shall breath into it and, by God's leave, it shall become a living bird." (Surah 3:49) and then Surah 5:10 says "When Allah saith: O Jesus, son of Mary! Remember My favour unto thee and unto thy mother; how I strengthened thee with the holy Spirit, so that thou spakest unto mankind in the cradle as in maturity; and how I taught thee the Scripture and Wisdom and the Torah and the Gospel; and how thou didst shape of clay as it were the likeness of a bird by My permission, and didst blow upon it and it was a bird by My permission, and thou didst heal him who was born blind and the leper by My permission; and how thou didst raise the dead by My permission; and how I restrained the Children of Israel from (harming) thee when thou camest unto them with clear proofs, and those of them who disbelieved exclaimed: This is naught else than mere magic."

Well, here are a few Questions in regards to the above Qur'anic references:

1. Who has power to create something from the dust and breathe life into it?
2. Who did the something similar somewhere else (when He created man from dust)?
3. Did Muhammad do such a life-giving miracle?
4. Did Muhammad heal those born blind and lepers?

(A full article of what Muslim theologians think and believe about the virgin birth and miracles of Jesus Christ is in Appendix III.)

Q#123—Do Muslims believe in Muhammad the way Christians believe in Jesus?

Answer: Well, it's little complicated because the Qur'an explicitly forbids the worship of Muhammad, since he was merely a man. However, the Qur'an teaches that Muhammad was the best in all the creation, and Muslims have to model themselves after him. According to the Qur'an whatever he does or says has already been approved by Allah.

Surat Al-Qalam (The Pen)—Sura 68:4

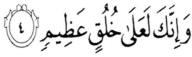

Sahih International Translation

And indeed, you are of a great moral character.

Muhsin Khan Translation

And verily, you (O Muhammad SAW) are on an exalted standard of character.

Surat An-Najm (The Star)—Sura 53: 2-5 with Sahih International Translation

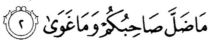

Your companion [Muhammad] has not strayed, nor has he erred,

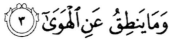

Nor does he speak from [his own] inclination.

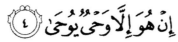

It is not but a revelation revealed,

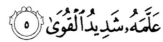

Taught to him by one intense in strength—

Surat Al-'Aḥzāb (The Combined Forces)—33:21

لَّقَدْ كَانَ لَكُمْ فِي رَسُولِ ٱللَّهِ أُسْوَةٌ حَسَنَةٌ لِّمَن كَانَ يَرْجُوا۟ ٱللَّهَ وَٱلْيَوْمَ ٱلْآخِرَ وَذَكَرَ ٱللَّهَ كَثِيرًا ﴿٢١﴾

Muhsin Khan Translation

Indeed in the Messenger of Allah (Muhammad SAW) you have a good example to follow for him who hopes in (the Meeting with) Allah and the Last Day and remembers Allah much.

Surat An-Nisā' (The Women)—4:80

مَّن يُطِعِ ٱلرَّسُولَ فَقَدْ أَطَاعَ ٱللَّهَ وَمَن تَوَلَّىٰ فَمَآ أَرْسَلْنَٰكَ عَلَيْهِمْ حَفِيظًا ﴿٨٠﴾

Sahih International Translation

He who obeys the Messenger has obeyed Allah; but those who turn away— We have not sent you over them as a guardian.

There are number of references such as Sura 48:10, 33:36, 9:29, 24:62, 49:15, 8:1, 4:59, 3:132, 24:56, all these verses prove that the ways and saying of Muhammad are the direct inspiration of Allah. Thus every faithful Muslim has to follow what the Qur'an commands and what the Hadith (the traditions of Muhammad how he lived, what he said, simply the ways of Muhammad) says. To answer your question, Muslims do believe that Muhammad was more than a prophet, but they claim that they believe him as a prophet who was just a human being.

Q#124—Is it true that extreme Muslims find justification of their actions in the Qur'an?

Answer: It is true that they find justification for their evil actions. According to the Qur'an:

"Fighting is prescribed for you, and ye dislike it. But it is possible that ye dislike a thing which is good for you, and that ye love a thing which is bad for you. But Allah knoweth, and ye know not" (Qur'an 2:216).

"And slay them wherever ye find them, and drive them out of the places whence they drove you out, for persecution [of Muslims] is worse than slaughter [of non-believers]…and fight them until persecution is no more, and religion is for Allah" (Qur'an 2:244).

"So fight them until all submit to the religion of Allah alone (in the whole world)" (Qur'an 8:39).

"He has sent His Messenger (Muhammad) with guidance and the Religion of Truth (Islam) to make it superior over all religions" (Qur'an 9:33).

"If anyone desire a religion other than Islam, never will it be accepted of him" (Qur'an 3:85).

Q#125—Are the majority of Muslims in the world moderate Muslims?

Answer: There are no moderate or extreme Muslims. There are only Muslims. The West has divided them into what we call "peaceful Muslims" and "radical Muslims." I do not know any moderate Muslims: if a Muslim is a moderate Muslim then he or she is not a Muslim. In Islam, either you are a Muslim or you are not. The average Muslim will consider those who are lukewarm Muslims to be a part of *Munafeqeen*, meaning that they have polluted the religion by adding or subtracting something from the teaching of Islam.

Q#126—Could you please give me a list of Qur'anic references that speak about Jesus in the same manner as the Bible?

Answer: Certainly. Here is a list of the Qur'anic and the Biblical references:

- He was messiah (Qur'an 4:171—John 1:41, 4:25-26)

- He was a Spirit from God [or of God] (4:171)

- He was the word of God (Qur'an 4:171—John 1:1-4)

- He was born of a virgin (Qur'an 19:16-35—Luke 1:26-38, 21:1-20)

- He created life and healed the sick (Qur'an 3:49—Matt. 11:1-6)

- He is a sign to mankind (Qur'an 19:21—Luke 2:25-32)

- He is illustrious in this world and the hereafter (Qur'an 3:45—Heb 1:3, Cal. 1:16-29)

- He was taken to heaven by God (Qur'an 4:158—Acts 1:9-11)

- He will come back and Judge the earth (Qur'an 43:61—)

- He was holy or faultless (Qur'an 19:19—Heb 7:26)

Q#127—Is it not true that the statement, "He was a Spirit from God [or of God] (4:171)" is very controversial?

Answer: The controversy exists because if Muslims accept that Jesus was the Spirit of God, then they have to recognize Him as deity. This contradicts the fundamentals of Islam's doctrine of "Towheed" that God has no companion. Ahmed Deedat is a well-known and a well-respected scholar in Islam. Ahmed in his short book, *Desert Storm has it ended: Christ in Islam*, writes the following:

> Though Jesus is mentioned by name in twenty-five places in the Holy Qur'ân, he is also addressed with respect as: *Ibn Maryam*, meaning

"The son of Mary;" and as the *Maseeh* (in Hebrew it is the *Messiah*), which is translated as "Christ." He is also known as *Abdullah*, "The servant of Allah;" and as *Rasul u Allah*, the messenger of Allah. He is spoken of as "The Word of God," as "**The Spirit of God**," as a "Sign of God," and numerous other epithets of honor spread over fifteen different chapters. The Holy Quran honors this mighty messenger of God, and the Muslims have not fallen short over the past fourteen hundred years in doing the same. There is not a single disparaging remark in the entire Quran to which even the most jaundiced among the Christians can take exception.

The point is this: in recent years Islamic theology and its apologetic approach have been changed. Muslim scholars have found ways to get around the translation of the Arabic text. Thus, replacing article "the" to "a" and the proposition "of" with "from" has changed the meaning of the verse in the Qur'an as well as the theology and the person of Jesus Christ in the Qur'an. Therefore, it is imperative to use names like Muslim scholar Ahmed or simply stick with the old translation and meaning of the verse regardless of the new Islamic theology about the verse.

Q#128—How many times does the Qur'an speak of Jesus?

Answer: In the Qur'an, Jesus is mentioned twenty-five times excluding the talking about Jesus with his title. The following are a few verses from the Qur'an talking about Christ:

- "We gave Jesus, the son of Mary, clear signs and strengthened him with the Holy Spirit" (The Holy Qur'ân 2:87)

- "O Mary! God giveth thee glad tidings of a Word from Him: his name will be Christ Jesus, the son of Mary..." (3:45)

- "...Christ Jesus the son of Mary was (no more than) an apostle of god..." (4:171)

- "...And in their footsteps we sent Jesus the son of Mary..." (5:46)

- "And Zakariya and John, and Jesus and Elias: all in the ranks of the righteous." (6:85)

Q#129—Is it true that all the religions are basically the same?

Answer: I would like to point to an answer provided by a friend of mine. He did some impartial research on other religions with a particular focus on Islam. Here is what he writes in his email to me:

All Religions are Basically the Same, or are They?

"All religions are the same, and therefore, you can't say that yours is the true religion," according to postmodern religious pluralists. However, this statement doesn't stand up to scrutiny.

Let's just take one instance—the marital relationship. The *Assembly of Muslim Jurists of America* (<u>amjaonline.com</u>) seeks to give authoritative explanations and judgments on shariah law to Muslims living in North America . One Muslim inquired:

> "Is a man permitted to FORCE his wife to have sexual intercourse with him? This is obviously when she is naashiz and unwilling to have coitus."

Here is AMJA's fatwa on the subject:

> "For a wife to abandon the bed of her husband without excuse is haram. It is one of the major sins and the angels curse her until the morning as we have been informed by the Prophet (may Allah bless him and grant him peace). She is considered nashiz (rebellious) under these circumstances. As for the issue of forcing a wife to have sex, if she refuses, this would not be called rape, even though it goes against natural instincts and destroys love and mercy, and there is a great sin upon the wife who refuses; and Allah Almighty is more exalted and more knowledgeable."

In contrast to this, any form of violence against the wife is never permitted by the Bible. Instead, the Christian husbands are required to love their "wives just as Christ also loved the church and gave Himself for her" (Ephes. 5:25), "giving honor to the wife, as to the weaker vessel, and as being heirs together of the grace of life, that your prayers may not be hindered" (1 Peter 3:7). While both the Qur'an and the Bible recognize that it is wrong for either party to withhold sex, the Bible (1 Cor. 7:1-5) never gives any sanction to the husband to force himself upon his wife.

I mention this distinction because it's reflective of the distinction between the two religions on many levels. If we fail to acknowledge this, we might be tempted to allow the Islamic community to impose shariah on their own people for the sake of peace. However, there are many problems with this strategy:

1. This indulgence will not produce peace any more than giving Hitler Sudetenland (Czechoslovakia) placated him. Faithful Muslims are required to impose shariah on everyone. This was the example of Mohammed, which they are mandated to uphold. Consequently, allowing them their own shariah courts merely represents a beachhead within a much greater conflict strategy.

2. Shariah de-criminalizes many things that the Christian West regards as criminal. It allows Islamic authorities to deprive human rights from those who are guaranteed them by their Western host nations. For instance, shariah sanctions honor killings and punishments (and sometimes death) for anyone choosing to leave Islam.

I write this way because we are not far from opening the door to shariah courts. Britain already has them, and this concession hasn't shown any signs of moderating Islamic radicalism. The Independent (UK) reports: "A senior Muslim cleric who runs the country's largest network of sharia courts has sparked controversy by claiming that there is no such thing as rape within marriage. Sheikh Maulana Abu Sayeed, president of the Islamic Sharia Council in Britain, said that men who rape their wives should not be prosecuted because "sex is part of marriage." And he claimed that many married women who alleged rape were lying." http://www.independent.co.uk/news/uk/home-news/rape-impossible-in-marriage-says-muslim-cleric-2106161.html

Are all religions the same? Only when you close your eyes!

You could also check my friend's blog on www.Mannsword.blogspot.com.

Q#130—What is Muhammadism?

Answer: It is the term that the West has given to Islam, but there is also a sect of Islam called Muhammadies. They claim to be strict followers of Muhammad. The term Muhammadism seems appropriate since 60% of Islam consists of studying Muhammad's life. In order to understand Islam and the Qur'an, you have to know Muhammad and his life. Every Muslim is supposed to follow the example of Muhammad in order to be a good Muslim. The Qur'an teaches the following traits of a good Muslim:

1. Most exemplary character (33:21) (68:4)
2. Sadiq (Truthful) (33:22)
3. Final judge and arbiter (4:65) (24:51)
4. Honored, Noble (69:40)
5. Forgiving (7:199)
6. He is Burhan (Clear Proof) (4:174)
7. Brave: Commands Muslims in battle (3:121)

Q#131—How did Muhammadism develop?

Answer: When Muhammad started his ministry as a prophet, for 13 years he did not have any success as a messenger of Allah. Some records say he had 70 followers and other say 150; either way it began as a very unsuccessful religion. However, the teachings were very similar to Judaism and Christianity. There was a call to follow one monotheist God. The proper name for God was determined as Allah and Muhammad was declared to be his prophet. If someone believes that Allah is the only God and Muhammad is his messenger he/she becomes a Muslim; and thus can be saved from hell fire.

The early part of the Qur'an teaches tolerance and peace. It was commanded to bear persecution for the sake of Allah. Muhammad was persecuted for his faith and his preaching of Islam but he did not respond to violence with violence. However, under persecution he moved to Medina and was given the opportunity to preach Islam without persecution and also was placed as a counselor to settle disputes of Medinians. Muhammad started a new Islam, which was the opposite of the previous Islam, which he preached and taught in Mecca for 13 years. A large portion of the Qur'an, 90 chapters out of a total of 114 chapters, were preached in Mecca and originated during the 13 years. It was in Medina that Muhammad's teaching adopted a new tone; a progressive development of a new Islam was shaping under the concept of Jihad.

According to Rev. Richard P. Bailey (http://www.answering-islam.org/Bailey/jihad.html), there are four stages in the Qur'an:

1. **No retaliation:** the early period of Islam e.g Sura 73:10-11, 52:4547,48 teaches be patient and wait upon God to punish those who deny truth.

2. **Defensive fighting was permitted:** (first instruction in Medina) e.g 22:39-41

3. **Defensive fighting was commanded:** but with the instruction to forgive and overlook unbelieving Jew and Christians and let God take care of them. e.g 2:190-194 is a command to fight until the persecution stops and Islam is the acceptable religion.

4. **Offensive war was commanded:** to kill the pagans and humble the Christians and Jews. e.g 9:1-6 says kill those who do not receive Islam.

Q#132—What else does the Qur'an teach about Muhammad?

Answer: This is actually a very good question because knowing what the Qur'an teaches about Muhammad is the basis for why Muslims idolize Muhammad. Most Muslims exalt the status of Muhammad almost as high as that of Allah. They do not say that outright, and may even formally even condemn it. The following division of Muhammad's status is taken from an Islamic source but you can check the verses from the Qur'an.

HIS EXALTED STATUS
1. He is Nur (Sacred Light) (5:15)
2. Allah blesses him (33:56)
3. Mercy for all the worlds (21:107)
4. His name is Muhammad (Meaning the Most Praised One) (47:2)

5. Allah has exalted his Zikr (remembrance) (94:1-4)

6. His exaltation on the Night of Mi'raj: his heavenly ascent (53:8-9)

7. His Station of Praise (Al-Maqam al-Mahmud) (17:79)

THE BELOVED OF ALLAH

1. If you want to gain the love of Allah, follow him (3:31)

2. Allah addresses him with love and affection (20:1) (36:1) (73:1) (74:1)

3. Allah says: Realize that My Prophetic Messenger himself is with you (49:7)

4. Allah describes him with His Own Attributes of Rauf (Most Kind) and Rahim (Merciful) (9:128)

5. Allah Himself praises him (33:45-47)

6. Possessor of Allah's Grace (4:113)

7. He is a special favour of Allah (Sub'hanahu wa Ta'ala) (3:164)

8. Allah does not punish people if he is in their midst (8:33)

9. Allegiance to him is allegiance to Allah (48:10)

HE RECEIVED THE HOLY QUR'AN

1. Allah gave him Surah al-Fatiha and the whole Qur'an (15:87)

2. Totally inspired (53:3-4)

3. Allah revealed the Noble Qur'an on his blessed heart (26:192-197)

4. The first revelation he received (96:1)

5. Teaches the Holy Qur'an and Hadith Sharif (Wisdom) and purifies people (62:2)

AMONG THE PROPHETS ('Alayhimussalam)

1. He is the Final Prophet (Sallallahu 'alayhi wa Sallam) (33:40)

2. Mentioned first among the greatest Prophets ('Alay-himussalam)(33:7) (4:163)

3. A Prophet whom Allah appointed with proven prophecies (30:1-6) (48:1) (48:27) (61:13)

4. Given the knowledge of the unseen (3:179)

5. Nabi Ibrahim ('Alayhissalam) prayed for his coming (2:129)

6. Foretold by Nabi 'Isa (Jesus) ('Alayhissalam) (61:6)

7. Allah asks all the Prophets to believe in him (3:81)

8. Confirms the previous (Prophetic) Messengers of Allah (37:37)

SERVES ONLY ALLAH (THE GLORIFIED AND THE EXALTED)

1. Worships only Allah (Sub'hanahu wa Ta'ala) (72:19-20)

2. Puts total trust in Allah (Sub'hanahu wa Ta'ala) (9:129)

3. Selflessly labours for Allah, asks for no reward (25:57) (42:23)

4. Rewarded by Allah (68:3) (108:1)

HIS EXEMPLARY CHARACTER

1. Most exemplary character (33:21) (68:4)

2. Sadiq (Truthful) (33:22)

3. Final judge and arbiter (4:65) (24:51)

4. Honoured, Noble (69:40)

5. Forgiving (7:199)

6. He is Burhan (Clear Proof) (4:174)

7. Brave: Commands Muslims in battle (3:121)

PREACHES ISLAM

1. Established the correct Message of Islam (6:161-163) (39:11-12)

2. Preacher to all humanity (4:170) (25:1) (34:28)

3. He is Bashir and Nadhir (Bearer of glad tidings and a warner) (5:19)

4. Invites people to Islam (12:108)

5. Even the jinn respond to his call (46:29-31)

6. He brought the truth (17:81) (39:33)

7. He brought a new law (Shari'a) (7:157)

8. A perfect guide to be followed (7:158)

9. He calls you to that which gives you life (8:24)

10. Brings people from the darkness (of Ignorance) to the Light (of Islam) (65:11)

11. His religion prevails over all religion (48:28)

HIS BLESSED FAMILY AND COMPANIONS (Rady Allahu 'Anhum)

1. His Family purified by Allah (Sub'hanahu wa Ta'ala) (33:33)

2. His Companions praised by Allah (Sub'hanahu wa Ta'ala) (48:29)

3. His Companions: The Muhajirin and the Ansar (8:74) (9:100) (59:8-9)

4. His Companions pledge allegiance to him (48:18)

BELIEVE, HONOUR, LOVE, RESPECT AND OBEY HIM

1. Believe, honour and respect him (48:9) (61:11)

2. Love Allah and His Beloved Prophet more than anything else (9:24)

3. He is closer to the believers than their own selves (33:6)

4. Respect him (49:1-3)

5. Obey Allah (Ta'ala) and His Beloved Prophet (Sallal-lahu 'alayhi wa Sallam)(3:132) (4:13) (4:59) (4:69) (4:80) (9:71) (24:52) (24:54) (24:56) (33:71) (49:14) (64:12)

6. Follow the Commands of Allah (Sub'hanahu wa Ta'ala) and of His Beloved Prophet (Sallallahu 'alayhi wa Sallam) (33:36)

7. Whatever he gives you, take it (59:7)

8. The reward of believing in him (57:28)

WAGED JIHAD AMIDST PERSECUTION

1. Non-believers plot to kill him (8:30)

2. His persecution (22:39-40)

3. Commanded to fight alone for Allah (Sub'hanahu wa Ta'ala) (4:84)

4. He led Muslims in prayer while in battle (4:102)

5. Allah asks him to seek peace (8:61)

6. Allah helped him in Jihad (33:9)

7. Allah made him victorious (110:1)

HIS MIRACLES

1. Living miracle: The Holy Qur'an (2:23) (17:88) (52:34)

2. Human miracle: he was the wasila (means) through whom people's hearts were transformed (5:83)

3. Heavenly miracle: Isra' and Mi'raj (his heavenly ascent) (17:1) (53:8-18)

4. Historic miracle: Hijra; escaped while surrounded (9:40)

5. The miracle of the Battle of Badr: Victory against all odds (3:123-125)

6. The splitting of the moon (54:1-2)

INTERCESSOR (SHAFI')

1. Allah appointed him as an intercessor to plead for people's forgiveness (3:159) (4:64) (60:12)

2. An accepted intercessor (19:87) (20:109)

3. His supplication a relief for hearts (9:103)

Q#133—Looking at these verses it seems to me that there are two types of teaching in Islam about Muhammad.

Answer: It would not be wrong to say that Islam is a dual religion. In Islam, we find both positive and negative teachings. Again, it is because of the life of Muhammad and the Qur'an. The Qur'an is not in chronological order, but if you study the life of Muhammad in the Qur'an you will see a clear connection between the Qur'an and the life of Muhammad.

Q#134—What do you mean by positive and negative teachings?

Answer: Every religion is supposed to teach good and positive things, which Islam does, but no religion is supposed to teach bad and negative teachings, which Islam in fact does. For example, killing, hatred, anger, lying (deceiving) and revenge are some of the pure evil characteristics, which can be found in the Qur'an. For a Muslim reader who is looking for justification to kill, hate, lie or take revenge of non-Muslims such verses provide a clear conscience.

Q#135—How can Muslims use a Qur'anic verse "if a Muslim kills one man it is as if he kills the whole world?" to condemn terrorist attacks and the killing of innocent people?

Answer: I am familiar with the verse to which you are referring. It is from Sura 5:32; "Because of this, we decreed for the Children of Israel that anyone who murders any person who had not committed murder or horrendous crimes, it shall be as if he murdered all the people. And anyone who spares a life, it shall be as if he spared the lives of all the people. Our messengers went to them with clear proofs and revelations, but most of them, after all this, are still transgressing."

Muslims all over the world use a tiny part of this verse to defend themselves, but they do not provide the full context of the verse. For example, if you ask them what they would consider a horrendous crime, you will be given a very long list, including anything and everything that does not fit in the structure of Islamic teaching and practices.

If you read the very next verse in the same chapter you will see how easily all the world except the Islamic world can be described as a community that has committed horrendous crimes against Allah and Muhammad by being non-Muslims. This particularly includes the Western world.

5:33] The just retribution for those who fight GOD and His messenger, and commit horrendous crimes, is to be killed, or crucified, or to have their hands and feet cut off on alternate sides, or to be banished from the land. This is to humiliate them in this life, then they suffer a far worse retribution in the Hereafter.

Western military attacks on Islamic countries are considered as direct combat against Allah and his messenger.

The following are a few verses on the negative commands:

SURA 9:5: Slay the idolaters wherever ye find them, and take them (captive), and besiege them, and prepare for them each ambush.

SURA 2:39: But they who disbelieve, and deny Our revelations, such are rightful Peoples of the Fire. They will abide therein.

SURA 2:191: And slay them wherever ye find them, and drive them out of the places whence they drove you out, for persecution is worse than slaughter. And fight not with them at the Inviolable Place of Worship until they first attack you there, but if they attack you (there) then slay them. Such is the reward of disbelievers.

SURA 2:194: And one who attacketh you, attack him in like manner as he attacked you. Observe your duty to Allah, and know that Allah is with those who ward off (evil).

SURA 2:254: …The disbelievers, they are the wrong-doers.

SURA 4:89: They long that ye should disbelieve even as they disbelieve, that ye may be upon a level (with them). So choose not friends from them till they forsake their homes in the way of Allah; if they turn back (to enmity) then take them and kill them wherever ye find them, and choose no friend nor helper from among them.

SURA 4:91: If they keep not aloof from you nor offer you peace nor hold their hands, then take them and kill them wherever ye find them. Against such We have given you clear warrant.

Q#136—I have spoken to a Muslim friend, and he argues that these verses are similar to the commandments in Torah.

Answer: Let me give you an example of verses Muslims use to justify violent verses in the Qur'an.

Exodus 21:17—"And he that curses his father, or his mother, shall surely be put to death."

2 Chronicles 15:13—"That whosoever would not seek the Lord God of Israel should be put to death, whether small or great, man or woman."

There are many other verses from the Old Testament that Muslims use. However, what they fail to mention is the context of the verses. In the Qur'an, the context will prove that the violent verses were not limited to Muhammad's society and the time. The verses intend a global implication for all people of all times. However, the Biblical verses are limited to a certain time and for a certain group of people. Most of the verses were for Jews and their relationship with God. Some verses are for the Gentiles, who were inhabitants of the Promised Land. However, once the Promised Land was secure, there was no more fighting and killing. In the Qur'an, fighting and killing is commanded until the whole world submits to Islam.

Q#137—How should I deal with the Issue of Trinity?

Answer: Before you deal with the issue of Trinity, you must know what the Trinity is according to Muslims. In my experience, this is the major issue Muslims raise when It comes to attacking Christianity and defending Islam. If you try to talk to a Muslim about the Issue of salvation or sin, they will bring up the issue of Trinity Moreover, most of the time they will win, because for Christians the concept of Trinity is hard to explain. There is no example or illustration good enough to justify the complex teaching of Trinity. Therefore, my advice to you is to study and understand what the Trinity is in Christianity; you must be well equipped with Christian theological knowledge about the subject before you study the Qur'anic argument against Trinity.

Q#138—I understand, and honestly I am not sure if I could explain the Christian concept of Trinity.

Answer: Unfortunately, many Christians can't. First, let me start by giving you the Islamic understanding of Trinity. The Muslim Jesus Isa is well respected among Muslims. The Qur'an condemns Jews for not believing in Jesus as a prophet and it also condemns Christians for believing in Him as the Son of God. As we read several verses earlier, Jesus and His disciples are considered true Muslims according to the Qur'an. Furthermore, a Muslim would not be a Muslim without believing in Christ as a prophet. Muslims indeed respect Christ as much as they respect Abraham, Moses, and David. The essence of Islam—willing submission to the will of God—was revealed to Adam, who was passed it on to his children. All the revelations which followed to Noah, Ibrahim, Moses, Jesus, and finally Mohammed (Peace Be Upon Them) were conformity with that message, with some elaboration to define the revelation between man and God, man and man, man and instruction. Thus, any contradictions among revealed religions is viewed by Islam as a man-made element introduced into these religions.

The position of Jesus in the three major religions—Judaism, Christianity, and Islam—should not be an exception.

In Islam. Jesus is the son of Mary, who is the sister of Aaron, and the daughter of Imran who is father of Mary and Aaron. According to the Qur'an, they lived during Pharaoh's time. Furthermore, the Holy Spirit is simply the Archangel Gabriel.

The Qur'an 3:45-47 (Al-Imran):

> When the angel said, "Mary, god gives you a good tidings of a Word from Him whose name is messiah, Jesus, son of Mary—high honored shall he be in this world and the next, near stationed to God. He shall speak to men in the cradle, and of age, and righteous he shall be, 'lord.'" Said Mary, "How shall I have a son, seeing no mortal has touched me?" "Even so," he said, "God creates what He will. When he decrees a thing He but says to it, 'Be,' and it is."

In the Qur'an, chapter three, "Al-Imran," is the story of Jesus and titled with the name of the Qur'anic character who is the father of Mary and Aaron who were the brother and sister of the Biblical Moses. Another Qur'anic chapter

(Surah) entitled "Maryam" (Mary), is dedicated to the story of Jesus and named after the Qur'anic mother of Jesus, Maryam the sister of the biblical Aaron and Moses. The Qur'an chapter 19 *Maryam* gives a detailed summary of who Maryam was and what Jews were accusing her of regarding the virgin birth. There is no objection regarding the virgin birth of Jesus Christ.

The Qur'an 19:29-33 (Maryam) says:

> Then she brought the child to her folk, carrying him, and they said, "Mary, you have surely committed a monstrous thing. Sister of Aaron, your father was not a wicked man, nor your mother a woman unchaste." Mary pointed to the child; but they said, 'How shall we speak to one who is still in the cradle, a little child. And he said, 'Lo, I am God's servant, God has given me the Book and made me a Prophet. Blessed He has made me, wherever/may be; and he has enjoined me to prayer, and to give the alms so long as I live, and likewise to cherish my mother; He has not made me arrogant and wicked. Peace be upon me, the day I was born, and the day I die, and the day I am raised up a live.

The story continues and points to the issue of Trinity. In the same chapter v. 34-35 says, "That is Jesus, son of Mary, in word of truth, concerning which they are doubting. It is not for God to take a son unto Him. Glory be to Him, He only says to it, 'Be, and it is. (Maryam 19:34-35)

Therefore Mohammad was given a mandate to call Christians to worship God alone, namely Allah, not the son of Maryam, Isa.: "Surely God is my God, and your God, so surely serve him. This is the straight path." (Maryam 19:36)

Q#139—So the Trinity is not mentioned directly in the Qur'an, correct?

Answer: Unlike the Bible, the Qur'an uses the word Trinity to condemn the Trinity. The Qur'an 4:171-173 Surah An-Nisaa (The Women)—O people of the Book! commit no excesses in your religion: nor say of Allah aught but truth. Christ (Maseeh) Jesus the son of Mary was (no more than) an Apostle of Allah and His Word which He bestowed on Mary and a Spirit proceeding from Him: so believe in Allah and His Apostles. Say not **"Trinity:"** desist: it will be better for you: for Allah is One Allah: glory be to him: (for Exalted is

He) above having a son. To Him belong all things in the heavens and on earth. And enough is Allah as a Disposer of affairs.

Christ (Maseeh) disdaineth not to serve and worship Allah nor do the angels those nearest (to Allah): those who disdain His worship and are arrogant He will gather them all together unto himself to (answer). But to those who believe and do deeds of righteousness He will give their (due) rewards and more out of His bounty: but those who are disdainful and arrogant He will punish with a grievous penalty; nor will they find besides Allah any to protect or help them.

Q#140—Are there any other chapters in the Qur'an other than Chapter "Al-Imran," and "Maryam" and also the above-mentioned chapter "An-Nisaa," which mention these things?

Answer: The Qur'an is filled with the story of Jesus—in every other chapter you can find reference to Jesus in terms of his virgin birth and the issue of Trinity. Let me try to provide a few in order that you can see some of the chapters. There are many references throughout the Qur'anic chapters:

Qur'an 2:135-141—Surah Al-Baqarah (The Heifer)

They say: "Become Jews or Christians if ye would be guided (to salvation)." Say thou: "Nay! (I would rather) the religion of Abraham the true and he joined not gods with Allah."

Say ye: "We believe in Allah and the revelation given to us and to Abraham Isma'il Isaac Jacob and the Tribes and that given to Moses and Jesus and that given to (all) Prophets from their Lord we make no difference between one and another of them and we bow to Allah (in Islam)." So if they believe as ye believe they are indeed on the right path; but if they turn back it is they who are in schism; but Allah will suffice thee as against them and He is the All-Hearing the All-Knowing. (Our religion is) the baptism of Allah; and who can baptize better than Allah? and it is He whom we worship. Say: Will ye dispute with us about Allah seeing that He is our Lord and your Lord; that we are responsible for our doings and ye for yours; and that we are sincere (in our faith) in Him? Or do ye say that Abraham Isma'il Isaac Jacob and the Tribes were Jews or Christians? Say: Do ye know better than Allah? Ah! who is more unjust than those who conceal the testimony they have from Allah? But Allah is not unmindful of what ye do!

That was a people that hath passed away. They shall reap the fruit of what they did and ye of what ye do! Of their merits there is no question in your case.

Qur'an 3:45-51—Surah Ale-'Imran (The Family of 'Imran)

Behold! the angels said, "O Mary! Allah giveth thee glad tidings of a Word from Him: his name will be Christ (Maseeh) Jesus the son of Mary held in honor in this world and the Hereafter and of (the company of) those nearest to Allah. "He shall speak to the people in childhood and in maturity and he shall be (of the company) of the righteous."

She said: "O my Lord! how shall I have a son when no man hath touched me?" He said: "Even so: Allah createth what He willeth; when He hath decreed a plan He but saith to it 'Be' and it is! "And Allah will teach him the Book and Wisdom the Law and the Gospel. "And (appoint him) an Apostle to the Children of Israel (with this message): I have come to you with a sign from your Lord in that I make for you out of clay as it were the figure of a bird and breathe into it and it becomes a bird by Allah's leave; and I heal those born blind and the lepers and I quicken the dead by Allah's leave; and I declare to you what ye eat and what ye store in your houses. Surely therein is a Sign for you if ye did believe.

"(I have come to you) to attest the Law which was before me and to make lawful to you part of what was (before) forbidden to you; I have come to you with a Sign from your Lord. So fear Allah and obey me.

"It is Allah who is my Lord and your Lord; then worship Him. This is a way that is straight."

The Qur'an 4:155-159—Surah An-Nisaa (The Women)

(They have incurred divine displeasure): in that they broke their Covenant: that they rejected the Signs of Allah; that they slew the Messengers in defiance of right; that they said "Our hearts are the wrappings (which preserve Allah's Word; we need no more);" nay Allah hath set the seal on their hearts for their blasphemy and little is it they believe. That they rejected faith: that they uttered against Mary a grave false charge. That they said (in boast) "We killed Christ (Maseeh) Jesus the son of Mary the Apostle of Allah;" but they killed him not nor crucified him but so it was made to appear to them and those who differ therein are full of doubts with no (certain) knowledge but only conjecture to follow for of a surety they killed him not.

Nay Allah raised him up unto Himself; and Allah is Exalted in Power Wise.

And there is none of the People of the Book but must believe in him before his death; and on the Day of Judgment He will be a witness against them.

Qur'an 5:112-115—Surah Al-Ma'idah (The Table Spread)

Behold! the disciples said: "O Jesus the son of Mary! can thy Lord send down to us a table set (with viands) from heaven?" Said Jesus: "Fear Allah if ye have faith." They said: "We only wish to eat thereof and satisfy our hearts and to know that thou hast indeed told us the truth; and that we ourselves may be witnesses to the miracle. Said Jesus the son of Mary: "O Allah our Lord! send us from heaven a table set (with viands) that there may be for us for the first and the last of us a solemn festival and a sign from Thee; and provide for our sustenance for Thou art the best Sustainer (of our needs).

Allah said: "I will send it down unto you: but if any of you after that resisteth faith I will punish him with a penalty such as I have not inflicted on anyone among all the peoples.

Qur'an 6:83-89—Surah An-An'am (The Cattle)

That was the reasoning about Us which We gave to Abraham (to use) against his people: We raise whom We will degree after degree: for thy Lord is full of wisdom and knowledge.

We gave him Isaac and Jacob: all (three) We guided: and before him We guided Noah and before him We guided Noah and among his progeny David Solomon Job Joseph Moses and Aaron: thus do We reward those who do good:

And Zakariya and John and Jesus and Elias: all in the ranks of the righteous: And Ismail and Elisha and Jonas and Lot: and to all We gave favor above the nations:

(To them) and to their fathers and progeny and brethren: We chose them. And We guided them to a straight way.

This is the guidance of Allah: He giveth that guidance to whom He pleaseth of His worshippers. If they were to join other gods with Him all that they did would be vain for them. These were the men to whom We gave the Book and authority and prophethood: if these (their descendants) reject them behold! We shall entrust their charge to a new People who reject them not.

Qur'an 9:30-35—Surah At-Tauba (Repentance)

The Jews call Uzair a son of Allah and the Christians call Christ the son of Allah. That is a saying from their mouths; (in this) they but imitate what the unbelievers of old used to say. Allah's curse be on them: how they are deluded away from the truth!

They take their priests and their anchorites to be their lords in derogation of Allah and (they take as their Lord) Christ the son of Mary; Yet they were commanded to worship but one Allah: there is no god but He. Praise and glory to him: (far is He) from having the parents they associate (with him).

Fain would they extinguish Allah's light with their mouths but Allah will not allow but that His light should be perfected even though the unbelievers may detest (it).

It is He who hath sent His apostle with guidance and religion of truth to proclaim it over all religions even though the pagans may detest (it).

O ye who believe! there are indeed many among the priests and anchorites who in falsehood devour the substance of men and hinder (them) from the way of Allah. And there are those who bury gold and silver and spend it not in the way of Allah: announce unto them a most grievous penalty.

On the day when heat will be produced out of that (wealth) in the fire of hell and with it will be branded their foreheads their flanks and their backs "this is the (treasure) which ye buried for yourselves: taste ye then the (treasures) ye buried!"

Qur'an 43:57-67—Surah Az-Zukhruf (Gold Adornments)

When (Jesus) the son of Mary is held up as an example behold thy people raise a clamor thereat (in ridicule)! And they say "Are Our gods best or He?" This they set forth to thee only by way of disputation: yea they are a contentious people.

He was no more than a servant: We granted Our favor to him and We made him an example to the Children of Israel.

And if it were Our Will We could make angels from amongst you succeeding each other on the earth.

And (Jesus) shall be a Sign (for the coming of) the Hour (of Judgment): therefore have no doubt about the (Hour) but follow ye Me: this is a Straight Way. Let not the Evil One hinder you: for he is to you an enemy avowed.

When Jesus came with Clear Signs he said: "Now have I come to you with Wisdom and in order to make clear to you some of the (points) on which ye dispute: therefore fear Allah and obey me."For Allah; He is my Lord and your Lord: so worship ye Him: this is a Straight Way." But sects from among themselves fell into disagreement: then woe to the wrongdoers from the Penalty of a Grievous Day!

Do they only wait for the Hour that it should come on them all of a sudden while they perceive not? Friends on that Day will be foes one to another except the Righteous.

Qur'an 61:14—Surah As-Saff (The Ranks)

O ye who believe! be ye helpers of Allah: as said Jesus the son of Mary to the Disciples "Who will be my helpers to (the work of) Allah?" Said the Disciples "We are Allah's helpers!" Then a portion of the Children of Israel believed and a portion disbelieved: but We gave power to those who believed against their enemies and they became the ones that prevailed.

Qur'an 66:11-12—Surah At-Tahrim (Banning)

And Allah sets forth as an example to those who believe the wife of Pharaoh: Behold she said: "O my Lord! build for me in nearness to Thee a mansion in the Garden and save me from Pharaoh and his doings and save me from those that do wrong;"

And Mary the daughter of 'Imran who guarded her chastity; and We breathed into her (body) of Our spirit; and she testified to the truth of the words of her Lord and of His Revelations and was one of the devout (Servants).

The above-mentioned verses are a few verses from the Qur'an that talk about Jesus but there are many more.

Q#141—Correct me If I am wrong, Isn't it true that the whole purpose of Jesus in the Qur'an is to show that Jesus was a mere man, and a prophet? Furthermore, that He denied that He was more than a prophet?

Answer: I would say that is a very fair statement. I would further state that the Jesus in the Qur'an actually invalidates Christianity. No crucifixion means no death and burial of Jesus Christ. If He did not die, then He accomplished nothing; there is no resurrection and no hope for Christians and for the world. The Jesus in the Qur'an seems so similar to Jesus in the Bible but yet because of a few things He is nothing like Jesus in the Bible. "If Christ hasn't been raised from the dead then your faith is useless and you are still guilty of your sins. Then those who have died in Christ are lost. If we only have hope in Christ for this life then we are to be pitied above all men" (1 Corinthians 15:17-19). How can He be risen If He never died?

But thanks to our Father in Heaven that Jesus in the Bible did die for the sins of men that we may have eternal life. Romans 5:6-8 says, " For while we were still weak, at the right time Christ died for the ungodly. For one will scarcely die for a righteous person—though perhaps for a good person one would dare even to die—but God shows his love for us in that while we were still sinners, Christ died for us."

Q#142—So how about a man who does not have a father, don't you think God could be considered his father?

Answer: First of all, that is very weak description of our Lord and Savior as the Son of God. Christians believe that Jesus was equally God, not a subordinate of God, but God. Therefore, although it makes sense that Jesus did not have a father, so God was His father, it will not fully justify the relation of Jesus and His Father in Heaven. Jesus claimed that He and His Father are one. When you are trying to explain to a Muslim, refer to the Qur'an:

> "And they say, The All-merciful has taken unto Himself a son. You have indeed advanced something hideous. As if the skies are about to burst, the earth to split asunder and its mountain to fall down in the utter ruin for that they have attributed to the All-merciful a son; and behaves not the All-merciful to take a son. None there in the heavens and earth but comes to the All-merciful as a servant" (Maryam 19:88-93)

The Qur'an recognizes the fact that Jesus had no human father, but they reject the idea that this makes him the son of God, or God himself. According to this criterion of "no human father," Adam would have been more entitled to be the son of God, because he had neither a father nor a mother, so the Quran actually addresses that in following words "Truly the likeness of Jesus, in God's sight is as Adam's likeness; He created him of dust, then He said upon him, 'Be' and he was." (Al-Imran 3:59)

Furthermore, since the Holy Spirit in Islam refers to the Archangel Gabriel they also reject the Christian belief in God the Father, God the Son, and God the Holy Spirit.

In the Qur'an chapter 4 *Surrah* entitled "An-Nisaa" (The Women) condemns the core belief of Christianity in the following words:

> People of the Book, do not go beyond the bounds in your religion, and say nought as to God but the Truth. The messiah, Jesus, son of Mary, was only the messenger of God, and his word (Fulfillment of his word (Fulfillment of His command, through the word "Be," for the creation of Jesus) that he committed to Mary, and a spirit originating from Him (was given life by God). So believe in God and His Messengers, and say not 'Three'. Refrain, better is for you. God is only one God. Glory be to him-that He should have a son! To Him belongs all that is in the Heavens and in the Earth; God suffices for a guardian.
>
> The Messiah will not disdain to be a servant of God, neither the Angels who are close to Him. Whosoever disdains to serve Him and walks proud, He will assuredly muster them to Him, all of them.
>
> As for the believers, who do deeds of righteousness, we will pay them their rewards in full, and He will give them more of His bounty; as for them who disdain and walk proud, them He will punish with a severe punishment, and they shall not find for them, apart from God, a friend or helper." (An-Nissa 4:171-173)

Moreover, the Qur'an 5-116 (Al-Maida) rejects and condemns the divinity of Christ. Muslims also assume that Christians believe that Mary was divine or God's wife per say. See the following verse the Qur'an 5:116:

> And when God said, 'O Jesus, son of Mary, did you say unto men, "Take me and my mother as gods, apart from God"? He said, 'To you be glory! It is not mine to say what I have no right to. If I indeed said it, you would have known it, knowing what is within my heart, though I do not know your knowledge; you know the things unseen. I only said to them what you did command me: "Serve God, my God and your God."

Q#143—How can I share about the Trinity, and particularly that Jesus is the Son of God and also God Himself?

Answer: First of all, you must follow the rules and techniques I have provided in the previous chapters. You must prove that the Bible never changes and that it is the infallible word of God. If you have the Bible as your source, then there is no problem. Second, let me share something from Ron Rhodes' quick reference guide to *Islam: What You Need to Know*.

He writes:

> It is important to understand what the doctrine of the Trinity is and what it is not.
>
> 1. It is *not* worship of three gods (that is tritheism).
>
> 2. It is *not* "three gods in one god" or "three persons in one person."
>
> 3. Rather, three is one God, and within the unity of the one God there are three co-equal and co-eternal persons—the Father, Son, and Holy Spirit.
>
> 4. The doctrine of the Trinity is based on three lines of evidence: evidence that there is only one true God (Isaiah 44:6; 46:9; John 5:44; 17:3; Romans 3:29-30; 16:27; 1 Corinthians 8:4; Galatians 3:20; Ephesians 4:6; 1 Timothhy 2:5; James 2:19); evidence that there are three persons who are called God-the Father (1 Peter 1:2), Jesus (Hebrews 1:8), and the Holy Spirit (Acts 5:3-4); and evidence of three-in-oneness within the Godhead (Matthew 28:19; 2 Corinthians 13:14).
>
> 5. Moreover, each of the three persons on different occasions is seen to prosess the attributes of deity. For example, all three are said to be *omnipresent* (everywhere-present): the Father (Jeremiah 23:23-24), the Son (Matthew 28:18-20). and the Holy Spirit (Psalm 139:7). All three are *omniscient* (all-knowing): the Father (Romans 11:33), the Son (John 16:30), and the Holy Spirit (1 Corinthians 2:10). All three are *omnipotent* (all powerful): the Father (Jeremiah 32:17), the Son (Matthew 28:18), and the Holy Spirit (Romans 15:19). Furthermore, *holiness* is ascribed to

each person: the Father (Revelation 15:4), the Son (Acts 3:14), and the Holy Spirit (John 16:7-14). And each of the three is individually described as the *truth*: the Father (John 7:28), the Son (Revelation 3:7), and the Holy Spirit (1 John 5:7).

6. Jesus is God's Son not in the sense that the Father procreated Jesus, but rather in the sense that Jesus Himself is *eternally God by nature*, just like the Father is. Ancient Semitics used the phrase "Son of..." to indicate *likeness or sameness of nature and equallity of being*. That is why when Jesus claimed to be Son of God, His Jewish contemporaries understood he was making a claim to be God (John 19:7; see also 5:18).

7. Note that to fully understand God's nature-including his triune nature-would require the mind of God Himself. Finite minds cannot fully understand an infinite God.

Q#144—It is very difficult to understand for a Christian like me, how a Muslim can understand that a Man could be a God?

Answer: That is precisely why I recommend keeping your focus on God rather than man. You see for Muslims, it is impossible to understand that the man Jesus could be a god, but there is no doubt that God Almighty, the all powerful, can do whatever He wills. Moreover, this includes His taking the form of a man and coming into this world.

Q#145—Do you think they will even allow me to start with this point since you mention it is a blasphemous to say that Jesus was God?

Answer: From a Muslim point of view, it is blasphemy to state that a man could be god. However, it is the power of God If He chooses to come in the form of a Man. Your focus should be to develop a friendship first. Remember, do not create unnecessary barriers. Be humble and emphasize the personal relationship with God. Furthermore, whatever you do, always commit to prayer before you engage in witnessing.

Personal Notes and Comments:

CHAPTER 12

Islamic Way of Life: Biblical Prophecies about Muhammad

In this final chapter, you will be able to recognize a clear difference between Islam and Christianity. Many Christians believe that Christianity is not a religion but a way of life. However, Muslims argue that Islam is also a way of life. This chapter will also provide a list of some of the verses from the Bible that Muslims believe are about their prophet Muhammad. They provide a very convincing argument; you must study the scriptures in its context. I will present that information with a Muslim perspective and interpretation so that you may able to understand what Muslims really believe. It is my intention that you read the Bible and commentaries to discover the true interpretation of the text mentioned by Muslims regarding the prophethood of Muhammad.

Q#146—Is it true that Islam is a way of life? Can you provide some verses to prove that Islam is a way of life?

Answer: Yes, it is! Let us examine the justice system. What does this world say? If one has committed a crime he or she must be punished. If someone hits you, you should strike back. What are the teachings of Christianity and the Qur'an? The Qur'anic and Biblical references are as follows:

Qur'an 2:194, "And one who attacketh you, attack him in like manner as he attacked you."

Matthew 5:39-42 "But if any one strikes you on the right cheek, turn to him the other also; and if anyone would sue you and take your coat, let him have your cloak as well; and if any one forces you to go one mile, go with him two miles. Give to him who begs from you, and do not refuse him who would borrow from you."

Q#147—I am sorry, I do not understand how "ISLAM" is the way of life and not "CHRISTIANITY"? One teaching cannot sum up the whole religion.

Answer: Actually, in Christianity it does. Christ summed up all of Christianity in two commandments: *Love your God and love your neighbor.* Obviously I am not preaching Islam but it is true that Islam is a way of *Worldly life.* In this life you pray five times a day, read the *Qur'an,* offer *Hajj,* and pay *Zokat* to earn forgiveness, all in one hope that one day you may receive your reward of paradise from Allah. Man's attempt to make God happy and change God's mind is a worldly way of life. There was a time when I used to use the famous phrase, "Christianity is not a religion. It is a way of life" until the day I heard a Muslim saying that about Islam, counting all the aspects of Islam: society, civilization, culture, politics, government, military, education, economics, family unit and on and on. All that Islam is concerned about belongs to this world and might be good for worldly life, whereas in Christianity it is different.

I believe that Islam can become a way of life, but it can never be "the way to life." Jesus Christ is the only one who said "I am the way and the truth and the life. No one comes to the Father except through me" (John 14:6). Thus, Jesus is our connection to heaven, not our way of worldly life.

Q#149—So what term should I use to describe such incredible phenomena?

Answer: It is simple. Jesus said, "I am the resurrection. **I am life**. If a man believes in me, even though he dies.... **I am life**," and also He said, "The thief cometh not, but for to steal, and to kill, and to destroy: **I am** come that they might have **life**, and that they might have it more abundantly." Thus all God wants us to do is to have a relationship with Him. Therefore, you could say, "Christianity is not about religion it is about a relationship." Jesus did not come to start a new religion or to promote the old religion of Judaism; He came to show us that life with God is not about religion (do and don't part of our hard work to please God) but it is about our relationship with God.

Q#150—Can I use the above answer to witness to a Muslim?

Answer: Yes, but I would suggest something like this:

I understand you believe that Islam is the way of life, because Islam offers everything that a person needs to live on this earth. For example, it has a proper educational, social, economical, military, political, governmental, and religious system, which is really good to have for this earthly life. I think that Islam offers some of the best ways that a person can live on this earth. But what about the heavenly life? What is the way to heaven? As far as we know from the Qur'anic teachings and Hadiths, even the prophet Muhammad himself never claimed to be life, a way of life, or a way to life. As a matter of fact, he asked for forgiveness from God in his life. Do you know that the Qur'an teaches about a man who in His earthly life never sinned or asked for forgiveness? Furthermore, He actually forgave others' sins. He was killed for that very reason because the only person who can forgive is God.

From here, you could start witnessing to a Muslim. Ask whether he or she would like to know about Him who is the only way of life: eternal life, and the way to heaven. Even the Qur'an says He is coming back (and add) *because He was resurrected from the dead.*

Q#151—What do Muslims say about that claim?

Answer: Muslims argue that Christianity does not offer those things that can help a man to live in this world. Some of the things are the following, where the unworldly Christian alternative is in parentheses:

1. Fight and war (all about love your enemy).

2. Eye for eye and tooth for tooth rule (all about turning to other cheek).

3. No proper financial system (everything about heaven and storing treasure in heaven).

4. No proper system to raise family and develop a society (all about pleasing God and thinking about God).

5. No worries about the work, how to make money (earn), do business (economics), run a family (all about the family of God and finding treasure in heaven).

6. No political guidance, how to interact with other government (all about what belongs to Caesar give to Caesar, and what belongs to God give to God).

There are many points that are raised by Muslims in support of Islam as the way of life here in this world.

Q#152—What if the person says, "No I do not want to know about Jesus"?

Answer: First of all, you will never mention the name Jesus or Isa before receiving permission from the person you are trying to reach; you could tell about **the man in the Qur'an.** Most likely, Muslims will never say something concerning Qur'an, but in case a person refused to continue conversation, acknowledge that you understand he does not have time or does not have interest to know about Him. But one day, as the Qur'an says, He will come back; and **When he comes back he will come as a judge,** so If you want to read about him later (hand him/her the pocket Gospel) here is his story.

Q#153—I know in the beginning you have already given a number of techniques to witness to others, particularly Muslims. Could you put the perspective of contrasting "way of life" and "the way TO life" through an illustration?

Answer: I would love to give you a simple illustration. I will introduce you to another way to witness to others. Whether the person is Atheist, Hindu, Buddhist, Muslim or something else, as in the **10 Steps Tale** approach, you will introduce yourself to a non-Christian and ask for permission to share the story of a man who fell in a hole. After formal permission, you should begin like this:

A man fell in a hole. He fell in a hole and he could not get out. A traveler passed by, he told the man to meditate to purify his mind. He said, when he will reach "Nirvana" he will receive a perfect state of mind that is free from craving, anger, and other afflicting states;

thus there would be no more suffering. The man in the hole did what he was told but he remained in the hole.

Another man appeared. He explained that the hole did not exist and neither did the man. He claimed that it was all an illusion, but the man who did not exist was still stuck in the hole.

Another visitor arrived and he instructed the man to perform good deeds to improve his "Karma," though he claimed that he would still die in the hole under the comfort that he may be incarnated into something magnificent and new.

Another man looked down from above. He told the man to pray five times a day facing the East and follow five important tenets. He claimed that if he was faithful, one day perhaps the Divine would set him free. The man prayed the best he could but he was losing strength; and in the hole he remained.

Another man then appeared, but there was something different about HIM; He called down into the hole and asked him if he wanted to be freed. This man then lowered Himself into the pit. He took hold of the man and dragged him into the light. The man in the hole who could not get himself out was saved.

Once you have finished the story ask in a very exciting voice, "**Do you want to know more about the last man?**"

(The story was adopted from www.Jesus.net for training purposes.)

Q#154—What if he/she says, "Yes"?

Answer: I would strongly recommend keeping the Gospel of John or Luke very handy. In this way, whether the person wants to know more about Him or not, just offer a free gift of the Gospel. You could say something like this: "If you would like to learn about the last man, what happened to Him, where He came from and where He went after saving the man in the hole," extend your hand with Gospel toward the person and continue "Please receive this free gift, it has all the answers you need." On the back of each pocket size Gospel you are given an empty spot. You could print or label your church contact information for follow up questions.

Q#155—Do you have any suggestions for memorizing the Qur'an or Biblical verses?

Answer: I am glad you asked! If you are interested in reaching out to a Muslim neighbor, here are a few verses to memorize (If you do not have a Qur'an you could use an online Qur'an it has a number of translations and commentaries http://www.quran.com):

1. The Qur'an 35:31"That which we have revealed to thee [Muhammad] of the book is the Truth-confirming what was revealed before it: For Allah is assuredly with respect to His servants well acquainted and full observant." (If Qur'an confirms what came before Qur'an which was Injil (the Gospels), Torah and the prophets (the Bible) then if the Bible was changed, what Allah is saying this verse can't be correct. See the two charts in the book.)

2. The Qur'an 6:93 "And He [Allah] is the One to cause the dead to issue from the living." (Then the question is this when Qur'an says Jesus gave life to dead what does that make Jesus?)

3. The Qur'an 10:37"This Qur'an is not such as can be produced by other than Allah; on the contrary it is a confirmation of that what before it [and that is the Bible], and fulfillment."

4. The Qur'an 2:256"Let there be no compulsion in religion."

5. The Qur'an 4:158 "Nay, Allah raised him [Jesus] up unto Himself."

6. The Qur'an 4:152 "Those who believe in Allah and his messengers and make no distinctions between any of the messengers [including Jesus] we shall sure give their reward."

7. The Qur'an 29:25"our Allah [God] and your Allah [God] is one."

8. The Qur'an 3:64 "O People of the Book! come to common terms as between us and you: That we worship none but Allah; that we associate no partners with him; that we erect not, from among ourselves, Lords and patrons other than

Allah." If then they turn back, say ye: "Bear witness that we (at least) are Muslims (bowing to Allah's Will)."

9. The Qur'an 10:37

10. The Qur'an 3:42-55

11. The Qur'an 4:171

12. The Qur'an 19:16-35

13. The Qur'an 3:45

14. The Qur'an 19:19, 19:21

15. The Qur'an 43:61

16. The Qur'an 3:48, 5:48-49, 10:95, 4:163, 21:07, 2:7, 2:113, 2:87, 7:157, 32:24

17. The Qur'an 46:11-12, 46:30, 2:89, 11:90, 4:172

18. The Bible Matthew 5:18

19. The Bible Isaiah 55:01

20. The Bible Revelation 22:18-19

Q#157—Could you provide a reference to the claim that Muhammad asked for forgiveness?

Answer: Previously we have discussed it in detail but here is an authentic Hadith saying that Muhammad asked for forgiveness. It is reported by al-Bukhari: "O people, repent to your Lord, for verily I [Muhammad] seek forgiveness from Allah and repent to him more than seventy times in a day."

It is reported in Saheeh Muslim that he said: *"I seek forgiveness one hundred times in a day"* [Muslim].

Also, the Qur'an 47:19 says, "So know (O Muhammad) that *La ilaha ill-Allah* (none has the right to be worshipped but Allah), and **ask forgiveness for your sin,** and also for (the sin of) believing men and believing women. And Allah knows well your moving about, and your place of rest (in your homes)" (Al-Hilali & Khan translation).

Today, many Muslim scholars will argue that Muhammad was sinless and will try to justify the verse. But for most Muslims, it is very clear, when you show them the text.

Q#158—Would you also provide a brief list of Christian scriptures that Muslims believe are a prophecy about the coming of Muhammad?

Answer: Rather than just providing a list, let me give you what Muslims say about each verse. I also recommend that you read the verses from the Bible with their context and conduct your own Bible study before you go and minister to a Muslim. A Muslim may tell you that the Bible teaches about Muhammad. So you must be prepared. Find a good commentary, and understand how these claims actually referring to the arrival of the Messiah not of Muhammad.

Isaiah 29:12—Or if you give the scroll to someone who cannot read, and say, "Read this, please," he will answer, "I don't know how to read." Muslims believe this verse about Muhammad because he was unlettered (The Qur'an, 96:1-5).

Isaiah 21:13-17—An oracle concerning Arabia:

You caravans of Dedanites, who camp in the thickets of Arabia, bring water for the thirsty; you who live in Tema, bring food for the fugitives. They flee from the sword, from the drawn sword, from the bent bow and from the heat of battle. This is what the Lord says to me: "Within one year, as a servant bound by contract would count it, all the pomp of Kedar will come to an end. The survivors of the bowmen, the warriors of Kedar, will be few." The LORD, the God of Israel, has spoken.

Muslims believe this was about Muhammad too and they provide the following explanation for their belief:

Ishmael's sons' (Kedar and Tema) descendants settled in Arabia. Medina was called Tema in Biblical times—next year an army of 1,000 Meccans marched against the Muslims. With only 300 (poorly armed) men, the Muslims defeated the Meccans at the Battle of Badr. Also Muslims believe Isaiah 42:10-11 is a prophecy about Muhammad and Islam.

Song of Solomon 5:16 reads—His mouth is sweetness itself; he is desirable in every way. Such, O women of Jerusalem, is my lover, my friend. Muslims take the middle part and claim that was a prophecy about Muhammad's prophethood. The Muslim response is as follows: "His speech is most sweet, and he is altogether desirable" ('Muhammad' means 'desirable').

Deuteronomy 18:18—I will raise up for them a prophet like you from among their brothers. And I will put my words in his mouth, and he shall speak to them all that I command him.

Again Muslims believe this was about Muhammad and because of the following reasons it cannot be about Jesus the Messiah:

Both Moses and Muhammad (peace be upon them both) had usual births, married and had children, and were forced to migrate [Moses to Median and Muhammad (p) to Medina]; they marched to battles against their enemies and won physical and moral victories in their lifetime; they were virtually kings, gave laws and scriptures, first rejected by their people and then accepted in the end; they were human beings with no divinity attributed to them by their followers, died a natural death and were buried in this earth. *Similarities between Moses and Jesus (peace be upon them both) are: threat to life in early infancy, both were Jewish lettered Prophets, and both performed miracles.*

John 14:15-16; 16:7-11—This is the famous passage where Jesus promised that He will not leave us as orphans, and will ask His Father to send us another Counselor (Comforter). Muslims argue: the Holy Ghost was already present with Jesus when he was alive, and the Comforter's arrival was conditioned upon Jesus' departure.

However, again Muslims do not look at the full text: "If you love me, you will obey what I command. And I will ask the Father, and he will give you another Counselor to be with you forever— the Spirit of truth. The world cannot accept him, because it neither sees him nor knows him. But you know him, for he lives with you and will be in you. I will not leave you as orphans; I will come to you. Before long, the world will not see me anymore, but you will see me. Because I live, you also will live. On that day you will realize that I am in my Father, and you are in me, and I am in you. Whoever has my commands and obeys them, he is the one who loves me. He who loves me will be loved by my Father, and I too will love him and show myself to him."

John 16:12-14—Muslims claim that Jesus' message was incomplete; therefore another Prophet was needed to guide mankind into all truth. The passage says: "I have much more to say to you, more than you can now bear. But when he, the Spirit of truth, comes, he will guide you into all truth. He will not speak on his own; he will speak only what he hears, and he will tell you what is yet to come. **He will bring glory to me by taking from what is mine and making it known to you.**

Q#159—What is the Gospel of Barnabas?

Answer: The *Gospel of Barnabas* is a substantial book depicting the life of Jesus; and claiming to be by Jesus' disciple Barnabas, who in this work is one of the twelve apostles. Muslims associate the writer of such a document to the person who is mentioned in **Acts 14:14; 11:24,** "But when the apostles Barnabas and Paul heard of it, they tore their garments and rushed out into the crowd…" Two manuscripts are known to have existed, both dated to the late 16th century and written respectively in Italian and in Spanish; although the Spanish manuscript is now lost, its text surviving only in a partial 18th-century transcript. *Barnabas* is about the same length as the four Canonical gospels put together (the Italian manuscript has 222 chapters); with the bulk being devoted to an account of Jesus' ministry, much of it harmonized from accounts also found in the canonical gospels. In some key respects, it conforms to the *Islamic interpretation of Christian origins* and contradicts the New Testament *teachings of Christianity.* This Gospel is considered by the majority of academics, including Christians and some Muslims (such as Abbas el-Akkad) to be late and pseudepigraphical; however, some academics suggest that it may contain some remnants of an earlier apocryphal work edited to conform to Islam, perhaps Gnostic or Ebionite or Diatessaronic. Some Muslims consider the surviving versions as transmitting a suppressed apostolic original. Some Islamic organizations cite it in support of the Islamic view of Jesus. There are two other documents associated to Barnabas: *Epistle of Barnabas* and *Acts of Barnabas. Epistle of Barnabas* was written between AD 70 and AD 135, but *Acts of Barnabas* and *Gospel of Barnabas* were forged during medieval times. Shamoun in his article on http://www.answeringislam.org/Shamoun/aboutbible.htm wrote:

> We must also point out that the idea of the Bible being corrupted was first promoted by Ibn Khazem (d. 1064 A.D.)

The following is a Muslim response concerning the Gospel of Barnabus:

The Gospel of Barnabus (written in 16th century) didn't get a place in the New Testament. Chapters 96 and 97 of his gospel read: "In the presence of a great multitude, the priest asked Prophet Jesus: 'Art thou the Messiah of God whom we expect?' Prophet Jesus answered: 'It is true that God hath so promised, but indeed I am not he, for he is made before me and shall come after me.' … Then said the priest: 'How shall the Messiah be called, and what sign shall reveal his coming?' Prophet Jesus answered: 'The name of the Messiah is admirable, for God Himself gave him the name when He created his soul, and placed it in celestial splendour… Muhammad is his blessed name.'"

Q#160—How can I get a copy of the Gospel of Barnabas?

Answer: You can find the full text of the pseudo gospel "The Gospel of Barnabas" online for free: http://www.answering-christianity.com/barnabas.htm).

Personal Notes and Comments:

_____

_____

_____

_____

_____

_____

_____

_____

_____

_____

_____

_____

_____

_____

_____

_____

_____

_____

_____

KEY TERMINOLOGY

9/11: September 11, 2001 when Muslim extremists flew two airplanes into the World Trade Center twin towers and killed about 3,000 people. This tragic incident began a new era of war—the war on terror.

Al-Hijra: It means to immigrate. It is an Islamic counterpart of to "A.D." The Islamic calendar starts with the date of Muhammad's immigration (Hijra) from Mecca to Medina. It is the emigration of Muhammad and his followers to the city of Medina in 622 CE, which marks the first year of the Islamic calendar, 1 AH (anno Hegirae). The Islamic calendar is a lunar calendar, and months begin when the first crescent of a new moon is sighted. The following are the names of Islamic months:

1. Muḥarram means "forbidden" in Arabic, so called because it was unlawful to fight during this month. Muharram is the second most sacred Muslim month, and includes the Day of Ashura.

2. Ṣafar means "void" in Arabic, supposedly named because pagan Arabs looted during this month and left the houses empty.

3. Rabīʿ I (Rabīʿ al-Awwal) means "the first Spring" in Arabic.

4. Rabīʿ II (Rabīʿ ath-Thānī or Rabīʿ al-Ākhir) means "the second (or last) Spring" in Arabic.

5. Jumādā I (Jumādā al-Ūlā) means "the first month of parched land" in Arabic.

6. Jumādā II (Jumādā ath-Thāniya or Jumādā al-Ākhira) means "the second (or last) month of parched land" in Arabic.

7. Rajab means "respect" or "honor" in Arabic. Rajab is another of the sacred months in which fighting was traditionally forbidden.

8. Shaʿbān means "scattered" in Arabic, marking the time of year when Arab tribes disperse to find water.

9. Ramaḍān means "scorched" in Arabic. Ramadan is the most venerated month of the Hijri calendar, during which Muslims fast between sunrise and sunset.

10. Shawwāl means "raised" in Arabic, as she-camels begin to raise their tails during this time of year, after giving birth.

11. Dhū al-Qaʿda means "the one of truce" in Arabic. Dhu al-Qaʿda was another month during which war was banned.

12. Dhū al-Ḥijja means "the one of pilgrimage" in Arabic, referring to the annual Muslim pilgrimage to Mecca, the Hajj.

Islam: (pronounced *al-ʾislām*) Islam is the official name of the religion followed by Muslims.

Imam: (pronounced Aʾimmah) It is an Islamic leadership position equivalent to religious leaders in other faiths. An Imam leads Islamic worship service and also provides religious answers to the issues a Muslim community might face. Different sects of Islam define the position differently. The major sect of Islam, Sunni Muslims, who make up about 90% of Muslim population do not have a clergy like Christian priests (pastor, father, etc.) or Rabbis. Therefore an Imam is not a cleric. The Shiʾa sect holds the position of Imam very secret and unique. To Shiʾa Muslims the concept of Imam is a much more central religious position.

Hadith: (pronounced /ˈhædɪθ/ or pronounced /həˈdiːθ/[2]; al-ḥadīth [ħaˈdiːθ]; pl. *aḥādīth*; *lit.* "narrative") It implies the narration of a saying, act, or an approval of the prophet Muhammad, irrespective of whether the matter is authenticated or still disputed. The Hadith is a model of behavior by Muslims (Muslim Internet Dictionary).

Hijab: (pronounced *he-zjab* or *hiʤæb*) In Arabic it literally means curtain or cover. Traditionally Muslim women use head coverings and many cover their faces with the same covering. It is a sign of modesty. It is also considered a part of Muslim women dress code.

Jihad: (pronounced *ǧihād* or *jihād*) Muslim Internet Dictionary (2009): "It is an Arabic word the root of which is Jahada, which means to strive for a better way of life. The nouns are Juhd, Mujahid, Jihad, and Ijtihad. The other are: endeavor, strain, exertion, effort, diligence, fighting to defend one's life, land, and religion." It is also defined as a struggle to promote Islam. In the West, it is known as the "holy war" by Muslims. The Qur'an teaches Jihad.

Muslim: (pronounced /ˈmʊslɪm/) A monotheist religious group that believes in Allah and an Arabian prophet Muhammad. Muhammad founded this religion in the 6th century.

Madrasah: An Islamic traditional school for Muslim children to learn the Qur'an and other religious subjects.

Madrases: (pronounced *madāris*) The plural form of Madrasah. Madris can also be used as plural of Madrasah.

- Madrasah 'āmmah translates as "public school."
- Madrasah khāṣṣah translates as "private school."
- Madrasah dīniyyah translates as "religious school."
- Madrasah Islāmiyyah translates as "Islamic school."
- Madrasah jāmi'ah translates as "university."

Mosque: Place of Islamic worship. Muslims call it "Masjid."

Mujahedin: (pronounced singular *muǧāhid* and plural *muǧāhidīn*) A Muslim who fights Jihad is called a Mujahid. The plural form of Mujahid is Mujahedin.

Militants: Islamic extremist train groups of Muslims for military purposes. These groups are officially unrecognized by the government.

Maccan: The most holy city (place) for Muslims and the birthplace of the Islamic prophet Muhammad. Also, this is the place where Muslims all over the world gather for Hajj, the Muslim pilgrimage.

Medinan: The second most holy city (place) for Muslims and the death place of Islamic prophet Muhammad.

Mullah: (pronounced *mawlā*) A Muslim priest who teaches the Qur'an.

Qur'an: (pronounced /kʊraʾn <u>kor-AHN</u>/qurʾa n) Muslims consider Qur'an the most holy book revealed to Muhammad from Allah.

Shari'a: (pronounced *šarīʿah*) Islamic law is derived from the Qur'an, the Sunnah, and the hadith.

Sunna: (pronounced *ʿsunna*) Also spelled Sunnah, it is the second source of Islamic jurisprudence, the first being the Qur'an. For Muslims, both sources are indispensable; one cannot practice Islam without both of them. In Islam, the Arabic word Sunnah has come to denote the way the Islamic prophet Muhammad lived his life (Muslim Internet Dictionary, 2009).

Suras: (pronounced *sūrah*) The verses of a Qur'anic chapter.

Shaheed: (pronounced singular *šahīd* plural *šuhadāʾ*) If a Muslim dies in battle while protecting a Muslim land or faith, Shaheed is the guarantee of entrance into paradise.

Shi'a: (pronounced *Shīʿah*) The second largest denomination of Islam, after Sunni Islam. Shi'a Muslims broke from the Sunni majority in a disagreement over who should have succeeded Muhammad. Those who wanted Ali to be the successor because he was Muhammad's cousin and son-in-law became Shi'a, and those who accepted the legitimacy of the caliphs who followed Muhammad became Sunni. While the differences between Sunni and Shi'a were historically political in nature, different religious and legal traditions have since developed to further set them apart.

Sufism: (pronounced *ṣūfi*) The mystical, esoteric dimension of Islam. Sufism can refer both to an approach to the practice and experience of Islam which cuts across sectarian divides, as well as more specific sets of practices propagated by Sufi orders.

Sunni: The largest denomination of Islam. The term is derived from the word Sunnah and refers to the example and traditions of Muhammad.

Ummah: According to Islamic theology this world is divided between believers and unbelievers. Believers are those who follow Islam, and the teachings of the Qur'an and prophet Mohammad. <u>The term is used to describe both individual communities, both great and small, of faithful Muslims. It also refer to the worldwide community of Muslims</u>—in the latter sense of the term it is synonymous with Dar al-Islam, or "The House of Islam," which refers to the world Islamic community. It is the prophet Muhammad that is the founder of the *ummah.*

Wahhabism: It is an Islamic religious movement that originated in Saudi Arabia. It is a particularly strict variant of Sunni Islam established in the 18th century by a Muslim cleric, Muhammad ibn Abd-al-Wahhab. Wahhabism is characterized by its call for a return to the traditions and examples established by the first three generations of Muslims and is often regarded as a form of Salafism. Wahhabism is the dominant form of Islam practiced in Saudi Arabia and this movement has spread all over the world due to the Saudi money donated by the government and the royal families of Saudi Arabia toward missionary work in the world.

Personal Notes and Comments:

APPENDIX I

Provided by Story Runner—a Project
of Campus Crusade

Story Crafting Tips

- Read the story from at least two different Bible translations.

- Look at the verses just before and after the story to make sure you understand the story better.

- Select stories that are consistent with the theme of the story set.

- Keep the story short and simple so that it does not take more than five minutes to tell.

- Use everyday language but don't use words that are offensive or hard to understand.

- Don't memorize the story. Tell it naturally like you were there when it happened.

- You may leave out parts of the story but don't add things that are not in the Bible.

- Do not use unnecessary names in a story.

- Connect two stories with no more than one to three very short transition sentences.

- Use an accurate interpretation of a word or phrase if needed to make the story clear.

    ✦ Example: Use "enter into a relationship with God" rather than "Kingdom of God."

- Use the same words throughout all the stories.

    ✦ Example: When you use the phrase "descendants of Abraham" DO NOT change to "Jews" or "Israelites" or "descendants of David" later in the story set.

- people can't remember your story then make it simpler and shorter so they can!

Words that can cause problems:

DO NOT use any words or phrases that your people will not understand. Here are examples of difficult words and phrases to explain, and some (different words or phrases) to use.

Angel (spirit God created and is faithful to him), Anoint (Pour Oil), Baptize/Baptism (dip under water and bring back up), Belief/Believe/Trust/Faith, Believers (Followers), Bless, Blessed, Blessing, Church (Group of Believers that meet together in one place), Christ (Promised Savior), Covenant (an agreement sealed with blood), Curse, Disciples (12 closest followers), Eternal Life (life that never ends), Demon (spirit God created and rebelled against him), Forgive, Forgiveness, Gentiles (people who are not descendants of Abraham), Heaven (God's dwelling place), Holy Spirit (God's Spirit), Jerusalem (city where the descendants of Abraham worshiped), Kingdom of God (enter a relationship with God), Master Messiah (Promised Savior), Most High God (the only God), Paradise (the place where God's people wait for him), Pharisees (religious leaders, educated men) Prayer, Prophet (spokesman or messenger), Righteousness (right relationship with God or trusting God), Redeem (buy back, win back, free from harm, ransom payment, release of debt, change for better, repair, restore, offset bad for good, make worthwhile, make worthwhile), Repent (turn away from disobeying God to follow the Promised Savior), Sadducees (religious leaders/educated men), Saved (escaped God's judgment which was due to disobedience), Sin (disobedience), Spirit, Synagogue (place where the descendants of Abraham worshiped), Temple (place where the descendants of Abraham worshiped), Tomb, Wisdom, Worship

Group Leader Tips

Group leaders must respond to many situations before, during, and after a Bible storytelling session. Here are some questions each group leader should be able answer before starting a Bible storytelling group.

1. How do you respond to people (Christians and non-Christians) who dominate the discussion or corrections of the story?

2. How do you respond to questions about the story?

3. What are the characteristics of a good group leader?

4. How do you deal with someone in the group that opens a Bible or takes notes during a story?

5. How do you get everyone to participate in the group discussion?

No group leader can prevent every problem that might happen but here are some suggestions that could help you prevent many problems:

1. Consider separate groups for Christians, non-Christians, women, men, husbands and wives.

2. When new group members are present, explain the rules before beginning for learning and discussing the Bible story. Explain that a Bible story is best learned and discussed by listening to the story without the distraction of reading a Bible or taking notes. For that reason Bibles will be closed and notes will not be taken during the session.

3. When someone asks you questions about the meaning of a story respond by asking them,

   ● "What does the story say about that?"

   ● "What do the other stories say about that?"

- "What does the rest of the group think about that?"

- "There are more stories later that will help us understand that better."

Do not attempt to answer questions about the meaning of a story. Trust God's Word and His Holy Spirit to guide the group even if the group is giving answers that you don't like. Anything you can talk them into believing, someone else can talk them out of believing. The Holy Spirit will give the right answer at the right time so they can receive it with great joy! If someone insists on getting an answer to a question tell them that you will discuss it with them privately at a later time. However, even when you discuss it with them later don't attempt to answer questions about the meaning of the story.

4. People will ask why you left out a part of the story. They will comment about the way you tell a story. Respond by saying you will answer their question for the whole group <u>after</u> the session has ended.

Personal Notes and Comments:

APPENDIX II

10 Step Tale Demo for Class Practice

H ello, my name is Alex and I am a storyteller. I tell stories for free.

You know how Allah created this world. God said and it happened (It is important to start with word "Allah" and then immediately use God. Also because Muslims believe Allah created everything by saying "Kun Faya Koon," which literally means "Be and it is."

And he wanted to have a personal relationship with his creation so He took dirt and formed a man…

(*act it out by pretending you are taking dirt from the ground. There are number of reasons why you have to say and do things in a particular way. First, when you say God took dirt from the ground and formed a man you are making a direct connection between the Christian story of the creation of Adam and the Muslim story. Second, by acting out, you are keeping him actively interested and attracted. Third, you are leaving a hint of God's way of creating the first man using dirt, because later when you share the story of the blind man, you will mention how Jesus took the dirt from the ground and spit to moisten it and then rub it on the blind man's eyes to give him sight/"new eyes." This will challenge a Muslim to connect the dots to recognize Jesus as the Messiah*).

God breathed life into Adam, and when He could not find a suitable partner for Adam God took one of Adam's ribs and built a woman.

And they had children. In time the population of the world increased and the people indulged in sinful behavior. They were wicked in the sight of God, thus God, thus God decided to wipe out the entire world. He made a promise to one man Noah that He would populate the earth again through him. So God commanded Noah to build an ark and take his family and a pair of each animal into the ark. There were 40 days and 40 nights of rain and everyone died except those who were in the ark. God did fulfill His promise and again the earth was populated and again they became wicked.

This time, rather than destroying them, God chose a man by the name of Abraham. God promised him that he would be the father of many nations and that God would give him a son. Ironically, Abraham was very old and could not have children. But God fulfilled His promise and gave him a son, and through his son God brought forth a mighty warrior and a king named David (Dawood in Arabic). David united the whole nation of Israel and God made another promise through the Jewish prophet Isaiah that He would give them the Messiah.

Now the Jews were waiting for the promised Messiah when one day, one young woman became pregnant by the power of the Holy Spirit. She was a virgin, and had never had any relationship with a man. Her name was Mary (Mariyam in Arabic). She gave birth to Isa-Al-Mesih (Jesus Christ). Jesus grew in knowledge and spirit. He performed many miracles. He healed the sick, gave life to the dead people (*mention that only God can do this*), cast out demons (Jinns) and provided food for thousands. But one day, while Jesus was walking in the street with many people around Him, a man shouted out (*be ready to act it out and shout as load as you can*), "Jesus, son of David! Jesus, Son of David!" The people asked the man to be quiet, but Jesus said, "Bring him to me." This man was blind. When Jesus looked at him, He asked, "What can I do for you?" (*now pretend the person is sitting on the ground looking up, you need to find someone who is the same gender and hold his/her head in your hand and lift his/her face, looking in their eyes saying, "What can I do for you?"*). The beggar could have asked for food, money, even a palace but he said, "I want to see." Jesus took dirt from the ground (*act it out exactly the way you acted it out for the creation of the man*) spit on it and rubbed it on the man's eye, and the blind man from birth was able to see for the first time in his life!

The religious leaders, just like today, did not like him because they wanted to be popular like him. They plotted against this innocent man. They arrested him and crucified him. When Jesus was on the cross, (*now act this whole thing out by stretching both your arms out making the sign of a cross)*, His hands and feet were nailed and blood was dripping from his hands and feet, yet He cried out, "FATHER FORGIVE THEM *(shout out)* FOR THEY DO NOT KNOW WHAT THEY ARE DOING." In addition, he gave his life. A solider pierced His side to make sure He was dead. He was buried and on the third day when two of his disciples came to perfume His dead body, they found an angel sitting by the empty tomb, and he asked them who they were looking for. The women said, "Our Lord Jesus' body." The angel reminded them that Jesus told them that He would rise from the dead on third day. The women went back and told the other disciples. They came and found Jesus' empty tomb. They became afraid and ran back, and the disciples were hiding in a room, which was locked. Lo and behold, Jesus appeared, they thought they were dreaming or maybe it was Jesus' spirit, but no, it was not! Jesus showed them the holes in his hands and feet and His pierced side. Over 500 people saw him alive. Then He went back to heaven and one day He will come back to reign on the earth.

Do you have any question or do you want to know more about this man Jesus?

Personal Notes and Comments:

_____

_____

_____

_____

_____

_____

_____

_____

_____

_____

_____

_____

_____

_____

_____

_____

_____

_____

APPENDIX III

Evidence for God's Existence
Greg Ganssle, Ph.D.

I. You Cannot Prove God's Existence

Since Immanuel Kant wrote his 'Critique of Pure Reason', it has been common for thinking people to insist that it is impossible to prove the existence of God. In fact this claim has been elevated to the level of dogma in American intellectual culture. The reason I know this is considered unquestionable dogma is the reaction I get when I call it into question. When someone says, "You cannot prove the existence of God," I want to ask, "How do you know? You just met me! How do you know what I can do?"

What do most people mean when they recite this claim? Most people mean that I cannot provide a philosophical argument for the existence of God, which will convince all thinking people. It is impossible, so the story goes, to provide an argument that will compel assent. If my argument will not convince the most ardent atheist, I have not proven God's existence. Since I cannot convince such an atheist to believe, my arguments do not count as proof. If they do not count as proof, what good are they?

I agree that I cannot provide an argument that will convince all thinking people. But what does this tell me? Does this tell me anything about God? No. This tells me more about the nature of proof than it does about whether God exists. I cannot provide an argument that will convince everyone, without a doubt, that God exists. You see, I cannot provide an argument for any interesting philosophical conclusion that will be accepted by everyone without possibility of doubt.

I cannot prove beyond the possibility of a doubt—in a way that will convince all philosophers—that the Rocky Mountains are really here. I cannot prove that the entire universe did not pop into existence five minutes ago and that all of our apparent memories are not illusions. I cannot prove that the other people you see on campus have minds. Perhaps they are very clever robots.

There is no interesting philosophical conclusion that can be proven beyond the possibility of doubt. So the fact that arguments for the existence of God do not produce mathematical certainty does not by itself weaken the case for God's existence. It simply places the question of God's existence in the same category as other questions such as that of the existence of the external, mind-independent world and the question of how we know other people have minds.

Does this mean that arguments for the existence of God are useless? Not at all. Sure, I cannot provide an argument that will convince all thinking people but this does not mean I don't have good reason to believe in God. In fact some of my reasons for believing in God may be persuasive to you. Even if you aren't persuaded to believe that God exists, my arguments may not be useless. It is reasonable to believe that the mountains are real and our memories are generally reliable and that other minds exist.

It is reasonable to believe these things even though they cannot be proven. Maybe some argument for God's existence will persuade you that belief in God is reasonable.

So how can we know that God exists? Instead of looking for indisputable conclusions, we weigh evidence and consider alternatives. Which alternative best fits the evidence? We will choose one alternative or another. There is no neutral ground.

II. Where Can we Find Information about God?

When you think about it, it seems that there are only two basic sources of information about God, if such a being exists. They are the following:

1. We can infer what might be true about God from what we observe in the universe. We look at the

physical universe, human nature and culture, and we observe things that may be clues to the existence or nature of the supernatural.

2. God may have entered the Universe and told us true things about Himself, morality, meaning and how to have a relationship with Him. This is called revelation.

Let me explain each of these. One year my wife and I drove from Los Angeles to Rhode Island. It took a long time. The country is pretty big. From this observation it makes sense to think that if there is some person or being who is responsible for making the physical universe, this being has a lot more power than we do. Now this is a rather simplistic example. Another observation we can make is that every culture has a deep sense that certain things are morally permissible and certain things are morally prohibited. This leads us to infer that if there is some supernatural being responsible for human nature, that being is personal. He has a moral aspect to His nature.

The second source of information is that God may have taken the initiative and stepped into the universe to reveal Himself. He may tell us true things about His nature, His purposes, and about human meaning and morality.

Christianity holds that both of these are good sources of information. We have clues to God's existence, which can be observed and God has entered the physical universe through the life and teaching of Jesus of Nazareth in history and told us about Himself.

Now in this article I am concentrating on the first source. Can we know anything about God from what we observe? Are there good reasons to believe in God based on these observations? I think there are.

III. Reasons to Believe in God

I want to pick two observations which I think give us good reason to think there is a God. First, the existence of the universe is better explained by the existence of God. Second, the existence of objective moral values is better explained by the existence of God.

A. The Existence of the Universe is Better Explained by The Existence of God.

I will begin by laying out the argument:

1. There are things that come into existence.

2. Everything that comes into existence is caused to exist by something else.

3. There cannot be an infinite series of past causes.

4. Therefore, there exists a first cause that did not come into existence. In other words, the first cause always existed.

Let us look at each of the steps in the argument:

PREMISE 1. "There are things that come into existence."

Many things have come into existence. This article is coming into existence as I write it. You came into existence and so did I. This premise is not controversial.

PREMISE 2. "Everything that comes into existence is caused to exist by something else."

It is obvious that nothing can cause itself to come into existence. Anything that causes itself to come into existence has to exist before it exists. This is impossible. Perhaps something can come into existence from nothing without any cause whatsoever. Can a thing just pop into existence with absolutely no cause? This also does not seem reasonable.

I have three children. If I walk into the dining room and see a picture of Pinky and the Brain that has been drawn on the wall in Permanent Magic Marker, I will ask, "Where did this picture come from?" My daughter Elizabeth (who is almost five) might say, "It came from nothing, Dad. Nothing caused it. It just popped there. I think it is quite strange — don't you?" Will I accept this? No! Things do not come into existence from nothing without cause. So, we have good reason to think that premise two is true. Everything that comes into existence is caused to exist by something else.

PREMISE 3. "There cannot be an infinite series of past causes."

Is the series of past causes infinite? Can the universe have an infinite past? The answer is that it cannot. First, there are philosophical reasons to think the past cannot be infinite. Second, there are scientific reasons that support this view.

PHILOSOPHICAL REASONS:

Why can't the past be infinite? The answer is that it is impossible to complete an infinite series by addition. The series of past events is complete. Think of this mathematical fact. Why is it impossible to count to infinity? It is impossible because, no matter how long you count, you will always be at a finite number. It is impossible to complete an actual infinite by successive addition.

The past is complete. This claim means that the entire series of past events ends now. It ends today. Tomorrow is not part of the series of past events. The series of past events does not extend into the future. It is complete at the present. If it is impossible to complete an infinite series by successive addition (as it is impossible to count to infinity), the past cannot be infinite. If the past is finite, that is, if it had a beginning, then the universe had a beginning. We have strong philosophical reason to reject the claim that the universe has always existed.

SCIENTIFIC REASONS:

I will not develop these. Rather, I will simply point them out.

1. The Big Bang theory does not prove that the universe had a beginning, but it supports this claim.

2. The second law of thermodynamics does not prove that the universe had a beginning but it supports this claim.

We can see that we have good philosophical and scientific reasons to reject the idea that the universe has always existed.

About the universe, there are only three alternatives:

1. The universe has always existed. It has an infinite past.

2. The universe was popped into existence from nothing with absolutely no cause.

3. The universe was caused to exist by something outside it.

We have strong reason to reject the first two alternatives.

Alternative three is the most reasonable. There was a first cause. This cause existed eternally. It initiated the Big Bang and created the universe. Now what can we know about this cause? Why think the cause is God? I will briefly sketch a few implications.

First, the first cause is not a part of the space-time physical universe because it caused the space-time universe to begin. Therefore it is outside of space and time. It is not physical. Second, it has great power. Third, it is a personal agent. This means it is not an inert force but it must have aspects of personhood; namely, that it wills. How do we know this? This is because it is the best answer to the question of why the Big Bang happened when it did. Why not sooner? Why not later? All of the conditions for producing the Big Bang existed from eternity. The only kind of cause we know of that can initiate an effect when all of the conditions are already present is the will of a personal agent.

I have not argued that it is logically impossible that the universe popped into existence from nothing without cause. I have argued that it is more reasonable to hold that it has a cause and that this cause is a non-physical personal agent—God.

So it seems that the first argument is fairly strong. The existence of the universe is better explained by the existence of God.

B. The Existence of Objective Moral Values is Better Explained by the Existence of God.

People experience a sense of morality that leads them to hold strongly that certain things are right or wrong for all people in all cultures. For example, it is wrong to torture another person just for fun. It is wrong for me today. It is wrong for a citizen of the Philippines and it was wrong for someone living in 500 BC. Our moral sense provides strong reason to believe in a personal God.

It will help clarify what I am saying if we put it into the form of an argument.

1. If there is no God, there are no objective moral values.

2. There are moral values that are objective.

3. Therefore, God exists.

Before I discuss this argument, I must make it clear that I am not claiming that one must believe in God in order to be moral. I am not claiming that statistically those who believe in God are more moral than those who do not. I am also not claiming that our knowledge of morality depends upon God. This argument is to the effect that objective moral values themselves are foreign to a universe without God. They do not fit.

DEFENDING PREMISE 1. "If there is no God, there are no objective moral values."

I have to admit that this claim is quite controversial and many philosophers disagree with me. I think, however, that objective moral values are not sufficiently explained in a universe without God. Many have agreed with this claim. For example, Dostoevski had Ivan Karamazov claim, "If there is no God, everything is permitted." Sartre wrote of Dostoevski's statement, "That is the very starting point of existentialism. Indeed, everything is permissible if God does not exist, and as a result man is forlorn, because neither within him nor without does he find anything to cling to." [See his essay Existentialism] John Mackie — probably the best philosophical atheist of the twentieth century recognizes this: "[Objective moral values] constitute so odd a cluster of qualities and relations that they are most unlikely to have arisen in the ordinary course of events, without an all-powerful god to create them. If, then, there are such intrinsically prescriptive objective values, they make the existence of a god more probable than it would have been without them" [The Miracle of Theism, pp 115-116].

Mackie recognizes that these objective values do not fit in the universe if there is no God. His answer, since he rejects God, is to claim that there are no objective moral values. His book on ethics is appropriately titled <u>Ethics: Inventing Right and Wrong</u>. I agree with Dostoevski, Sartre and Mackie. If there is no God, there are no objective moral values.

DEFENDING PREMISE 2. "There are objective moral values."

We know there are objective moral values. By this I mean that the content of morality is not determined by the individual, or by culture. Rather some things are objectively wrong. Other things are objectively obligatory. Actions such as rape, racist discrimination and torturing an innocent baby to death for no reason are really wrong. Furthermore, It is wrong for me to do these no matter when I live and no matter from what culture I come.

Now many people believe that morality is not objective. This view comes in three basic varieties.

1. **The individual determines morality.**

If the individual determines morality, then if I believe it is morally permissible to steal your stereo and beat up your girlfriend, it is permissible for me to do it. But it is not permissible for me to beat up your girlfriend. Therefore, the individual does not determine morality.

2. **Society determines morality.**

   If I lived in a completely racist society, would racism be right for me? Not at all. When an American university student protested against South Africa's former policy of apartheid, he was assuming that morality is not determined by society. It is transcendent of cultures. All of our greatest heroes have been men and women who have stood up to society's wrongs and appealed to a morality that is transcendent to society in order to demand change. If society determines morality, it is always morally wrong to criticize society. There is no morality outside of society that can form the basis of a moral critique.

3. **Morality has survival value.**

   Some people claim that the reason we have this moral sense is that it helped the human race survive. Those individuals with moral sense grouped together for mutual protection and these did better than those without the moral sense. This is a kind of prehistoric social contract theory of morality. The problem with this is that we do not need morality to survive today. In fact, if you and I know that morality has no objective validity and the rest of our culture still thinks it is valid, we can take advantage of this to get the most we can. There is no moral reason to refrain from rape, robbery and murder.

These inadequate objections show that there is a morality that is trans-personal, trans-cultural and trans-temporal. The existence of a personal God is the best explanation for this. It is not up to the individual or the culture to decide if it is permissible to rape simply for fun. Any individual who believes it is morally permissible to rape for fun has a false belief. Any culture whose moral guidelines include the claim that it is permissible to rape for fun has simply got it wrong.

If it is true that Hitler was morally wrong, it is true that there are objective moral truths that are trans-cultural. If it is true that it was wrong for Romans to leave baby girls to die on the trash heaps — simply because they were girls, then morality is not determined by culture. If it is true that Martin Luther King was a moral hero because he criticized his own culture by appealing to objective morality, then it is true that morality is not determined by culture.

Now, it is true that Hitler was wrong. It is true that the Romans were wrong. It is true that Martin Luther King was right — heroically right. So, we know there are objective moral truths. But objective morality makes no sense in the universe if there is no God. Objective moral values point to the existence of a moral being who created the universe. His moral character is the standard for objective right and wrong.

Summary

I have briefly presented two arguments for the existence of God. These show that it is more reasonable to believe that God exists than that He does not exist.

A. The Existence of the Universe is Better Explained by The Existence of God.

B. The Existence of Objective Moral Values is Better Explained by the Existence of God.

So we see that some of the things we observe about the natural world give ground to a strong inference to the claim that God does exist. This gives us reason to consider with renewed openness the possibility that God has entered the space-time universe and revealed Himself through the person and life and death of Jesus of Nazareth.

I have not claimed to prove with mathematical certainty that God exists. I have, however, provided good reasons to think that He does. If someone wishes to argue successfully that God does not exist, he must first provide an answer for each of my arguments and second, he must offer arguments that God does not exist. Until He does this, we can conclude that we have good reason to claim that God does exist.

Greg Ganssle holds an MA from the University of Rhode Island and a Ph.D. from Syracuse University, both in Philosophy. He is a faculty member of the Rivendell Center for Christian Thought, adjunct professor of Philosophy at the International School of Theology and has been a teaching fellow at Yale University. Greg has served on staff with Campus Crusade for Christ since 1978. He has published several papers in the areas of Philosophy of Religion and Metaphysics and is editing a book for Oxford University Press.

Personal Notes and Comments:

APPENDIX IV

Muslim/Islamic Understanding of the Virgin Birth of Jesus

The following article shows the Islamic understanding of Virgin Birth of Jesus Christ and his miracles.

The Virgin Birth of Jesus

Muslims believe in the virgin birth of Jesus. When the angels announced to Mary (peace be upon her) Allah's promise that she would have a son, she was surprised, since she was a virgin. "How can this be?" she thought. She was reminded that it is easy for Allah to create whatever he wills.

She said: My Lord! How can I have a child when no mortal hath touched me? He said: So (it will be). Allah createth what He will. If He decreeth a thing, He saith unto it only: Be! And it is (Qur'an 3:47).

It is not difficult for Allah to do anything he wants. He can create a child either with both human parents or only one. No miracle is beyond His power. After all, He had created Adam (peace be upon him) from neither a man nor a woman. He created the rest of us from both man and woman. What is so hard if Allah decides to create a human being from a woman only? He only commands, "Be!" And it occurs.

Some people think that since Jesus, peace be upon him, had no human father then God must be his father. The Qur'an rejects this view. The position of Jesus with Allah is comparable to the position of Adam with Allah. Just because Adam had no human parent does not mean we should call him the Son of God.

Lo! The likeness of Jesus with Allah is as the likeness of Adam. He created him from dust, and then He said unto him: Be! And he is (Qur'an 3:59).

According to the Qur'an, everyone, except Allah, is His servant.

And they say: the Beneficent hath taken unto Himself a Son. Assuredly ye utter a disastrous thing, whereby almost the heavens are torn, and the earth is split asunder and the mountains fall to ruins that ye ascribe to the Beneficent a son when it is not meet for (the Majesty of) the Beneficent that He should chose a son. There is none in the heavens and the earth but cometh unto the Beneficent as a slave (Qur'an 19:88-93).

The Miracles of Jesus

According to the Qur'an, Jesus, on whom be peace, performed the following miracles by Allah's permission:

1. Spoke while he was only a baby.
2. Healed those born blind.
3. Healed the lepers.
4. Revived the dead.
5. Breathed life into a bird made of clay.

In the Qur'an Allah quotes Jesus, peace be upon him, as saying:

Lo! I come unto you with a sign from your Lord. Lo! I fashion for you out of clay the likeness of a bird, and I breathe into it and it is a bird by Allah's permission.

I heal him who was born blind, and the leper, and I raise the dead, by Allah's permission. And I announce to you what you eat and what you store up in your houses. Lo! Herein verily is a sign for you if you are to be believers.

And (I come) confirming that which was before me of the Torah, and to make lawful some of that which was forbidden unto you. I come unto you with a sign from your Lord, so keep your duty to Allah and obey me. Lo! Allah is my Lord and your Lord, so worship Him. That is a straight path (Qur'an 3: 49-51).

Again, in the Qur'an Allah tells us about the situation on the Day of Judgment:

In the day when Allah gathers together the messengers and says: What was your response (from mankind)? They say: We have no knowledge. Lo! Thou, only Thou art the Knower of Things Hidden.

When Allah says: O Jesus, son of Mary! Remember My favour unto you and unto your mother; how I strengthened you with the holy Spirit, so that you spoke unto mankind in the cradle as in maturity; and how I taught you the Scripture and Wisdom and the Torah and the Gospel; and how you did shape of clay as it were the likeness of a bird by My permission, and did blow upon it and it was a bird by My permission, and you did heal him who was born blind and the leper by My permission . . . (Qur'an 5:109-110).

Not all of these miracles are recorded in the canonical gospels, the four gospels contained in the Christian Bible.

The fact that Jesus spoke while he was yet a baby is not written anywhere in the Bible. This should not be surprising, because none of the Gospels can claim to recover every single event in the life of Jesus. Instead, the gospel, according to John, seeks to emphasize that the events were too many to record.

Similarly, the miracle of breathing life into a bird made of clay is not attested by the Christian Bible. This too should not make us wonder. It is obvious that the writers of the gospels **************could write down only the tradition that was available to them.*************** Furthermore, they could not write down everything they knew about Jesus for they were writing on papyrus material that was very limited in length.

What is worthy to notice here is that the Prophet Muhammad, may peace and the blessings of Allah be upon him, was honest enough to promulgate this information about Jesus. The religion taught by God through Muhammad would deny the divinity of Jesus. Any human being, therefore, who wished to deny the divinity of Jesus, would have tried to belittle Jesus. Since Christians looked upon the miracles of Jesus as a proof of his divinity, we might expect that any human being who tries to deny the divinity of Jesus would not have informed people of miracles not previously known to them. He might have even tried to deny some of the miracles recorded in the canonical gospels. On the other hand, the prophet Muhammad honestly conveyed the message delivered to him from Allah. (May the peace and blessings of Allah be upon him.)

Allah tells us the truth without fear. Human beings trying to win followers tell us only what is conducive to winning us over. They usually withhold information that could lead to opposite conclusions. On the other hand, Allah informs us about the miracles of Jesus even if people use this information to support their prior commitment to the doctrine of the divinity of Jesus. Allah does not need to win worshippers. Those who worship Allah do so for their own good. And those who worship false gods do so to their own detriment.

What Allah emphasizes, though, is that the miracles of Jesus do not prove he was divine. The miracles he performed were a sign, a proof, that he was God's messenger. He performed them with God's help and permission. Those who use his miracles as proof of his divinity choose to forget the following words of Jesus:

> I can of my own authority do nothing (John 5:30).

They also forget the declaration of Peter:

> Jesus of Nazareth, a man approved of God among you by miracles and wonders and signs, which God did by him in the midst of you, as ye yourselves know (Acts 2:22 KJV). These passages suggest that Jesus did not do miracles on his own. These, rather were accomplished by God's leave. Allah reminds us of this. Jesus also constantly repeated to his audience that the miracles he performed were by God's permission.

Personal Notes and Comments:

_____

_____

_____

_____

_____

_____

_____

_____

_____

_____

_____

_____

_____

_____

_____

_____

_____

_____

_____

_____

APPENDIX V

The Issue of Mosque, Western Civilization
and Legitimate Concerns

The Media and the Mosque
by
Daniel Mann

Why has Western civilization turned so viciously against its own Christian roots? Why do our institutions that started as Bible schools—Harvard, Princeton, Yale, Columbia, Brown, and Dartmouth—now mock the mother that gave birth to them? The latest manifestation of Western self-contempt is the embrace of Imam Rauf who is now a USA paid emissary.

In regards to Rauf, the president of ACT for America.org and Lebanese immigrant to the USA, Brigitte Gabriel writes,

> "More Americans now know that Rauf, as recently as March, said in Arabic that he opposes interfaith dialogue. They know he is a vocal supporter of Sharia law, that he says governments that do not employ Sharia law are 'unjust' and that he has refused to label Hamas a terrorist organization. They know he has refused to sign the 'Freedom Pledge,' issued by Former Muslims United, which pledges to oppose retaliation and punishment toward Muslims who leave Islam. The more Americans learn, the more concerned they become."

It wasn't our mainstream media that has disclosed these unsettling but important facts. Gabriel explains that instead it was "investigative reporters, bloggers and watchdog organizations."

Meanwhile, the mainstream media largely paints those who raise questions about Rauf and his mosque as simply fearful or, even worse, as instruments of hate. They are also referred to as "extremist elements" or just "ignorant."

However, is it hate that causes us to question Rauf's rationale for rejecting Donald Trump's generous offer to buy their property so they can relocate the mosque at a less contentious site? Rauf explained that this option couldn't be considered because it would anger Muslims! Is it extremism that causes us to be concerned about what else might anger Muslims? Wouldn't transparent dialogue about the real nature of Islam also anger Muslims? And what does this say for the future of interfaith dialogue? Is it ignorance that would lead us to question moderate Muslims about their understanding of certain ******Koranic****** verses such as:

[3:27] Let not the believers take the disbelievers for friends rather than believers. And whoever does this has no connection with Allah…

[5:54] O ye who believe, take not the Jews and the Christians for your friends and protectors. They are but friends and protectors to each other.

Or is it extremism that would lead us to inquire about the Islamic doctrine of "Taqiyya," which authorizes lying to the infidel in order to promote Islam? Perhaps it is a legitimate fear that would engender concerns about other verses impacting our 1st amendment rights:

[33:59-61] [59]Prophet, tell your wives, your daughters, and women believers to make their outer garment hang low over them, so as to be recognized and not insulted: God is most forgiving, most merciful. [60]If the hypocrites, the sick of heart, and those who spread lies in the city [Medina] do not desist, we shall arouse you [the Prophet] against them, and then they will only be your neighbors in this city for a short while. [61]They will be rejected wherever they are found, and then seized and killed.

Should we be concerned about how such a teaching might impact free speech? Why are we so willing to gloss over these verses and the potential threat of these teachings to Western civilization, while our Bible is customarily torn to shreds in the very academic halls it had once founded? One Nigerian woman privately lamented, "The media is crazy. They just don't know Islam. They have no idea what it's like living under Sharia law." I think she's wrong. The media does know, but their lens prevents them from clearly seeing what seems to be alarmingly ever-present—the intolerant Jihadist core of Islam.

Imam Rauf comes across as grandfatherly and reasonable, but as Gabriel points out, this seems to be no more than a neatly cultivated veneer for his naïve multi-cultural, religiously-pluralistic Western audience. Indeed, he endorses Sharia law, which reduces non-Muslims to a *********tertiary******** status and relegates Muslims who deny their faith to the sword. Gabriel concludes:

> "Terrorists are only one manifestation of radical Islam. As Americans look even closer they will come to realize that the same ideology that produces a terrorist also produces a seemingly moderate Muslim who is dedicated to the advancement and imposition of Sharia law. They will learn that the Islamist in a suit and tie, who wants to replace the Constitution with Sharia law, differs from the terrorist only in the means to the end, not the end itself."

Why aren't we coming to terms with what has already become so obvious around the world? I don't understand much about the European Union. However, no one seems to dispute the fact that they have criteria for membership. The Union just doesn't receive every nation into membership. Instead, there has to be a fit. Is it therefore unreasonable to examine the fitness of Islam?

However, when Islam's fitness is called into question, those who do so are dismissively labeled "Islamophobes." Meanwhile, the media is happy to give time to any radical who has a new angle on how to deconstruct the Christian faith. Why this discrepancy? Is it a matter of crucifying Christ all over again? The Christ Himself might agree:

> "If the world hates you, keep in mind that it hated Me first. If you belonged to the world, it would love you as its own. As it is, you do not belong to the world, but I have chosen you out of the world.

That is why the world hates you. Remember the words I spoke to you: 'No servant is greater than his master.' If they persecuted Me, they will persecute you also. If they obeyed My teaching, they will obey yours also" (John 15:18-20).

Ironically, it is the Biblical revelation alone that provides the indispensable foundation for the freedoms that secularism values. It is only the revelation that we are created in the image of God (Genesis 1:26-27), and therefore have certain unalienable rights that can provide an adequate philosophical foundation for the Bill of Rights. Even the skeptic, Thomas Jefferson, confessed:

> "And can the liberties of a nation be thought secure when we have removed their only firm basis, a conviction in the minds of the people that these liberties are the gift of God? That they are not to be violated but with His wrath?" (Notes on the State of Virginia)

Can secularism also insist on these liberties? Well, it can, but not in a way consistent with its anti-theistic position. If all it has is a materialistic orientation, then we are coerced into regarding one another materialistically! Consequently, all aren't equally deserving of society's freedoms and protections. Some of us are a credit to society, while others are a financial drain on society. Some are deserving; some aren't! On the basis of what should each have an equal vote or protection? There is no secular basis! So it must secretly borrow from its hated parent.

As secularism continues to wage its auto-immune war against Christianity, it fails to see that it consumes itself in the process. Welcome Islam!

Personal Notes and Comments:

FINAL THOUGHTS FROM DR. JAVED

Without discipleship, evangelism cannot sustain the desire and excitement of a new convert to pursue the will of God in his or her life. A convert must be taken care of before and after the conversion experience. Moreover, Muslim Background Believers need strong Christian families around them. In Islam, the family is the strong anchor to hold on to during times of a need. I would ask you to consider the example of a bridge. What does a bridge have in common with a Muslim Background Believer? The strong support on both ends. If you remove one of the ends, the bridge will collapse. Moreover, Muslim Background Believers need a smooth transition. It is important to remember that when they accept Christ, they lose their families. Thus, relationship is the key. If there isn't a fast and smooth transition to the next family (the body of Christ), the life and faith of a MMB will collapse.

Thus, I recommend the following:

Islam

Islam is not a religion but a movement, culture, ideology, an educational, economical, millitary and political system. Therefore, every effort to minister to Muslims must be culturally sensitive. Most Muslims are unaware of what the Qur'an really teaches. Thus, it might be an excellent idea to study the Qur'an, Hadith and Sira in order to use the Qur'an to share some of the significant portions of the Qur'an that nullify the Muslim claims against the death and resurection; the doubts about the validity of the Christian scriptures; and the deity of Christ. However, my recommendations should be received with great caution. First, study the Bible well before you study the Qur'an. If you do not have a well grounded faith and a clear understanding of the Bible, I ask you not to read the Qur'an at all. Second, use the Qur'an to initiate conversation only. The Qur'an should not be your primary text to share Christ with a Muslim friend. The sooner you are done with using the Qur'an, the better the chance you have to win a soul to Christ. Therefore, do not rely on the Qur'an for more than a few minutes. Third, begin your conversation with a prayer if possible, certainly pray before you are going to meet up with a Muslim friend. Lastly, close with a prayer, and continue praying for your Muslim friend on regular basis.

The Best Weapon

Prayer is the best weapon you have in spiritual warfare. More prayers produce better results. Ask others to pray for you and the person you are trying to reach out to. Furthermore, never forget this is our Lord's fight. No spiritual fight has ever been won without the Holy Spirit. I would say 75% prayer (although there is never enough prayer) + 25% personal witnessing (but you must be lead and directed by the Holy Spirit) = conversion of a lost soul. God always wins, and He is determined to bring all nations to the saving knowledge of Jesus Christ. Our job is to be obedient to our calling and with prayers execute the little faith we have that He might increase our faith by bringing more flock through us.

Culture

The Western understanding of Islam cannot and will not bridge the gap between Muslims and non-Muslims living in the West. Muslims enjoy a very different type of food, clothing, values, and belief system. Moreover, the Muslim worldview is very different than the Western worldview. Furthermore, their thought process and philosophy of life is much different than the West. Therefore, writing, talking, and sharing with and about Muslims from an Eastern perspective is much different than the Western perspective. Christians whether they are in the East or the West have been given something unique and valueable that no one else has: the Holy Spirit. Christ promised us that we will be given words to say at the appointed time. The Holy Spirit directs us to rise above and beyond racial, and clutural differences to embrace the lost in the world.

Apologetics

Christian apologists need to get a fresh look at the Islamic literature and the claims Muslims make about Christ, Christianity and the Bible. Moreover, Christian apologists must respond responsibly. In the past, what was considered to be an effective apologetic dialogue with Muslims has already been studied by the Muslim apologists/scholars. Today, Muslims are trained in Mosques and houses regarding how to answer and raise specific questions about Christianity. I provided an example earlier, that in the Qur'an, Jesus is called the Spirit of God (Rohullulah) and the Word of God (Kalimatullah). The classic argument was that Jesus is the Spirit of God and His Word incarnated into a human form. Today, many Muslims, not all, have learned from their scholars how to answer to this apologetic question. Their answer is that the proposition "of" is wrong and that it should be "from." Thus, Jesus was a created being. Of course this is a new distortion, but if we study well we know how to avoid such complication. The Church constantly needs to work on studying the old and new religions/cults and develop proper apologetic answers.

I also talked about the Islamic claim that Jesus or God never promised to protect the Bible from alteration or corruption. Apart from my above apologetic answer, here is something else that I would like to suggest. Do not validate any claim Muslims make regarding Christ, the Bible and Christianity without the studying the word of God. If you do not know the answer at that moment, ask if you could come back after studying the scripture. Moreover, with respect to the promise of protection of the Bible: First, both Jesus and the Qur'an state clearly that God's Word can never be altered. In Matthew 5:18 we read "For truly I tell you, until heaven and earth disappear, not the smallest letter, not the least stroke of a pen, will by any means disappear from the Law until everything is accomplished." Jesus also said, "Heaven and earth will pass away, but my words will never pass away" (Matthew 24:35). The Qur'an testifies that God's word never changes "Perfected is the Word of thy Lord in truth and justice. There is naught that can change His words. He is the Hearer, the Knower" (Sura al-An'am 6:115).

Thus, either the Bible and Qur'an are wrong, or those Muslims who claim that the Word of God *the Bible* has been changed or altered by humans. Is it possible that the God of the universe, the might creator of man becomes weaker to protect His Word? Of course not! Furthermore, as I have previously stated, Muhammad and the Qur'an claimed the validity of the Bible: the Torah, Zabur (Psalms), and the Gospels. Muhammad quoted many verses from the Bible. Why is it hard for Muslims to understand that God would not ask Muhammad to read from a corrupt Word of God as he was commanded in the Qur'an 10:94-95? (the Torah, Psalms, and the Gospels).

Here are a few verses about the Old Testament's and New Testament's unchangeability: **"Do not add to what I command you and do not subtract from it, but keep the commands of the LORD your God that I give you" (Deuteronomy 4:2). No one would be foolish enough to alter the Torah. God promised to destroy them just like He destroyed those who worshipped idols (Deuteronomy 4:3). Since God's Word is perfect, we are reminded not to change it. "Every word of God is flawless; he is a shield to those who take refuge in him. Do not add to his words, or he will rebuke you and prove you a liar" (Proverbs 30:5-6). "If anyone adds anything to them, God will add to that person the plagues described in this scroll. And if anyone takes words away from this scroll of prophecy, God will take away from that person any share in the tree of life and in the Holy City" (Revelation 22:18b-19).**

The Trinity

The most difficult concept of Christianity is the belief in the Trinity. Although the word "Trinity" is not found in the Gospels, it certainly does not mean that that the concept is not taught in the Scriptures. Two Church fathers and theologians Athanasius (c. 296-373 A.D.) and Augustine (354-430 A.D.) are among those who saw the concept of Trinity in the Bible and developed the doctrine for us. No one was supposed to be able to explain it in a comprehensive human way. It is a divine mystery that can be understood and explained through Holy Spirit in faith. I do not expect Muslims to understand that unless the Holy Spirit resides in them. However, Christians can simply refer to the baptism of Jesus as the prime example of the Trinity. The Father, the Son, and the Holy Spirit were all present at once. When Jesus came up out of the water, "he saw the Spirit of God descending like a dove and alighting on him. And a voice from heaven said, 'This is my Son, whom I love; with him I am well pleased'" (Matthew 3:16-17).

You should invite Muslims to read the Bible even though they do not believe in the Bible. Moreover, the following reasons will interest them: First, Muslims are required to believe in all the holy books *the Qur'an* 4:136. Second, there are a number of unfinished stories in the Qur'an about previous Old Testament characters. For example, most of the prophets that Muslims believe in and are required to believe in are mentioned in the Bible. Please see the list of the prophets in Question no. 68 of this book. The Bible can tell the life stories of all those prophets whose names are only mentioned in the Qur'an. Third, the nation of Israel. Muslims throughout the world hate Jews because the Qur'an has commanded such hatred until the end of this world. Muslims might want to read about Israel and what has been happening to the Hebrew nation for over 5000 years. In the Qur'an, you can read about the story of the plagues that God sent to Egypt to show Pharaoh that He is the God of Israel. The Qur'an says there were nine plagues but mentioned only six. For the rest of plagues you may want to invite a Muslim to read from the Bible.

The Four Gospels

It is important to note that Muslims claim that the four gospels of the present day have many discrepancies, whereas the Qur'an is pure and has none. I would suggest that the readers of this book keep in mind the stories about Jesus were told orally but were written down within the first century A.D. To be correct, the Gospels were originally written from about 50-95 A.D. Each gospel was written with a specific audience and with a unique emphasis in mind. However, the message was, and still is, timeless. If the written text of the Qur'an is God's Word, then the Bible is God's Word too. The question remains: if God's Word is in a book form, then what can stop God's Word from being in human form? The Gospel of John 1:14 is the clear presentation of such dwelling of the Word of God among human beings in the form of a man, **"The Word became flesh and made his dwelling among us. We have seen his glory, the glory of the one and only Son, who came from the Father, full of grace and truth" (John 1:14).**

Authenticity of the Scriptures

There are a few tests one can perform to know whether a book is the Word of God or not. I have already mentioned a few earlier in this book, but I would like to emphasize that God authenticates His holy books too show if they are God's Words or merely human genius. The manner in which God does that is through prophecies which are foretold events. In the Bible, you can find event after event that prove the Bible to be the authentic Word of God. One of the more famous examples is the destruction of the city of Tyre. In Ezekiel 26, you will find that the prophecy states the city would be torn down and its debris will be thrown into the sea. Alexander the Great fullfilled this prophecy by destroying the city of Tyre, and using the rubble of the city of Tyre to form a land bridge to attack a tower on an island. The Qur'an does not stand up to such authentication by God. The second best test is the historical, archeological and geographical test. For instance, the places, the historical time line, and the characters in the Bible can be verified through historical, archeological and geographical evidences. However, the Qur'an lacks such evidences. For example, as previously mentioned, the Qur'an talks about Mary the mother of Jesus as the sister of Aaron, the brother of Moses who lived in Pharaoh's time! Besides, Allah and the Qur'an clearly declare the Bible as an authentic source of God's revelation for Muslims. I have provided a number of verses such as 5:48. One verse I would like to mention here is:

Quran 5:47

وَلْيَحْكُمْ أَهْلُ ٱلْإِنجِيلِ بِمَآ أَنزَلَ ٱللَّهُ فِيهِ وَمَن لَّمْ يَحْكُم بِمَآ أَنزَلَ ٱللَّهُ فَأُو۟لَـٰٓئِكَ هُمُ ٱلْفَـٰسِقُونَ ﴿٤٧﴾

Sahih International

And let the People of the Gospel judge by what Allah has revealed therein. And whoever does not judge by what Allah has revealed—then it is those who are the defiantly disobedient.

According to the above verse, Allah validates the copy of the Gospel available during Muhammad's time. The verb in present tense indicates that people of the Gospel were commanded to be judged by the Gospel available during Muhammad's time. It shows that either the claim Muslims make today about the corruption in the Bible is wrong or Allah was unable or unwilling to maintain and uphold the Bible available during Muhammad's time. But, of course, the ample manuscript evidence for the Bible shows that it is the same Bible in use during Muhammad's time. So God HAS maintained it, and Christians and Jews may still be judged by it as a standard.

There are many other examples, but let's examine the only Gospel Muslims believe to be the true Gospel.

The Gospel of Barnabas

We examined this gospel in Question no. 158-160. If one analyzes the manuscript of the Gospel of Barnabas, it will be clear that it fails all the tests of God's authentication. Moreover, it fails as a reliable historical piece of literature. First, it is a cheap knock-off of the Gospel and Gnostic gospels. Second, historically both manuscipts of the gospel of Barnabas were written in 14th-16th A.D. There are two existing manuscripts one in Spanish and the other one in Italian. Third, the Gospel of Barnabas contradicts both the Gospels as well as the Qur'an. Some highlights of the Gospel of Barnabas are:

1. It denies the crucifixion of Jesus Christ. That agrees with the Qur'an but contradicts the Bible.

2. It prophesies about Muhammad (Muhammad was born in the 6th century and prophcey was made between 14th-16th century when Islam was a powerful religion). So this prophesy after the fact once again agrees with the Qur'an but contradicts the Bible.

3. It proclaims Muhammad as the long awaited Messiah, not Jesus. However, the Qur'an clearly uses the word Messiah for Jesus, the son of Mary. Therefore, here it contradicts the both the Bible and the Qur'an.

4. It teaches that Hell is a temporary place for sinners. Once again, this document contradicts Christianity and Islam.

5. It teaches that Mary gave birth to Jesus without any pain, where in Qur'an 19:23 Mary suffered great pains at the birth of Jesus. The Gospel of Barnabas not only contradicts the Bible and Qur'an; but fails God's authentication for being the Holy Word of God, and does not match the Historical time line. Furthermore, it fails the geographical test as well. Here are a few examples:

   ● Nazareth is a village on the shores of the Sea of Galilee. Wrong! Nazareth is located on the top of a hill. It also states that Jesus climbs up from the Sea of Galilee to Capernaum. Wrong! He didn't because Capernaum lies directly on the shore of the Sea of Galilee. The Gospel of Barnabas reports that Jesus boarded a ship to sail to Jerusalem. Wrong! You do not need a ship to sail to Jerusalem because Jerusalem lies inland and cannot be reached by ship.

   ● Here is another big historical error that does not match the time line. The Gospel of Barnabas mentions a golden coin, the dinari worth 60 minuti (RR, LIV/128). This coin was only used for a short period in medieval Spain. Since the Gospel was created in Spain that makes sense. It also mentions wooden barrels to store wine, whereas in the Middle East bags made of leather were commonly used.

Validity of the Qur'an

The Qur'an regardless of the claims Muslims make has a number of errors or other difficulties. Some of them are as follows:

1. The Qur'an does not prophecy about the future.

2. The Qur'an 40:36-37 says Haman was Pharaoh's prime minister but Esther 3:1 tells us otherwise. It states that Haman lived in Babylon 1000 years after the Pharaoh in Egypt was shown miracles by Moses.

3. The Qur'an 20:85-88 states the Samaritans were responsible for making a golden calf when Moses went up on the mountain to meet God. Historically, Samaritans did not exist until after the Babylonian exile.

4. The Qur'an 19:23 says Mary gave birth to Jesus under a palm tree, that is also false. Christian records show Jesus was born in a manger.

5. The Qur'an 7:54; 41:9; 41:1; 41:12 provides two different accounts of creation. One account states the creation was completed in 6 days and the other says 8 days. There are many other errors that one can find.

6. The Qur'an wasn't given to the prophet of Islam directly from Allah. Muhammad claimed it was an unidentified spirit which appeared to him in the cave of Hira in 610 AD. Later his wife Khadija and her causin Waraka Ibn Nawfal, a Chrisitian Ebionite priest, told Muhammad that the spirit was Angel Gebrael. Thus, the claim Muslims make about the Qur'an that it is a revelation directly from God is not valid, according to the Qu'ran itself.

7. In the book of Revelation in the Bible God commanded to "write" (Rev. 1:11) 12 times and one time do not write (Rev. 10:4). It shows that John was guided to write word by word and not from his own memory some time later. However, in the Qur'an you cannot find an explicit command to Muhammad or anyone else to write. Muhammad tells his story and also the Qur'an testifies the story by saying that Muhammad was commanded three times to "read" or "recite," not to write.

8. Before the third Caliph, Uthman, there were at least two different copies of the Qur'an that were already used publically. Ubayy bin aK's codex and Ibn AMU's codex. One became the standard text for Syria and the other for Kufa in Iraq.

9. In 1972 one of the oldest copies of Qur'an was found in Yemen. The manuscripts prove beyond a reasonable doubt that before the recension of Uthman's Qur'an the available copies of the Qur'an were very different.

The Coming of Muhammad

Muslims believe that the Bible predicted the coming of the prophet Muhammad. This belief has become one of the major teachings in Islam. Muslims quote the following references: Deuteronomy 18:18 "I will raise up for them a prophet like you from among their fellow Israelites, and I will put my words in his mouth. He will tell them everything I command him." and "Since then, no prophet has risen in Israel like Moses, whom the LORD knew face to face, who did all those signs and wonders the LORD sent him to do in Egypt—to Pharaoh and to all his officials and to his whole land." Muhammad was neither an Israeli nor did he meet God face to face like Moses. He claimed, and the Qur'an testifies, that it was the angel Gabriel who brought the Qur'an to him from God. However, this has nothing to do with the story of Mirage where Muhammad claims he went to the seventh heaven to meet God. Muhammad did not perform any miracles. The one person who was able to do all that was prophesied was Jesus. In the New Testament, Muslims claim that John 14:16-26; 15:26; 16:5-15 are about Muhammad's coming. First, if this is true, then Muslims must believe that Muhammad was sent by Jesus in His name because it is written "I will send him to you," "in my name." Second, Muslims must believe that the Bible is not changed and that it is the Word of God. Also, the Paracletos (the helper, assistance, the Holy Spirit) was not supposed to be seen (John 14:17) but Muhammad was a living being who had flesh.

The biggest group of non-Christians

There are 6.8 billion people in the world, only 2 billion of whom are Christians. 4.8 billion are non-Christians. 97% of non-Christians believe in a god but they do not know Jesus as resurrected Savior, the Son of God. Billions need Him, but they are looking for God in the wrong place. Jesus says, "I love you," "I'm calling you." Yes, we are His hands and feet. If we are going to bring billions to Christ, don't you think we should start with the biggest group? The ones who are seeking a god and want to know the Truth. What is the biggest group? The biggest group of non-Christian people in the world today is Muslims. **40% of non-Christians are Muslims.**

An Opportunity to Serve

If you want to serve with *Love For Muslims*, let us know so that we may send you the catalog regarding our ministry. Following a training session, you may qualify to run a chapter for *Love For Muslims* in your church or area. You should contact our office in Virginia or New York City. We would love to help you get the full training you need. If you want us to come to your church or small group, we would love to come and share the correct knowledge about Islam. If you have any questions, contact us through www.themuslimnextdoor. info. Dr. Alfonse Javed is available on facebook too. We would love to help you to understand why we modified some of the well known Christian evangelistic tools and techniques. To obtain free pocket size Gospels Contact:

THE POCKET TESTAMENT LEAGUE

P.O BOX 800

LITITZ, PA 17543

www.pocketpower.org

What can you do?

Three things:

1. Pray for our ministry and promote this book.
2. Invite us to come to Church, Sunday school or ministry.
3. Find us on facebook: **The Muslim Next Door by Dr. Javed**

Personal Notes and Comments:

_____

_____

_____

_____

_____

_____

_____

_____

_____

_____

_____

_____

_____

_____

_____

_____

_____

ABOUT DR. JAVED

Background

It was not a remote, isolated area in some Islamisized tribal village of Kanddar, Afghanistan but the populous city of Lahore in the heart of Pakistan. It was there that a massacre took place under the new secular government. The victims were Pakistani Christians and the perpetrators were Pakistani Muslims. Both had lived in peace for generations until Sharia Law was implemented in the Pakistani courts. Many such incidents occur everyday unnoticed by the national and international media, as if the lives of Pakistani Christians were disposable, worth nothing.

Early Life

In this diverse but hostile environment Dr. Alfonse Javed was born to a pastor and his wife. Being the second oldest son among five siblings, he never learned to cope with his identity as a "choora," a derogatory word for Christians. As an untouchable, it was not possible to drink from the same cup as other Pakistanis. He was determined to break through the social barriers of racism, and religious differences. Regardless of the treatment he received, he always found a reason to believe that one day things would change for the beter. Having a soft spot for Muslims, he looked for ways to prove himself worthy of respect. In 1998, at the age of 18 he started an after school program that turned into a successful high school activity within one year. The same year, he founded a non-profit organization that continues to fight for peace, justice and equality. It also provides humanitarian aid to the Pakistani people.

Fame

His success and fame became a curse when he was chased by some Muslims. Before his adversaries could become a nightmare for his family, he was disowned by them. A man who had everything was left with no choice but to escape. The thorn of hatred against him was so deep in the soul of his own countrymen that he was forced to live in exile and make a foreign land his new home.

New Life

The root of the sort of evil that turns good friends against friends and relatives against relatives was the new frontier that he was about to discover. He has since devoted his life to the study of Islam and learning about its history. His culture and background gave him a unique perspective on Islam.

Education and Abroad

In 2003, he planted a church in Athens, Greece among Indians and Pakistanis. The church continues to grow. In the following year, he also ministered in Iran and Afghanistan. In 2006, coming from a country of almost 200 million people that has less than a 1.8 % Christian evangelical community, he started a new life in the US, where 80% of the population claims to be Christian. Dr. Javed was saved as a result of his family's miraculous deliverance from an intense wave of persecution.

He is a graduate of Liberty University in Lynchburg, Virginia and holds several degrees: BA, BS, BRE, MS, MBA, Ed. S and Doctor of Education degree in Leadership and has served in two churches as a pastor, one in Binghamton, NY and the other in Pennsylvania. Currently, he is the director of Outreach and Evangelism at Calvary Baptist Church, a historical church in New York City. He is a dynamic speaker who travels around the world to preach, teach and train leaders.

New York City Life

In New York City, Dr. Javed has served as the director of Love for Muslims, a ministry of Advancing Native Missions, out of Hephzibah House. His unique understanding of both Eastern and Western cultures allows him to interpret the Qur'an in its true context. His doctoral research on Muslim students in the New York school system has given him a different perspective on Muslim youth living in New York City. He has been invited nationally and internationally to present his research work. Under his ministry leadership at Calvary Baptist Church, with the collaboration of Advancing Native Missions, the church is developing a model to reach out to Muslims for other churches in the New York metropolitan area. The Muslim next door by Dr Alfonse Javed is one recommended resource by Christian leadership.

If you would like to invite Dr. Javed for a secular or Christian event, please contact us via: www.themuslimnextdoor.info, or through facebook. He teaches regularly at New York School of the Bible, as well as teaching at Davis College's Brooklyn New York site. For more:www.dralfonsejaved.info.

Personal Notes and Comments:

Personal Notes and Comments:

CPSIA information can be obtained at www.ICGtesting.com
Printed in the USA
BVOW062157080412

287032BV00001B/3/P